Mind, Body, and Spirit

Praise for The Necktie and The Jaguar

"Carl Greer has written a moving testimonial to the reality of transformation in life's journey toward psychological and spiritual wholeness. This narrative of his personal experience should be an inspiration and encouragement to others who find themselves also along the Way."
—Murray Stein, PhD, Jungian analyst, past president of the International Association for Analytical Psychology and author of *Jung's Map of the Soul*

"Carl Greer is an explorer who clearly throws himself wholeheartedly into every angle of himself that he chooses to invest in. The result of his life search is this powerful narrative, which is a testament to his journey through the material, psychological and spiritual realms. Looking back on his eight decades on this planet, he has uncovered gold in unexpected places. This book will offer insight and inspiration to its readers."
—Malcolm Stern, psychotherapist, author of *Slay Your Dragons with Compassion*, and cofounder of Alternatives

"Carl Greer's memoir of making radical changes in his life shows that working with various states of consciousness can be extremely helpful in a creative process of personal transformation. With journaling questions to support readers in their own self-reflection, The Necktie and The Jaguar is an engaging story and a strong testament to the power of a mindful approach to decision making, leadership, and living authentically."
—Ronald Alexander, PhD, psychotherapist, and author of *Wise Mind, Open Mind*

"Chronicling the seasons of a man's life—from child to sage, Carl Greer shares his remarkable journey as businessman, psychologist, Jungian analyst, shaman, and philanthropist, hence bridging the moral and the numinous on his path toward individuation. In reading his memoir, you get the real sense of being in the presence of a wise man with a fulfilled spiritual existence. His life story will inspire you to become your possibilities and develop a deeper sense of grounding and purpose connected to something greater than ourselves. What a truly extraordinary life."

—Jon Mills, PsyD, PhD, ABPP, Postgraduate Programs in Psychoanalysis & Psychotherapy, Adelphi University; author of *Inventing God*

THE NECKTIE
AND THE
JAGUAR

A memoir to help you change
your story and find fulfillment

CARL GREER, PHD, PSYD

CHIRON PUBLICATIONS • ASHEVILLE, NORTH CAROLINA

www.ChironPublications.com

Interior and cover design by Danijela Mijailovic
Printed primarily in the United States of America.

Some material in this book originally appeared in Carl Greer's unpublished thesis, "Warrior Principles Amplified by the Martial Arts as Metaphors for My Life, Individuation, and Analysis."

Some of the text on "suddenlies in life" was previously published on Carl Greer's blog and the *Spirituality & Health* website.

The descriptions of Carl Greer's first encounter with the matrix and his shamanic journey in which he encountered a Mycenean village and nearly entered the Holy of Holies, the description of the chapters in our life stories, and the poem "Letting Go" by Carl Greer previously appeared in his book *Change Your Story, Change Your Life*, published in 2014 by Findhorn Press in Scotland.

The description of Carl Greer and his wife, Pat, working with shamanic techniques to address her health issues related to breast cancer previously appeared in Carl Greer's book *Change the Story of Your Health*, published in 2017 by Findhorn Press in Scotland.

ISBN 978-1-63051-903-2 paperback
ISBN 978-1-63051-904-9 hardcover
ISBN 978-1-63051-905-6 electronic
ISBN 978-1-63051-906-3 limited edition paperback

Library of Congress Cataloging-in-Publication Data
Names: Greer, Carl, author.
Title: The necktie and the Jaguar: a memoir to help you change your story and find fulfillment / Carl Greer, PhD., PSYD
Description: Asheville, North Carolina : Chiron Publications, [2020] |
Includes bibliographical references. | Summary: "The Necktie and the Jaguar is an interactive memoir- the story of Carl Greer reinventing his life as a result of honoring his longings for meaning and purpose. As you read his story, you might wonder how you would tell yours and how those who know you would tell it. You might never have asked yourself, "What is my story, really, if I'm honest about it?" or "How did that story-my thoughts and perceptions about what I have experienced-come about?" Answering these questions can help you acknowledge your truth and begin to break out of old, constricting patterns and live according to your soul's needs. You might well find yourself listening to the call of the jaguar-the call to let go of any fears of transformation and step into the unknown as you begin to change your life"-- Provided by publisher.
Identifiers: LCCN 2020049168 (print) | LCCN 2020049169 (ebook) | ISBN 9781630519032 (paperback) | ISBN 9781630519049 (hardcover) | ISBN 9781630519063 (limited edition paperback) | ISBN 9781630519056 (ebook)
Subjects: LCSH: Greer, Carl. | Psychologists--Biography. | Philanthropists--Biography. | Jungian psychology. | Shamanism.
Classification: LCC BF109.G74 G74 2020 (print) | LCC BF109.G74 (ebook) | DDC 150.19/5092 [B]--dc23
LC record available at https://lccn.loc.gov/2020049168
LC ebook record available at https://lccn.loc.gov/2020049169

Table of Contents

Disclaimer

I'm grateful to many people whose stories have enriched my own. Out of respect for the privacy of some living individuals I wrote about in this book, I have changed some names and identifying details.

Acknowledgments

As I approached my eightieth year, which I have now entered, I came to understand that my story could serve as a vehicle for others to reflect on their own. I have been fortunate to embark on what seem to me to be uncommon adventures and to receive illuminating teachings that widened my worldview and allowed me to be a more effective healer for those who have sought my assistance. Through years of extensive Jungian and shamanic training, I have been privileged to be able to gain tools and insights that I have enjoyed sharing with readers and followers of my work.

Many I've encountered on my journey have influenced my life in positive ways, and to them, I am grateful and appreciative. Among those I wish to thank are my teachers and professors, my business associates at the various companies with which I've been involved, the family of Harold Martin of Martin Oil (who have been my good partners for more than fifty-three years), and my Jungian, psychology, and shamanic colleagues as well as those I have worked with in my philanthropic activities. I want to thank Don Waterlander and Lisa Sanchez for their outstanding work on behalf of the Greer Foundation. And thank you to Don and to Tom Floyd for staying with me for more than thirty-five years, helping me manage my various business interests.

I am indebted to many people for joining me in bringing this book to life and light. Charlotte Kelchner, Sue Baugh, and Gladys Burow—who worked with me for more than fifty-two years and was an indispensable and exceptional assistant—helped me organize the extensive material. Nancy Peske's insights and guidance as an editor and book publishing consultant were of great value.

I'm thankful for the clients and students I have worked with and for my friends, many of whom I've known for more than sixty-five years.

I'm thankful for my parents, Joe and Gene Greer, my stepmother, Mary Anne Greer, my brother, Kirk, and his wife, Rita, and my grandparents, aunts, uncles, cousins, nieces, and nephews. I'm also thankful for Jerri Greer, my first wife and the mother of my children.

As always, and perhaps in increasing measure over time, I want to acknowledge my children, Caryn, Michael, and Janet, and my stepchildren, Michael, Susie, and Jeannie, as well as their significant others, Rudy, Jenny, Joe, Leslie, and Mike, who have all been an important part of my life. I'm grateful for my fourteen grandchildren, who continually remind me that new generations will be the light bearers of change. Finally, I celebrate the contributions of Pat—my love, my wife, and my partner in past, present, and future endeavors. She has supported me throughout many chapters of my life and when I was writing this book. Her careful reading of the drafts and her comments helped make this memoir better.

Dedication

To all who are consciously reflecting on their lives and making changes so their journey is more pleasing to them and Spirit

A Note to the Reader

The Necktie and the Jaguar is my story of reinventing my life as a result of honoring my longings for meaning and purpose. As you read my story, you might wonder how you would tell yours and how those who know you would tell it. You might never have asked yourself, "What is my story, really, if I'm honest about it?" or "How did that story—my thoughts and perceptions about what I have experienced—come about?" Answering these questions can help you acknowledge your truth and begin to break out of old, constricting patterns and live according to your soul's needs. You might well find yourself listening to the call of the jaguar—the call to let go of any fears of transformation and step into the unknown as you begin to change your life.

Many people find they are uncertain at first of what they want their future to look like and who they want to become. Fear of the unknown can send you back into the familiar ways that weren't working for you. In my experience, while the work of transformation can be uncomfortable at times, it can also be deeply rewarding. Accessing "jaguar" power for change can help you to fully inhabit a new way of being.

When we are children, we don't mentally and emotionally process our experiences the way we do as adults. We can't always find appropriate words to describe them. We can't put them in the context of a lifetime of experiences. We only know what we know, and events shape our perceptions of ourselves, our families, and the outside world. These early experiences make up our conditioning, setting up how we will act and react going forward into adulthood. Even if in adulthood we become aware of behavior patterns that have been set in place and some of the experiences that set them in motion, we might not appreciate the power of the stories we were told growing up. Some of those stories were found in books, television programs, or movies, but some were family and community stories about what a "good man," "good woman," or "good child" does. Exploring these stories, which may be mostly hidden in our unconscious, can free us from the pain they cause. They are stories others wrote for us that we might want to replace.

Because of my training and work as a Jungian analyst and shamanic practitioner, I know that people can change their stories by relating differently to the archetypal energies within them. These energies include the young hero, the warrior, the teacher or master, the fool, the nurturer, the healer, and so on. They reside in our unconscious and influence how we think, act, and feel.

If you have always thought of yourself as a warrior, you might want to be a different type of warrior—or reduce the influence of that warrior energy affecting you so that you can be a better teacher or nurturer. You might stop fearing the fool within you and allow yourself to be innocent, trusting, and playful again, unafraid of "making a fool of myself." Using Jungian and shamanic techniques can help you learn from and work with archetypal energies that influence you and your story. By relating differently to these energies, you might find it easier to transform your life.

How our memories live within us can change as we reexamine our stories. We can write a new story that integrates the same events but is a different interpretation of them. For example, my story of "It's best not to talk about unpleasant things—best to keep your anger and sadness to yourself," learned in my childhood home, had to change so that I could live a more fulfilling life. I had to start to acknowledge painful events I'd experienced and better understand how they had affected me for good or bad. They now live differently in my memory. They have new meanings for me, and that allows me to live more freely and consciously.

The Necktie and the Jaguar is what I call an interactive memoir because at the end of each chapter, I've provided questions for you to ponder. Self-reflecting with the help of these questions, you can start—or continue—the process of self-discovery. That can lead to healing old wounds, letting go of old habits, and experiencing personal transformation.

When you think about your answers to the questions, consider whether there are things you wish you'd done differently. Think about whether there is anything you can do today to make up for what you did or didn't do in the past. Could you reclaim an aspect of yourself that you became disconnected from? Could you consciously choose a new story for yourself, one that is more empowering than the old one?

You might want to write your answers in a journal or record them in a document or an audio file, perhaps transcribing them later. You might find yourself rewriting your story as you remember new details or gain insights into your experiences past and present.

If you do some self-exploration using this book, I think it might help you become more aware of any unconscious influences on the choices you make day to day—and begin thinking about how you can change those influences. Then, you can free yourself to live a more fulfilling life according to a new story you have written consciously and that is pleasing to you and Spirit.

Preface

Twinkling stars danced in the clear black sky as the light of the full moon pooled around us, illuminating our ritual. I stood silently next to a shaman who had brought me here to a secluded spot high in the mountains so we could summon and engage helpful energies, including that of the jaguar. I hoped the shamanic work we planned to do tonight would awaken me to my spiritual nature and my connection to all of Creation—that it would help me to evolve into a new way of being and live with greater purpose and meaning. The theme of emotional constriction had been influencing my story for too long.

Before beginning, the shaman and I called on Source to assist and guide us. I had been warned that journeys like this one can prove very uncomfortable—even frightening. I knew I might feel myself falling off a cliff into a void of uncertainty. Even so, curiosity and eagerness outweighed any trepidation about what I might experience in the hours ahead of me. Who might I become as a result of this shamanic journey? How might my life change? As I stood in the sacred space the shaman and I had opened together, I surrendered to whatever Spirit might have in store for me. *Thy will be done.*

I could already feel myself entering a state of nonordinary reality: My rational mind with all its biases no longer had me in its grip. Everyday awareness gave way as I entered a realm beyond the limitations of my senses.

In my hand was a jaguar stone that held the energy of the sleek, big cat, infused in it hundreds of years before by a powerful medicine man. Something compelled me to look at the carved rock the shaman had given me to work with tonight. I felt its weight and its coolness in my palm. I sensed my soul opening up to the possibility of transformation.

Suddenly, the stone started to pulse and throb as if it were breathing. The jaguar eyes began to open and close.

"It's alive! It's alive!" I shouted to the shaman.

"Feed it! Feed it! Before it feeds on you!" he exclaimed.

Quickly, he pressed into my other hand my bottle filled with Florida water, used for blessings, ceremonies, and cleansings. "Feed it! Hurry!" he cried. Knowing what he meant, I took some of the liquid into my mouth and sprayed it out in a mist toward the jaguar before it could devour me.

Instinctively, I knew the beast hungered for me just as I had hungered for its essence—the alchemical potential I had yearned for as far back as I could remember. I waited, transfixed. Had my offering been accepted? Then, the jaguar's threat lifted like a fog and floated away into the night air. I felt the wet stone in my palm, sinister no more yet still alive, warm, and breathing. My heart still pounded, but I realized the danger had passed.

Feed it. So simple.

My soul had craved nourishment, yet I had denied it again and again. I had been taught that what I like to call "mythopoetic tendencies" are inconvenient and impractical. Life was hard work and responsibility, not a poem or a mystery—that's what I'd learned from my family and the midwestern culture in which I'd been raised. Conforming to these values, I suppressed my yearnings for many years.

It's said that the unseen world can exact a price on those who neglect their spiritual nature. What would be the cost of this stingy, starvation diet I'd inflicted on my long-suffering soul?

This much I knew: A sated jaguar has no reason to attack a human.

Feed it. Feed it well.

Thy will. My will. No more denial.

CHAPTER ONE

A Boy in the Woods

A spillover of families from Pittsburgh filled mostly modest houses along the suburban streets of Mount Lebanon, Pennsylvania. The town was edged by farms and untamed woodlands where as a small child, I spent many hours alone without supervision—and where I first discovered the secrets hidden behind the ordinary.

My father, Joe Greer, had moved my family here but had grown up in Kentucky's bluegrass country around Lexington. He had met my mother, Gene Crawford, at Northwestern University, where he worked as a waiter at her sorority house to help pay for his college expenses. Dad and Mom married shortly after they both graduated, and societal norms would shape their lives as a couple: His domain would be the world of work and hers would be the world of their home. Each would take easily to their new habitat—or so it seemed.

Dad became an executive at U.S. Steel, and by the time he and my mother moved to Mt. Lebanon, she was taking care of her first child: me. The local steel mills had employed many of the men in the area until World War II when their wives, daughters, and aunts took the places of many of them temporarily. Smoke spewed day and night as the mills turned molten metal into shining sheets that would be used to build airplanes. Not until after the war would the steel go into making cars again. In the meantime, there was plenty of work at the mill, and Dad's salary allowed him to provide his family with a modest home at the outer edge of a suburban neighborhood.

When I was not yet old enough for kindergarten, I would often leave behind my baby brother, Kirk, who was still in cloth diapers and in need of my mother's watchful eye, and wander off by myself to explore the town and countryside near my home. Neither of my parents realized that my sense of adventure bordered on the foolhardy.

Oblivious to the possibility of being hit by a speeding streetcar or falling onto the road below, I played on a dangerous trestle that spanned a nearby road. Confident I could navigate using only my homing sense, I didn't announce when I was going out for a walk that might take me far from our house. Since I always showed up in time for lunch or supper, my distracted mother apparently didn't worry about whether I was somewhere in the woods or upstairs in my room.

On one of my excursions, I decided to visit my maternal grandparents—Elsie and Carl-Carl, as I called them. The two of them lived a couple of miles away from us and offered a home filled with laughter, homemade cookies, and stories Elsie told that sparked my imagination. Drawing on my memory of the route my parents drove to their house, I made my way along the sidewalks of numerous streets without taking a wrong turn. Mom and Dad, who didn't know I had set off alone, began to search for me frantically as day slipped into evening and my chair at the kitchen table sat empty. Finally, they received a call from my grandmother, who reported that I had shown up at her door. When my father came to pick me up, his eyes blazed, and my own grew wide as I realized the consequences of taking this journey would be harsh. Impressed by my courage and successful navigation, my grandmother quickly pleaded, "Don't punish the boy, Joe." To my relief, he listened and calmed down rather than pull his belt out of his pants loops.

My father warned me never to venture off so far again—but I was already determined to forge my own path. My boundaries were made clear to me, but within them was much territory to traverse. I didn't know what I would find, but the call to adventure seemed to pull me forward into the unknown spaces far from the familiar.

Among my discoveries was a stream that ran through a valley about a mile away. Thickets lined its banks, and I picked my way through them to stand and watch the water leaping and lifting over stones in its path. The trunks of the trees were covered in lichen that to my eyes seemed like maps from an ancient world. The buckeyes yielded a prized harvest of nuts that I would collect and carry home.

During one particularly cold winter day, I trudged through the snow to forge a path through the bramble, hoping to discover any secrets the stream might reveal. When at last I reached it, I became fascinated by the contrast of black water against the white snow and stood in silent awe. Suddenly, a single glove floated by on the dark river. My imagination and excitement were triggered. What if a body followed? I waited expectantly, peering upstream as far as I could, but nothing else appeared. I would have to come back another day to see whether new mysteries would reveal themselves.

I also felt the urge to investigate the small farm that bordered the hillside at the end of our street. One day when I was five, I stepped onto the property and suddenly, a glowing, ethereal light appeared to encircle the apple tree in front of me. Time seemed to be suspended as my mind struggled to grasp what was happening. The tree, the sky, the land, and I were one, connected by the light. Was I alive? In a world of dreams? The light seemed to weave together everything in the field, including me, unifying all that existed. There was no separation, no aloneness. All were intermingled in a field of energy, every tree aware of its every leaf and every leaf aware of every insect, bird, and ray of sunlight. I had never felt anything like this before.

Then, just as abruptly, the light around the tree faded, and I was back in the ordinary world. Before me was just a tree like any other. The magic and sense of safety, comfort, and love had completely evaporated. Where had it gone? How could I get it to return?

I had no idea what had just happened or why, but to this day, I can recall that undeniable feeling of being interconnected with all living things. This awakening would be the first of many such experiences, whether invited or spontaneous, that would break through into my ordinary, everyday life and remind me that there is so much more to our existence than what the eye can see.

I would later come to understand that this had been my first view of the energetic, luminous light body that surrounds and connects everything. A shaman might say it marked the beginning of my shamanic education—my recognition that our world and the hidden realm of the transpersonal coexist alongside each other, separated only by a veil of perception that can be pulled aside if our consciousness shifts into a nonordinary state. Back then, I only knew that I wanted more of this magic to touch me, but I didn't know how to make that happen. Part of me must have recognized that time alone in the natural world would help me find it again—that sense of connection and oneness and the understanding that I belonged to something large and wondrous with potential yet to be discovered.

Two Very Different Houses

Our family seemed to mirror the wider conflict that raged around the globe in those very early years of my boyhood. Home was a place where meals were predictable, but moods were not. Times of peace were often punctuated by ferocious arguments between my parents—usually, after they had hosted parties where glasses were refilled again and again so people could loosen up for a few hours before returning to lives of conformity, duty, and worries about loved ones fighting overseas.

Often, I would lie in my bed at night as my parents entertained downstairs. Indistinguishable conversations, punctuated by laughter, drifted up the stairs. After the parties began, I would sometimes make an entrance so my parents could introduce me to their guests. Pungent perfume and cigarette smoke mingled with the smell of alcohol on the breath of the adults who greeted me with smiles, having been freed from the cares of the day. Later, as I began to drift into sleep, I would hear car engines starting and the guests driving off. Then, too often, the air of gaiety would disappear entirely as my parents would begin to quarrel. Their arguments would sometimes crescendo into shouting, doors slamming, and bitter accusations that I could hear even with my door closed. Was my mother unhappy? Was my father cruel or disrespectful? The substance of their disagreements is lost to time, but I have not forgotten that in those late hours, it was clear something was wrong between them. The next morning, the tension hung in the air like a cloud of stale cigarette smoke.

In hindsight, there were probably strong connections between their cocktails, my father's quick temper, and my mother's emotional withdrawal from my brother and me. She was home with us all day, but it was as if an invisible wall stood between her and her sons. Whether the bricks in that wall were made of depression, sadness, regret, or anger, I don't know. Too young to make sense of my parents' behavior, I felt my mother was present physically but not emotionally.

The sense of being disconnected from her made me appreciate even more the relaxed sense of security I felt at her parents' home nearby.

My grandparents provided all the warmth that my mother did not. My grandfather taught me woodworking, showing me his workshop and tools and patiently explaining how to use them. I also remember walking down a street in Mt. Lebanon with him when I was around seven years old. He greeted everyone we walked by, whether he knew them or not, and told me, "Carl, it doesn't cost a nickel to say hello." My grandfather expressed his friendliness and kindness easily, and I loved spending time with him.

At Christmas, my grandparents would gather us around the piano my aunts played and encourage my mother to sing "O Holy Night" in her beautiful contralto voice before we all joined in on more jolly carols like "Deck the Halls." The air was rich with the smell of gingerbread cookies, and I would awaken to a plate full of buttermilk pancakes, syrup, and bacon my grandmother had prepared. I suspected my mother felt overshadowed by her own mother's culinary abilities. Whenever my mom cooked liver with bacon and onions, a meal I loved when my grandmother made it, the meat was always tough. I kept my complaints to myself, however. I also made sure my mother didn't hear me tell my grandmother she was the best cook in the world. It was true, I was certain, and I proved it by cleaning my plate every time she served me a meal.

As I ate at my grandparents' house, my grandmother often transformed before me from cook to storyteller. She told the tale of Frank, her brother, who went missing one day only to be discovered alive at the bottom of an abandoned well, having fallen in while out walking across their farm. Her friend Effie Lemon's near-fatal adventure was an even more riveting story. Effie was determined to take a shortcut across a river, so she picked her way across the ties of the train track on the bridge high above its waters, only to be startled by the sound of a train barreling toward her. Realizing she couldn't outrun it or survive the fall if she jumped into the river below, Effie threw herself between the metal tracks just in the nick of time before the train roared over her, leaving her shaken and scared but unhurt.

My grandmother retold these tales many times, with great mastery and suspense. She may have embellished them a bit with each repetition, but no matter how familiar they were, I never tired of them and their themes of heroism and death-defying adventures.

She was marvelous at bringing to life fairy tales, too. Her narration of "The Goose Girl" by the Brothers Grimm, with its description of the princess's horse, Falada, having its head chopped off and nailed to a gate, made me cry. It wouldn't have occurred to my grandmother to protect me from such grisly details that were a part of fairy tales. I suspect she believed that a child has to learn about pain and ugliness through stories in books, all the better to prepare them for the world they would enter when they would leave home and go to school.

My emotional fortitude was challenged each year on Valentine's Day when schoolteachers would pass out the homemade valentines we children had placed in a box decorated with hearts cut out from red construction paper. Like my classmates, I would wait for that moment when I could breathe a sigh of relief as I heard my name called, allowing me to walk to the front of the class and pick up the proof that at least one other child wanted to "Be Mine." We all wondered who would end up with the greatest number of cards. If your pile was no match for the other kids', that was simply how it was. Maybe the practice was a bit more like *Lord of the Flies* than is healthy. Then again, it may have inoculated us somewhat against the heartache and betrayal everyone experiences at some point. I would become especially fond of one little girl, and then another, so the ritual of the elementary school Valentine's Day box was fraught with drama for me.

The midwestern culture I was raised in expected children to toughen up in preparation for a life that could be filled with difficulties from the sting of winter's chilly winds to the paucity of affection from those who felt that saying "I love you" was unnecessarily effusive. Many people, including my father's family, had roots in the frontier, where livestock could die of diseases and crops could be destroyed by weather, leaving parents and children to become desperate and hungry and ashamed of their dependence on others.

My father's family had risen from humble beginnings and hardship. As a high school athlete and scholar, my dad, Joe, was spoken of with respect by his neighbors in Paris, Kentucky, where his father was an optometrist who owned a small jewelry store and his mother was the daughter of a small-town doctor. If anyone doubted that my father had mettle, he proved it by winning a scholarship to Northwestern University and by being a good athlete who could handle the rigors of training and competition. He set the foundation for a solid career at a time when men who were diligent and self-sacrificing, unafraid to compete and willing to set aside their emotions to get the job done, could make enough money to feed the dream of supporting a family and secure their footing in the middle class.

Dad was very serious about his career but wasn't a workaholic. Whenever I was sick, I looked forward to him coming home after work to spend some time with me and ask me how I was feeling. I had many bouts of illness when I was little, taking my turn with measles, mumps, chickenpox—and even polio, according to some family stories. I contracted ear infections so serious and painful that the doctor punctured my eardrum on more than one occasion to release the fluid buildup, an excruciating procedure that, in theory, would offer relief from the pain. It seemed to have worked, but it was a big hurt for a little kid. At those times, I was much comforted by my dad's presence. I don't remember my mom's soothing touch when I was sick, however. I am sure she took care of me, but memories can be distorted and even erased by time, and I always felt more connected to my father than to my mother.

Illnesses simply had to be waited out, I realized. I would take whatever concoctions the doctor recommended after coming to our house to check on me. Then, I would crawl under my covers, hoping for relief. In my bed, I often distracted myself by reading stories that spoke to my imagination. I loved classic novels in comic book form— and I lost myself in the stories of Scaramouche and Captain Blood, identifying with these heroes whose swashbuckling adventures filled the pages of hardcover books and could hold me in their spell for many hours.

I also listened to radio shows that gave life to my sense of drama and mystery: *The Lone Ranger, The Green Hornet, The Squeaking Door, Suspense,* and *The Shadow.* My imagination created a vivid world for each story as I hung on the suspenseful endings to each episode, wondering if they could find a way out of their latest scrape. The next week, I felt a comforting sense of relief when their cleverness proved the key to surviving. Then, the action-filled plotline, as always, would weave its way to another exciting cliffhanger at the end of the hour. A few years later, I was able to watch some of the television shows made from the radio serials and was just a little disappointed that the images didn't match the ones in my mind when I was under the quilts and envisioning the Lone Ranger and Tonto fighting—and outwitting—the bad guys.

Hidden Undercurrents

My parents took us on some family vacations (mostly trips to visit relatives), and weekends were filled with yard work and repairs around the house. On his days off, Dad sometimes brought me to the ballpark to see the Pittsburgh Pirates play. Just like in the lyrics of the song, he would buy me some peanuts and Crackerjack—caramel corn and peanuts packaged with a small toy I couldn't dig out from the bottom of the box until I had eaten enough to uncover it and fish it out with my fingers.

At home, my father would often be in a jolly mood. I can remember him singing folk songs that my mother would join in on. "Go tell Aunt Rhody" he would sing, "the old gray goose is dead! Died in the morning with a pain in her head." He also sang a song about drinking corn liquor with lyrics about getting drunk, put in jail, and having no one to pay your bail. And both my parents sometimes sang:

> You'll take the high road
> And I'll take the low road
> And I'll be at Scotland before you
> For me and my true love
> Will never meet again
> On the bonny, bonny banks of Loch Lomond.

I also remember they sang the Yale "Whiffenpoof Song," toasting to the tables down at Mory's and the place where Louie dwells, and the dear old Temple Bar we love so well. My parents had no connection to Yale, but clearly, they enjoyed singing that drinking song together.

Looking back, I am struck by the fact that most of the songs I remember my parents singing were about drinking, loss, and death. However, they also sang "She'll be coming around the mountain when she comes" and the line about "we'll have chicken and dumplings when she comes." It's a song that reminds me of happy times with my extended family.

Afternoons at the ballpark, singing with his wife, and having cocktails after work followed by drinks with dinner all softened the edges of my father's irritability. Despite his sometimes-jovial nature, patience was not one of his strengths. Now and then, he would erupt into violent outbursts that swept away his rational self in a gust as strong as any produced by a furnace at the steel mill.

If my younger brother, Kirk, or I misbehaved or broke a rule, Dad's belt might come out. The sting from the whipping brought tears to my eyes, but I tried my best not to cry until my father had walked away to cool down. I learned that his rages simply had to run their course, and we tried to stay out of our father's way when he seemed to be near to a flare-up.

If my mother objected to his behavior when he was upset, I don't remember. But she was capable of out-of-control anger as well. One day, when Kirk was two, she pushed him into the front seat of our car as I stood watching from the edge of the driveway, confused about what I was seeing. My mother seemed very angry about something. She quickly climbed into the driver's seat, furiously turned the key, and hit the gas pedal. The car lurched backward, and Kirk, whose door must have been left open, tumbled out and hit the cement. He suffered no lasting damage, at least to his body, but the incident awakened me to the reality that both my parents could end up inadvertently hurting Kirk and me.

Whenever he punished me, my father would try to reconnect afterward, the softer tone in his voice making it clear that his dark mood had passed and he didn't want me to be upset with him for losing control. Once, when I was six, Dad started coming after me for some transgression. I dashed into the bathroom, locked the door, and threatened to scream out the open window unless he promised not to spank me. The shame of the neighbors possibly hearing all this somehow convinced him to calm down. He promised not to punish me and kept his word. I learned the power of using my wits to protect myself and made a mental note to remember that when he was raging, I needed to think fast and be as cool-headed as he was angry. I couldn't count on his self-control, so I would have to learn to tame the beast whenever I sensed it was stirring.

In June 1948, my father was promoted to a higher position at U.S. Steel. That required us to move to Gary, Indiana. By August, the moving boxes had been unpacked, and I was beginning to get to know the neighborhood kids who would be my classmates in the fall. Then, one morning, the pungent smell of gas awakened me and brought me downstairs to the kitchen, where I found my mother lying in her nightgown on the linoleum floor, unresponsive. Frightened, I hurried upstairs to tell my father. He leaped out of bed and ran down to the kitchen with me in tow—and saw that the gas stove was fully on but the pilot light was out.

Dad knelt beside my mother and felt for a pulse.

"She's gone."

My story starts, as do many shamanic stories and fairy tales, with a child facing the world essentially on his own. In a traditional culture, the elders might regard a child who consistently wanders alone into nature as receiving a call to the shaman's way. They might start such a child's training at an early age. But how does someone today hear a shamanic calling and respond to it if they do not live in a culture that has a tradition of shamanic training and lineages? How do you get the training you need? Where will you find opportunities? It's difficult, but not impossible, to have what you need show up for you—as my story shows. A Jungian would say that when we are ready, our unconscious will help us to see a path forward.

As you consider the questions about the themes in this chapter, I hope you'll begin to understand how your earliest experiences contributed to your story.

Questions for the Reader to Ponder

Earliest memories. As you remember your early years, what experiences stand out? What lessons did you learn as a result of those experiences? What decisions, if any, did you make having learned those lessons? How did those decisions affect your life from that point on? As you think about your earliest memories, do you see any connections to your life today? If so, what are they?

Solitude. Do you enjoy solitude, avoid it, or both, depending on circumstances and how you're feeling? What are the payoffs to being a loner or limiting the amount of interaction, or the amount of intimacy, you have with others? What are the downsides? If you rarely spend time alone or avoid doing so, why do you think that is? If you have positive memories of being in solitude, what were those experiences like?

Emotional volatility and anger. Do you feel in control of your anger, or do you fear what might happen if you felt it and expressed it? If you experienced emotional volatility, anger, and even violence in your home growing up, what lessons did you learn from your childhood about how to handle other people's anger? What lessons did you learn about handling your own anger? Did those lessons serve you in some ways but not others? Have you changed your ideas about anger and aggression since then, and, if so, how have your ideas changed?

Using activity to distract from difficult emotions. Do you anesthetize yourself by keeping busy and always striving to achieve? Does it work? What payoffs to this habit are there? Imagine achieving freedom from anger, grief, or fear without being as busy as you are and working as much as you do. What would that look like?

Nature as a healing, peaceful place. Do you seek out nature as a refuge and a place for restoration? Are there particular places in nature where you have felt that you are being healed simply by being in those places? What are they, and why do you think they have been such healing places for you? If you are not inclined to seek out nature as a refuge, how do you seek solace in your life? (You might want to consider spending time in nature to see how it affects your mood and sense of well-being and writing about your experience.)

CHAPTER TWO

A New Family

I've often wondered what would have happened to Dad, Kirk, and me if I hadn't been awakened by the smell of gas and decided to get out of bed and investigate. My dad was a smoker, and his habit was to light up a cigarette first thing in the morning before coming downstairs. If he had followed his usual routine, would enough gas have accumulated to blow up our house once he struck a match? And while the coroner's report listed the cause of death as "accidental," there was some speculation among the extended family that my mother had been depressed for a long time and had taken her own life that night. Just what happened and why has remained a mystery all these years.

In an eerie coincidence, when my mother was two, her father, who like my dad was employed by U.S. Steel, came home from work one day to his home in Gary and found his wife and daughter unconscious on the floor. He managed to call the police before he passed out. The whole family suffered from carbon monoxide poisoning, traced to a faulty furnace, and were rescued just in time. Could the story, passed around for years, have given my mother the idea about how to end her life when it became too painful for her to tolerate?

A Jungian would say that exploring these synchronicities, tied together through an invisible thread stretching across time, might reveal insights about my past that could help me understand what really happened to my mother. However, there is no way of knowing what was in her mind and heart that night. I was only eight, and all these decades later, I still ponder the complexity of the story.

I have only a few memories of those late summer days the year my mother died: the train ride to the funeral in Ladoga, Indiana, where her mother had grown up; the cloying scent of the flowers; and going to the gravesite. I distinctly recall telling my father in those days following her death, "I don't want anyone else in our family. I want it to be just you, me, and Kirk."

The mysteries around what had happened would be set aside. With my mother in the ground, we stopped talking about her death. We stopped talking about her life, too.

War Games

As I started to make friends, I could see right away that Glen Park, the suburb of Gary where my father had relocated us, was a rougher place than Mt. Lebanon. I didn't mind. To the neighborhood boys, a few scrapes and even broken bones weren't such a big deal. Their fearlessness was infectious. We would play tag on our bicycles, aiming to ram each other's bikes and knock them down onto the pavement.

I joined the other boys on my block in battling the boys who lived on another street. When playing soldiers fighting each other, we had an assortment of weapons: BB guns, pellet guns, slingshots, and crab apples on a stick embedded with cherry bombs that we hurled at our "enemies." It's a wonder there were no serious injuries. Our parents probably had no idea how violent our games were. I suspect we were saved by poor aim and a desire to do no real harm. We only wanted to stir up excitement and a little fear in the other kids.

On my own, I cut saplings to make bows and arrows that I shot off into the woods. My dad brought home some tin sheets that I fashioned into armor held together by leather straps. I was always making rough swords and loved using all kinds of knives, careful not to cut myself as I played at being a warrior.

With the war over and peace secured, the adults in Gary seemed content to live lives that may have lacked excitement but were comfortably predictable. The men in our neighborhood worked hard in the steel mill, and after the day shift was over, they went home and drank beer out of bottles while awaiting supper. I would sometimes see their babushka-wearing wives walk out their back doors to their chicken coops to gather eggs or find a hen to serve for Sunday dinner. With a sharp and efficient twist of the wrist, a woman would wring the chicken's neck before disappearing back into her house to begin the process of plucking and cooking.

Children were expected to work hard at school, to do what the teachers told them and not complain about grades or unfair treatment. Kids filtered out into the streets and woods when they got home and knew to make their way back from wherever they were when it grew dark at the end of the day. Following these simple rules meant the steady clockwork of life could carry on uninterrupted just like the shifts at the mill.

My home and family life still had some structure despite my dad's need to be at the office or traveling for work—sometimes remaining out of town overnight. After my mother died, we had a succession of house-keepers who cooked, cleaned, and stayed with Kirk and me whenever our dad was gone. None of the women Dad hired expressed much interest in us, and I saw them as little more than visitors in our house.

Dad was stoic when it came to grieving his wife, and my brother and I followed suit. In fact, I saw my father cry only once during those years we lived in Gary. It was during a visit to my grandparents in Mt. Lebanon, and he was standing in front of a mirror shaving. I was really mad at him for something and suddenly declared, "You're no good, like Mom said!" I wanted my words to hurt him as he had sometimes hurt me. I saw his eyes instantly well up with tears, and he quickly turned away from the mirror so I couldn't see his face.

My anger disappeared. Shame took its place. Why had I let myself lose control, as he had done with me and Kirk? I had never fully realized the power of words to inflict emotional pain. I don't recall apologizing, but I remember that afterward, the guilt clung to me for some time. I vowed I would be more careful and catch myself before I went so far again.

Other than his rare displays of softer emotions, my dad kept hidden what was going on inside him. He modeled to me to suppress my feelings, shut pain away, and be wary of loving or bonding with anyone too much. *The more you feel,* his behavior seemed to say, *the worse the loss. Watch out, because your emotions can run away from you. Remain in your head, thinking and expressing your opinions so people respect you and your wisdom. Don't open your heart too widely, don't love or feel too much, and you'll be safe.* Something in my father had changed, and his volatility seemed to give way to an acceptance of sorts. The lesson he was teaching me was clear: A man could become irritable, and even shout at others, as long as he didn't completely lose control.

"Want to buy some peat moss?"

With my father off at work and our housekeeper busy with chores and caring for my little brother, I could disappear for most of the day without anyone noticing or scolding me afterward. I yearned to be a part of something larger than myself that would give me a feeling of home, so I sought adventure outside my door.

The street we lived on in Gary ended at a railroad track, and even now, the sound of a train whistle still evokes a nostalgic feeling in me, reminding me of days when I felt free of all responsibilities. On one side of the road was a wooded area with dunes and a peat bog, and I spent hours playing there. In summer, I would join my friends in digging up the peat moss to sell for fertilizer to the neighbors who did gardening. I liked how it felt to do something that led to a clear reward.

As a nine- and ten-year-old, I would ride my bike miles from home to fish in Lake George nearby, or I'd take the bus to downtown Gary to the movies, roving wherever my curiosity took me. To earn money, I mowed lawns, raked leaves, and shoveled snow. During the Korean War, scrap paper was valuable, so I often walked down the street pulling my wagon and knocking on doors to ask people if I could haul away any old magazines and newspapers they didn't want. I transported the papers home by wagon and stored them in our garage next to our car until the stacks took up so much space that my father would call the paper recycler for me. Once the recycler had loaded up all my papers on the truck's open bed, I'd climb up and perch myself on top of the stacks, holding on as he drove off to a spot downtown where they would determine the paper's value. They would put me on the scale with my load, subtract my weight, and pay me—typically, around $20 to $30. That was a lot of cash for a small boy in those days. Earning money and having the choice to save it or spend it gave me a sense of independence.

Tippy, my dog, used to tag along with me on my rounds. One day, he raced across the street to be with me, got hit by a car, and was killed.

I was devastated as I brought him home in my wagon and later, buried him in my yard. I'd had other pets before—dogs, cats, and hamsters—but Tippy was special.

Each summer, I rode the bus to the county fair, hoping to win some prizes at the carnival games. I had plenty to spend throwing balls to knock down stacked tenpins or shooting a pellet at a target to win a prize. I had pretty good hand-eye coordination and usually brought home a teddy bear or a maybe a small painted plaster statue.

Often, I would head to the movie theater to watch comedies—Abbott and Costello films were favorites—or dramas such as *Drums Along the Mohawk, Captain Blood,* and *The Adventures of Robin Hood.* I remember one scene in *Captain Blood* where the heroine looks contemptuously at the captain and tells him, "You, sir, are a pirate and a thief." Not knowing all the obstacles he had overcome and the suffering he had experienced, she harshly misjudges him. I was deeply frustrated. Why couldn't she see him for the heroic, good man he was? Why condemn him just because he broke some rules and operated differently from everyone else? And why didn't he defend himself? By the end of the film, the captain's actions proved to the heroine that she had been wrong. I left the theater admiring how he had not pleaded with her to understand him or allowed his expression to betray how hurt he was. That's how I wanted to be when I grew up. True, Captain Blood's face may have flinched ever so slightly, but his pride was strong. As I rode the bus home, I replayed the scene in my mind, and it soon settled into a memory that would shape how I thought about vulnerability and a man's response to feeling misunderstood and having the woman he loves wound him.

"We put a TV in Carl's ear"

That first summer after my mother died, when I was nine, I experienced a period of enforced solitude because of a series of surgeries I underwent. Everything started while my family was on vacation at my grandparents' house in Mt. Lebanon. We were all gathered for a family barbecue, and for some reason, my five-year-old brother stuck a berry in my ear before I could stop him. It went in deep. Aunt Joan, my mother's sister, attempted to pry it out with a sharp pencil. That didn't work, so later in the evening, she took me to a doctor, Dr. Black, who had only recently graduated from medical school.

He tried to remove the berry with a set of instruments that looked like the picks used to strip walnuts from their shells. As I yelped, he ripped out part of my ear canal and eardrum and damaged some of the tiny bones in my middle ear known as the hammer, anvil, and stirrup. I've experienced pain in my life, including multiple kidney stones, but this was more excruciating than anything I've ever suffered. The next day, my father brought me to an ear specialist, who had to operate to clear blood clots. Soon afterward, I developed a life-threatening infection in that ear. It took so long to recuperate that I missed the first months of fourth grade—and when the infection finally cleared, they found the berry was still wedged deep into my ear's canal, requiring another surgery to remove it.

Unfortunately, future operations many years later never were able to restore my hearing—there was simply too much damage. A surgeon did manage to close the hole in the eardrum and reduce my risk of serious effects like meningitis. The medical bills for my ear surgeries put a strain on the family finances, keeping us from buying a television for a while. We used to joke that Kirk had put a TV in my ear. In social situations even today, I position myself for better hearing so I don't miss out on conversations. As I've grown older, my hearing in my good ear has deteriorated. I'd like to think that straining to hear has helped me become a better listener in some situations.

During my long convalescence at home as a child, I was mostly alone and devoured books as I always had. Mountain men like Jim Bridger and Jedediah Smith intrigued me, and I read about Geronimo and Sitting Bull and tribes like the Sioux, Cheyenne, Comanche, and Apache. I was fascinated by their courage, strength, resourcefulness, and ability to live off the land. The books planted in me a deep respect for the heroes' traditional way of life and their close relationship with nature. The stories echoed the way I felt about nature when I was deep in the woods, walking across a field, or sitting by a lake.

I didn't realize how much impact these stories would have on me until much later when I started on a shamanic path and began to realize how early the seeds for my shamanic explorations had been planted. Someday, I would come to work with North and South American shamans and recapture that sense of connection to something vast and extraordinary. My shamanic adventures would prove to be as exciting as those I vicariously enjoyed as a boy reading the tales of heroes found in books.

Manners Don't Buy Affection

When I was living in Gary, my father began dating a woman who was employed at U.S. Steel in Pittsburgh. He probably met her through her brother, John, who worked with my father at the nearby mill. While I was recuperating at home from the latest assault to my ear, Dad handed me a book on dogs that I paged through as he explained it came from a friend of his who worked at U.S. Steel—a nice lady named Mary Anne. I thought it was kind of this female stranger to give me a get-well gift but didn't understand why she would go out of her way like that. Soon afterward, I met her for the first time—a woman in her forties with short gray hair who was wearing a plain dress. Mary Anne seemed neither hot nor cold emotionally—polite, but aloof.

Looking back, I think she and my dad had dated for a few months at this point. When soon afterward he announced that the two of them were getting married and Mary Anne would move into our Gary home, I felt unsettled. I sensed life as I knew it would never be the same.

I started to call Mary Anne "Mom" because I felt I should, but the name didn't seem to fit. Even so, I tried to be nice to her since she was my new mother.

Although she showered affection on her niece and nephew, Jan and Elliot, Mary Anne was different with Kirk and me. She seemed to have had no idea how to raise two energetic boys and emphasized rules and decorum over warmth and caring. Whenever our family would eat a meal together, she would cut off any conversation between Kirk and me with a curt rebuke such as, "Let's not talk about school at the dinner table." My brother and I were bewildered. What else were two boys supposed to discuss? Mary Anne wanted to talk about what her relatives were doing—who married whom and what job someone had taken. I hadn't met these people and her tales lacked drama or adventure, so I listened with feigned interest and let my mind wander.

She had no questions for Kirk and me, so family dinners centered on the task of eating and politely listening, nothing more.

At one point when her mother was visiting us, I asked Mary Anne, "Do you think you'll ever love Kirk and me as much as you love Jan and Elliot?" I can still remember the answer: "Maybe if you mind your manners and do what you're told." Years later, my father told me that his mother had said of Mary Anne, "She is good with manners, but I wish she would be warmer toward the boys."

There was very little gaiety in our house after Mary Anne arrived, and if she became upset with my father, she would become silent and leave the room. Later, she would act as if nothing had happened. The emotional temperature of our home was set at awkward, making it difficult for me to feel any connection to her.

In retrospect, I feel compassion for Mary Anne. Maybe she didn't intend to come across to me and my brother as withholding, disinterested, and cold and was simply following her mother's example of formality. Also, Mary Anne may have been struggling with a new role she never expected to find herself in. She was in her forties and back then, many women were married by their early twenties and starting families before they turned thirty. With no prior mothering experience, Mary Anne became part of a family system that had predated her inclusion by many years. Where did she fit into this family of males with their interests in sports and the outdoors?

Having a stepmother who was emotionally closed off, I lived with an unsettled feeling whenever I was in my family's house. I am grateful that even though I didn't get maternal nurturing from Mary Anne, I got it from my grandmother.

After Mary Anne, my dad, Kirk, and I had lived together in Gary for a year, my dad was promoted again, and we moved back to Mt. Lebanon. Although we once more lived close to my maternal grandparents and had seen them often when my mother was alive and in the months after her death, the visits I had enjoyed so much tapered off because Mary Anne was uncomfortable around my late mother's family. Even Christmastime lost much of its magic as the wrapped packages under the tree yielded socks and shirts instead of Erector sets and toy water guns. Giving and receiving gifts became a joyless chore. Years later, when I became an analyst, I worked with clients who told similar stories, and I could strongly empathize with them. It took me a long time to get over having mixed emotions about giving and receiving presents—and the forced enthusiasm the ritual often seems to require. The practice also brought up feelings that what I had received came with a price I would have to pay to balance the emotional books between the gift giver and me.

During Dad's marriage to Mary Anne, we only went on one family vacation other than visiting relatives—a week on the Jersey Shore. I caught a flounder, and Mary Anne cooked it for dinner. It wasn't the most exciting or luxurious vacation—the cabin we rented was infested with bugs. But I remember this trip as being filled with family fun, one of few such memories I have.

On the whole, rules, unspoken but understood, seemed to constrict me. It would take many years for me to open my heart more fully and free it from the restrictions created by living in a home where practicality triumphed over sentiment. The emotional nourishment I craved would have to be found elsewhere—and my independence gave me the courage and motivation to seek it out.

I recognized that my skills, hard work, and willingness to focus on my goals could pay off in a tangible way. That gave me a sense of satisfaction, security, and pride. I had adventures that boys with a different family situation would probably be denied, and that taste of independence was often intoxicating. I wanted more! Experiencing self-reliance, earning money through odd jobs, and spending time alone in the woods were all good training for someone who wanted to make his own way in the world and maybe, someday, live by his own rules rather than someone else's.

Although I didn't have any clear ambitions about what I wanted to be when I grew up, I assumed that my job would allow me to provide a home and stability to a family of my own someday. The script had been written, and the men around me lived according to its dictates—at least, the men I looked up to. Mine was a simple dream and not one I consciously crafted as I thought about my future. Only many years later would I come to realize how limited my capacity for dreaming was back then. I would have to experience more heartache and loss, and more battles would have to be fought before my courage to take a different road would arise.

When I was a child, the radio programs I listened to, the movies I saw, and the books I read about heroes gave me a hunger for adventure and a yearning to explore the larger world. According to most mythologies, following the hero's path is necessary to grow beyond childhood and become an adult. That means going out into the world and encountering foes, hardships, and experiences beyond our imagining that expand our understanding of others and help us discover qualities and skills we didn't know we had.

As you remember your childhood, you might want to think about why certain memories stay with you. Some will be memories of activities that were common for you, such as my memory of gathering old newspapers and magazines in my wagon and selling them to the scrap dealer for pocket money. Others will be memories of specific incidents that made an impression on you. I will never forget seeing my dad's image in a mirror as he began to cry, for example, because he almost never cried and because it taught me the power of words to hurt others. I also remember a line from a movie that captured a female character's misunderstanding of the fictional adventurous hero, Captain Blood, although many scenes from that movie have faded from my memory. If you remember a specific scene from your childhood that seems to be random, you might want to explore your memory more closely. Maybe it has more meaning for you than you realize.

Looking at photographs or videos of yourself in your youth, or listening to recordings that someone might have made of your voice and reading any journals or diaries you might have kept, can help you examine your memories. Questioning how you remember events might give you insights you might otherwise not have had. You might also find yourself remembering long-forgotten details that did not get integrated into the narrative you have held on to. Rediscovering them can be eye-opening.

Questions for the Reader to Ponder

Home and nurturance. What do you remember about being at home as a child? Was it a nurturing place? Why or why not? If your home was not a nurturing place, what did you do to experience a sense of nurturance? Do you feel nurtured in your life today? Why or why not? What do you do to generate that feeling of being loved and cared for? Did you, as I did, need kindness, believe you couldn't get it, and convince yourself that you could live without it? If so, how has that worked for you? If you would like to have more kindness in your life, how could you receive more of it? Would expressing kindness toward others help you? Do you have the ability to express kindness easily? Why or why not?

Growing up and role models. What did you believe you had to do or be in order to be considered "good" when you were a child? What did you think you would have to do to be considered a "good" man or woman as an adult? Were there any kids or adults you looked up to as role models? What did you admire about them? Did you have negative role models who helped you see what you didn't want to do or be? Do you still look at those role models as "bad" or "failures" or can you now see them in a different light?

Money. What were your earliest experiences of making or having money, or both? What did you spend your money on? What lessons did your experiences of earning, having, or spending money teach you? Did they contradict what your parents told you about earning, managing, spending, and giving away money? What connections do you see between those childhood experiences of money and your relationship to money today?

Giving and receiving gifts. Are you comfortable receiving gifts? If not, what about it makes you uncomfortable? Do you feel obligated to the giver after you've received gifts? Do you enjoy giving gifts? Why or why not? Do you feel you're looking for payoffs when you give gifts? What are those payoffs? Would you like to change the habits or rituals of giving and receiving gifts in your family? If you did, what would that look like?

Being listened to. As a child, did you have someone in your life that you felt truly listened to you? What did this person teach you about listening to others? Did you have someone significant in your life you wished would listen to you but who seemed to not value your opinions and ideas? If so, how did you compensate for not feeling that this person cared to listen to what you had to say?

Myths and stories. What fictional or family stories you heard as a child inspired you in some way? Do you remember wanting to be, meet, or befriend a fictional character? Who was it, and why did you want to interact with this character? What did you admire about these characters you looked up to as a child? Did you do anything to be more like these characters? As you look back at the stories you loved as a child that helped shape your ideas, what if anything do you see now that you didn't see then?

CHAPTER THREE

Keeping My Own Counsel

Rocks, logs, and branches from saplings I had chopped off with my knife and hatchet redirected the waters of the stream to form a large pool. I stocked it with fish caught in a pond a few miles away, transported to my private sanctuary by a bucket that I hung off my bike's handlebars. Alone at this spot near my home in Mt. Lebanon, I found any tension I had drained out of me into the earth as I sat and watched the slowly drifting clouds reflected on the surface of the water. I was in middle school now, and the shift into adulthood was beginning. Spending time in nature helped me feel connected to something larger than myself, something that was there long before me and would be there long after I had moved on.

Echoes of That Terrible Summer

My home was somewhat more peaceful than it had been when I was very young, even though my father continued to lose his patience and temper on occasion. His fights with Mary Anne involved hurt feelings, silences, and withdrawals. It was an uncomfortable atmosphere to grow up in.

Dad's promotion to general manager of production planning at U.S. Steel had brought us back to Mt. Lebanon the summer before I entered sixth grade. Our three-bedroom house had a big backyard, and at the point farthest from the back door were raspberry and gooseberry bushes intermingled with wild strawberry plants. They yielded sweet fruits I could pop in my mouth before returning to play football with my friends on the grass. The new neighborhood was more middle class than our neighborhood back in Indiana: There were no chicken coops in anyone's backyard. And while I didn't reconnect with any of the kids I had known a few years back, making new friends seemed easy enough.

On the surface, the move didn't upset me, but Dad was traveling out of state a lot and often was absent all week long. That summer was an echo of the summer I lost my mother, with the move and starting a new school and getting used to a new house. My dad's presence had been stabilizing for me, and I was affected by his being gone more than I realized.

Soon after we arrived in Mt. Lebanon, I started to be jolted out of sleep at night by the sensation of my heart racing and my lungs gasping for breath. It was frightening, and I didn't know what to do. When the spell passed, I felt embarrassed. I didn't want to tell my dad about it. I remember one night after it had happened again, I was trying as hard as I could to wait for my anxiety to subside so I could go to sleep without bothering my father. Finally, I succumbed to phoning the house where my dad and Mary Anne were attending a party. I explained what happened and asked them to come home, which they did.

My father seemed to have compassion for my situation—he didn't scold or lecture me—but he also didn't have any answers for why I was having what I now know were panic attacks. On my own, I discovered that lying next to my seven-year-old brother helped me fall asleep and sleep soundly. And spending time in the woods felt healing. I was finding ways to deal with my anxiety. After a month or so, my panic attacks disappeared, never to return, and I was sleeping alone in my own bed again.

Snakes, Frogs, and Sports

Although I grew up in the suburbs, I feel equally at home in small towns and even rural areas, which I believe has helped me relate to the wide variety of people I have met, befriended, treated in therapy, or worked with in my life. Every summer, we visited my father's extended family in Paris, Kentucky, which had a population of about 7,000 when I was growing up. My cousins and their friends took to the outdoors as I did, disappearing from their house for hours. We would wake up to the sound of a rooster crowing, eat breakfast, and go out to play, leaving our shoes and socks indoors. We ran around in the woods and looked for snakes in nearby creeks.

A few times, my Uncle George woke me up in the middle of the night at my grandparents' house to go frog gigging. We went out with a burlap sack, a knife, a three-pronged spear, and a flashlight to a pond nearby, following the sounds of frogs calling to each other. "Shine the light right into their eyes, and they'll be too stunned to move," my uncle instructed, and sure enough, the frogs were dazed by the brightness. We killed them with the spear, cut off their legs, which we then threw into our sack, and tossed their bodies aside. Back at my grandparents' house, we would fry the frogs' legs for breakfast.

Time spent in Kentucky getting to better know my cousins and listening to my aunts, uncles, and grandparents tell stories about their everyday lives provided emotional color and vibrancy that contrasted with what I typically experienced back home. It helped me to see that the emotional connection I yearned for with my dad and Mary Anne could be found elsewhere.

While summers meant visits to our relatives, long hot days riding my bike, and hanging out with neighborhood kids, from sixth grade through high school, my school year was defined by sports seasons. In the fall, I played football starting in sixth grade and ending in ninth—but later switched to cross-country when I realized my medium-sized, 140-pound frame, inherited from Dad, was too small to allow me to compete in Western Pennsylvania high school football. Winter was basketball season, and, in the spring, I ran the mile and the half-mile on the track team. While many parents attended their sons' or daughters' sporting events, my dad and Mary Anne never came to any of my games or meets—even the state championship I competed in.

Playing sports appealed to me because I was motivated by competition. I like to win. I liked seeing my hard work pay off—and if I lost, I would push myself to do better next time and usually did.

"Congratulations to a real fisherman"

When I was five or six, I fell in love—with fishing. I made my first catch while with my grandfather at a man-made lake near Pittsburgh. The seeds were sown for a lifelong hobby of sitting in a boat or standing on a shoreline enjoying nature and the outdoors while waiting for a fish to take my bait.

Whenever I'm fishing, I enter the space of the unknown, trusting that deep below the ripples of the water are plenty of fish ready to bite. Out in a boat, I immerse myself in the moment, fully present, my senses alert to the sounds around me and the sunlight on my skin. I feel close to Source. As I cast my lure into a lake and reel it in slowly, trying to sense whether the fish are active, I reconnect to the rhythms of the earth, the plants and animals, and the seasons. Time seems to move more slowly. Then, after reeling in a bass, walleye, or northern pike, even if it is big enough to keep, I almost always release it back to the water after unhooking it. My joy isn't in the prize as much as it is in the experience of the calming ritual and the excitement of landing a fish.

Most summers during high school, I would spend a week or so up at my grandparents' cottage by Deer Lake, Pennsylvania, and take the rowboat out by myself for hours. If there was a day when I was initiated into the world of fishermen and fisherwomen, it was back when I was a sophomore, staying just with my grandfather at Deer Lake. One evening, I caught several good-sized largemouth bass, and when I was reeling in the largest one, I exclaimed, "Oh, Lordy!" My grandfather said, "Carl, don't swear!" To him, I had just taken the lord's name in vain! The next morning at dawn, when I was heading out to the lake to fish, I spotted on the dining room table some of my grandfather's prized fishing gear with a note alongside it that said, "Congratulations to a real fisherman. This gear is yours." It was the best present he ever gave me.

A Sense of Connection and Belonging

Some evenings after I came home late from sports practice in my preteen or teenage years, I would join my father and Mary Anne in the living room, where they liked to sit and smoke, one on either side of the fireplace. Our conversations skimmed the surface of what was happening with all of us. We talked without emotionally engaging each other and then would fall into silence. After that, I was off to do my homework or listen to some records in my room.

I socialized with the kids at school and in the neighborhood, became a Boy Scout, and joined the Beverly Heights United Presbyterian

Church, where our troop held its meetings, even though my father and Mary Anne had joined a different Protestant congregation. My church offered teen programs and events, and I felt a sense of belonging whenever I went there or joined my peers to socialize or do service projects. I remember delivering Christmas gifts to kids from the poorest areas of Pittsburgh and singing Christmas carols to older people in nursing homes, experiences that helped me feel a sense of gratitude for my own good fortune and made an indelible impression on me about the importance of helping others in your community.

The low-income areas of Pittsburgh were like parts of my old neighborhood in Gary—the houses were small and run down, crowded with family members. Many people had come up from the South to work in the mills, leaving behind the coal mining life for a life that was hard, yes, but didn't lead to early death from mining accidents or black lung disease. Even so, many of the local men and women, working class or wealthy or in between, smoked. Just about everywhere, people would casually light up: in public buildings, workplaces, and even cars that had the windows rolled up to keep the heat in during the winter. The surgeon general had yet to issue a warning about the dangers of smoking. People saw it as a relaxing habit, and my guess is that at least some believed the old cigarette advertisements that claimed smoking helped with circulation or digestion. Smoking was as American as apple pie, football, and church on Sundays.

I didn't smoke—but I loved apple pie and football and went to church almost every Sunday. Once, my church group of teens traveled together to an arena to see Billy Graham speak. He was the superstar preacher of the day, and we had all watched him on television, so our excitement ran high. I quickly became caught up in the energy and spirit of the event as he worked the crowd into a crescendo with his passionate words and his call for us to repent and receive Jesus's forgiveness. Some made their way into the aisle and briskly walked up to the front for the altar call, ready to declare their dedication to Christ.

The altar call was a ritual I was familiar with through my grandparents in Kentucky, who belonged to a Baptist church. In fact, I had answered the call when attending church with them. That day when

Billy Graham spoke, I felt embraced by a church filled with the spirit of love.

I liked singing the hymns I came to know well—although I preferred the livelier Baptist ones I sang at my grandparents' church in Kentucky to the more sedate ones we sang in my own. My main interest in Christianity, however, was that I hoped it would answer the bigger philosophical questions I had, such as how much does faith count when it comes to salvation? And what if that faith isn't accompanied by works that reflect Christian values?

I believe in Christ's divinity and his messages, such as following the Golden Rule, helping those less fortunate, and being nonjudgmental and forgiving. I never became caught up in the conflicts between Christianity and other religions. Such conflicts, and self-righteousness, seem to me to miss the point of Jesus's messages regarding love, compassion, generosity, gratitude, and kindness.

Since those days, I have attended and belonged to different Protestant churches and for many years, I have attended Catholic services with my wife. Even so, my relationship to Spirit is increasingly about having a reciprocal relationship with the all-loving force that I sometimes call Source, acknowledging that ultimately, "thy will be done"—and realizing I'm just one small participant in a dance much larger than myself. Taking communion or singing the doxology feels familiar and comforting to me. It also gives me a sense of belonging—to a community of people who recognize and honor the larger spiritual forces that I honor as well.

But now I also try to experience or create rituals drawn from other traditions, some taught to me by elders who wanted to share their ways with people respectful of their spiritual beliefs. Some might be puzzled by how I blend metaphors, teachings, and practices from seemingly contradictory wisdom traditions. But if I and the apple tree in the farmer's field were one, with no separation, then why should I separate myself from others through embracing this and not that? Religion and church, for me, are about finding connections with other people and with God and nature—and recapturing that feeling of oneness that I had felt as a child in the farmer's field.

"I guess we'll just have to postpone our fight"

Back in the 1950s when I was in middle school and high school, I had no idea how big the world was and how much there was to explore and learn. I knew little about how other people lived, what challenges they faced, or what their biggest concerns were. Television was a box in the living room with five or six channels that signed off late in the evening, and phones could not take messages or be taken any farther than the cord to the wall could stretch. Communication was mostly face-to-face and through words, not screens or devices. I had some exposure to what lay outside the confines of Mt. Lebanon, but even those sources were limited. What was invisible to me—racism, sexism, suffering in impoverished places—wasn't present in my imagination either. I only knew what I knew, and my awareness and understanding of national and international events were very limited.

Overall, my suburban life in the Midwest of the 1950s seemed relatively tranquil. It's fair to say I lived in a bubble. There wasn't much to pierce it, no harsh realities crashing through beyond what we read in the newspapers or heard about on the TV news. In Mt. Lebanon, there wasn't a lot of juvenile delinquency or boys and girls "getting into trouble." I probably would have defined "getting into trouble" as being sent to the principal's office, something I never experienced even though I got into some fights in junior high and high school.

Although I was a daydreamer, I had an aggressive and even somewhat violent side that came out on occasion. If someone insulted me, I was not going to back down and be called a coward. I remember once in the seventh grade after another boy and I exchanged words, we felt compelled to fight after school. The two of us went searching for a good spot to have our fistfight as a crowd of our classmates followed us, excited about their chance to see us go at each other. Suspicious about what was happening, a teacher interrupted us and stopped us from following through on our plan. The next day, the other kids had forgotten all about the fight, and I think the other guy and I were both relieved that no one mentioned it.

I learned from fights I was in that the worried anticipation beforehand takes a lot of energy. The fight itself was not as bad as the dread I felt thinking about how well I would handle myself in the encounter. It's said that if we are looking at a pack of worries down the road, we could spend a lot of time looking at them, but many of the situations we fear might not show up—or they might be very different when we do meet up with them.

That middle school fight was the only one I got out of. A couple of times in high school, I overreacted violently to some slights and actually started fights in school. Both happened in my English class. The first time, another student purposely poked a pencil into my leg, breaking off the tip. I grabbed him, slammed him into the blackboard, and started beating his head against it. My teacher shouted at me to stop, and I did, but she only told us to take our seats, so there were no real consequences. Another time, the school tough guy purposely jostled me, and I popped up from my seat and slammed him hard against the wall. My teacher stopped us from fighting further, and that was the end of it—no trip to the principal's office, no forms to fill out, detention, or suspension. My parents probably never knew it happened because nothing more came of it. Fights in the school buildings were mostly unheard of, and maybe the teacher never reported me because she was too shocked to know what to do.

The other fights I had were outside of school and involved me and the person I was going to fight going someplace relatively private, accompanied by lots of kids who would egg us on. We would fight until one of us won, and then we would go home to take care of our wounds and bruises.

I learned at a young age to try to control my rage and was generally successful. I wasn't always able to remain cool-headed, however. Over the years, sports, martial arts, and spending time in nature have helped me manage my aggression.

The warrior in me helped me stand up to my father, particularly in defense of my younger brother, Kirk, when Dad was being impatient. There were times when I'd find him berating Kirk for something, and I'd say, "Dad, quit being so hard on him." Even if my father turned his anger on me, at least he was leaving my younger brother alone.

A defining moment came one day when my dad and I were arguing heatedly, almost coming to blows. He shouted, "Carl, you'll never be as tough as me!" I was fourteen or fifteen at the time and had a sudden insight into why he said that: Despite his protestation, if he felt compelled to say those words, he must really think of me as tough! It was a coming-of-age moment when I knew I had earned his respect as a man who could stand up for himself and challenge others.

Mythopoetic Me

Alongside that warrior aspect of myself was a mythopoetic aspect that I had discovered as a child reading adventure stories and imagining myself as a swashbuckling and romantic hero. Mythopoetic me is the self that is connected to my spiritual, soulful nature, to a sense of mystery and awe at the existential questions about the human experience. At school, I was a good student and liked to read historical novels and imagine what it would have been like to live in a different time and place. I also enjoyed and memorized a few poems, and I wrote a couple for my honors English class that ended up being published in an anthology. One was about the tranquility of fishing in the early morning on a still lake with the mist lifting, frogs croaking, and fish jumping; the other was about the pain and the joy of long-distance running.

While that English class was probably the most memorable of my high school career, I didn't envision myself becoming a writer, storyteller, or poet. Poems and music often stirred my emotions, but creating art outside of what I had to do for school assignments wasn't on my agenda.

Three other boys and I had our own singing group, whose name expressed our talent, skill, and seriousness about our craft: the Inepts. But it was fun to practice harmonizing and, occasionally, perform. At our senior dance, the Inepts performed their swan song: "Book of Love" by the Monotones, and afterward, a classmate came up to me and said, "That sounded great, Carl. Really."

It was the tough guy I had slammed against the blackboard.

A Familiar Path

The socialization I experienced at school and church allowed me to build a life outside my family, with friends I could confide in, including girls, some of whom I dated. High school also offered me opportunities to show I could play by the rules, study and do my homework, and be rewarded with mostly As. I knew that would take me to any college I chose and, I hoped, a good job in industry after that. I didn't aspire to something different, although part of me wondered what else might be out there. Living in Pennsylvania suited me, and the steel industry offered a working man a sense of security whether he was in the union and employed at a mill or a white-collar worker with an office and perhaps a company car.

The summer after my junior year, I first sampled the grown-up world of work. My father arranged for me to have a job at U.S. Steel's Homestead Works, where I was placed in the engineering department. I proved reliable as I delivered and filed papers, and I got along with all the men and the few women I interacted with. Every week or so, a runner would come around to see if anyone wanted to play the numbers for fifty cents—which bought you one guess at what the last three digits in the volume on the New York Stock Exchange would be at closing. Playing the numbers was a small ritual that made me feel that I was part of the world of working adults, so I usually bought a guess. I never won a dime.

That same summer, I took Pat, a girl who had been in my honors English class, on our first date. We went to Kennywood Park (an amusement park) and rode the rides, including the rollercoaster. I won some prizes for Pat by shooting baskets and throwing balls. After that, we continued dating through our senior year and went to dances, movies, and parties, sometimes on our own and sometimes with other couples.

When Pat decided to go to college in Philadelphia, I decided to go to Lehigh University—an all-male college an hour away in Bethlehem, Pennsylvania. I thought this would allow us to keep our relationship going. Plus, Lehigh had a good program in metallurgical engineering, which was my intended major.

As it turned out, Pat and I broke up, and it was too late for me to attend any other colleges where I had been accepted. Even so, I was content with my choice of where to go to school.

I graduated high school and turned eighteen in the same month, and with a very structured life ahead of me for the next few years, I was now focused on one particular goal: to feed my soul's craving for adventure before heading off to Lehigh in the fall.

Being outdoors in the woods or fishing on a lake made me feel relaxed, invigorated, and connected to my spirituality and to nature. This was important for me given that my home did not feel like a nurturing place. Even as I made friends and became more involved in community activities, I valued my independence and solitude—which is not the case for everyone.

I also was attracted to competitive sports, which gave me an outlet for my aggression and opportunities for competing with others along with clear, mostly predictable results for my efforts.

I remember participating in fights as a boy and having panic attacks when my father was on the road—and how the adults around me responded to both. I wasn't made to feel ashamed of what I can now see were emotional, primitive reactions to troubling or even traumatic experiences. When identifying your story, it can be easy to overlook or forget what your memories are tied to, whether it's a pattern of feeling a certain way in your body (out of control, for example), a pattern of how adults in your life responded to you, or something else.

As you look back at your own childhood and teenage years, you might want to think about how you handled your anger or aggression, what replenished you, what gave you opportunities to socialize or be by yourself, and what gave you a sense of familiarity, comfort, and control.

Questions for the Reader to Ponder

Fighting and conflict. Have you had verbal or physical fights in your life? How did you feel before such encounters, during them, and afterward? What, if any, fights, physical or verbal, do you remember from your childhood and teen years, whether you were directly involved in them or simply observing them? What lessons did they teach you about conflict? For example, do you tend to stand up for yourself and for others? If not, how could you learn to do so?

Competition. What, if anything, do you like about being in competition with others? Are there any types of competition you don't like and, if so, why? If you don't generally enjoy competing with others, what motivates you to develop new skills or greater mastery in areas you'd like to improve in?

Hard work and perseverance. Have hard work and perseverance paid off for you? If you haven't worked hard, or have a pattern of giving up too quickly, how has that habit affected you? If you would like to change your patterns regarding hard work and perseverance, what do you think would change in your life if you were to do so?

Replenishing your soul. Have you ever felt you have been neglecting your soul—your essential self? What was going on at the time? What choices did you make that helped you feel replenished and connected to Spirit and your soul? Are you currently living a life that doesn't feed your soul? If so, how can you feed your soul, even in small ways?

CHAPTER FOUR

Westward Bound

"Wanted: young men and women between the ages of 18–25 to sell professional publications. Willingness to travel a must, so Go West, young man!"

The ad didn't actually say all of that, but it felt as if it did. It included an impressive weekly figure that could be earned, and I was young enough not to question whether it was a realistic one. The promise of travel triggered my sense of adventure.

The summer I graduated from high school and turned eighteen, I was eager to get outdoors and work. Originally, I'd thought I would be able to find employment harvesting tobacco or bluegrass in Kentucky but soon discovered it was the wrong time of year to be looking for that type of work. With my family gathered around my grandparents' breakfast table in Paris, I decided to check the morning newspaper's job listings, saw the ad for selling professional periodicals, and made up my mind to apply. After breakfast, I took a bus to Lexington to be interviewed at the hotel whose address had been included in the notice. They hired me, and later that day, I boarded a bus to Louisville, where they'd told me training would begin and I would be put up overnight. I didn't ask many questions and simply set off with my suitcase in hand.

Around 9 p.m., I stepped out of the bus into the soggy, sweltering air. I walked down a dimly lit street to my destination, the Colonial Hotel, a decaying building whose best years were clearly in the distant past. Inside, a heavyset man sweating profusely through his dirty, sleeveless undershirt described the job I'd been hired for. I discovered that instead of selling periodicals to professionals—I had been thinking doctors, lawyers, and businessmen—I would be peddling subscriptions to *Life*, *McCall's*, and other common magazines door to door. I was told I would sleep at the Colonial Hotel that night and breakfast would be provided the next morning. There was no need to worry about paying for meals after that, I assumed, because the dollars would be rolling in quickly.

I heard what I wanted to believe.

I saw several people in the hotel's public areas who seemed to be disfigured, sweaty, and dressed very casually—and in some cases, speaking a foreign language I didn't recognize, which I found curious. I rarely heard other languages back in Pennsylvania and didn't recognize the one they were speaking. "These folks are the regular crew," the man I was talking to explained. "You can learn a lot from them." I soon discovered that the crew members who were disfigured would commonly use their impairments to wring pity out of their customers and elicit sympathy sales. Some were immigrants who had fled the 1956 Hungarian uprising; some had been injured during the fighting. Presenting themselves as poor refugees—from Hungary or elsewhere—helped them to make sales, too.

I couldn't blame the immigrants and disabled people for making the best of their circumstances. But how was I, a healthy, young American teen, going to convince people to commit to subscribing to magazines they could purchase at any newsstand? What story could I tell that was honest but effective? And did I really want to manipulate prospective customers' emotions just to make a buck? The optimism that had propelled me to eagerly pack my suitcase back at my grandparents' place was wilting. I figured I might as well stay the night and give the job a try for a day or two, even if I didn't think it would work out. I hadn't any other plans.

I climbed the stairs to my assigned room, and when I opened the door, I smelled a heavy stench of sweat and manure hanging in the stagnant air and saw a heavyset man lying in the bed. After a short exchange, we realized we were to be roommates—and I learned that the man was the source of the manure smell, as he had recently been working in a fertilizer plant. Tired and not seeing him as a threat, I asked him to move over and climbed into the bed to go to sleep. I dozed off and didn't wake up until morning.

The weirdness of what I had gotten myself into was further revealed when I joined the rest of the sales crew to eat breakfast at the hotel. The sales manager, Mr. Mullins, was introduced, and he tried to pump up the energy by encouraging us to sing a familiar gospel song that had the lyrics, "I'll take Jesus as my savior/you take him, too"—only we were asked to substitute "Mullins" for "Jesus."

That blasphemy ringing in our ears, we were next given our instructions for the day. Newcomers would be paired with experienced and presumably successful people so we could learn from them.

Shortly afterward, I was dropped off with a partner at the entrance to Fort Knox military base, and together, we walked to the first house we saw. "Watch and listen," my partner said as he leaned forward to push the doorbell. I stood a few feet behind him while he turned on the charm and offered his pitch to the lady of the house, which went something like this:

"Hello, ma'am. I'm Joe Jones, and I'm a junior at the University of Kentucky in the veterinary school. I just love animals—and I can see you do, too, judging by your cat. What's her name? Boots? That's a great name. So, here's the thing, ma'am. I can earn points toward a scholarship for every question I ask that you answer. Would you mind my asking you a few brief questions? Thanks. First, do you read magazines? You do? Terrific, because that gives me ten points. Does anyone else in your family? Yes? Oh, that's ten more points." He posed a few more questions like this and asked if she read particular magazines. He would tell her the number of points he would get if she would order some of those. And so it went, with him playing on the poor woman's sympathy and maybe even her longing for human contact while her husband was working. Again and again, he got these women to sign up for subscriptions they didn't need and probably couldn't afford.

My assigned mentor, who looked to be in his midtwenties but had enough charm in his voice to overcome any suspicions about the college student story, walked briskly to the next house, proud that he had mastered a successful spiel. We visited a number of homes before I spotted a military police vehicle approaching and realized they wanted to talk to us. Apparently, our solicitation was illegal, so they carted us off to the jail on base and locked us up. It was a shock to be behind bars, but it was just my new partner and me, sitting on a bench—no other hardened criminals sharing our space. Evening fell before a crew boss showed up to spring us. The MPs allowed us to go on our way as long as we promised to stay off the base.

The next day, having completed my "training," I set out alone, going door to door in rural Kentucky, past the horses and hay fields to one house after another. Whenever a homeowner opened the door, I began my own admittedly bland pitch:

"Hi, my name is Carl Greer. I'm selling magazine subscriptions. Would you be interested in buying any of these magazines?" Then I'd show them my list.

My soft-sell approach was a complete bust, but my conscience wouldn't let me follow the example my trainer had provided. Before each woman closed her front door, I asked her if she knew of any work I might apply for in the area, but no one offered me any leads. After two days of completely striking out at finding a job or selling magazines, I decided I'd had enough.

The company didn't want to lose any salespeople, and I'd heard a rumor that to discourage it, they roughed up anyone who tried to quit, so I got up in the middle of the night and quietly walked out of the hotel, hoping that some better opportunity would present itself.

Thumbs Up to a Bigger Adventure

I could have returned to my grandparents' place, but as long as I had come this far, I decided to go west on my own. I walked along the dark highway and each time I heard a vehicle approach, I stuck out my thumb, hoping to get picked up. I'd never hitchhiked before, and it seemed like a good way to get to see the country before making my way back home eventually. I didn't have a clear idea of where I wanted to go and didn't dwell on any possible danger. At some point, I had probably heard or read some alarming tales of hitchhikers being hurt or killed. But naively, I didn't think anything would happen to me.

It may seem strange to have so much faith that I would find food and places to stay. But just as I had trusted being in nature's woods, streams, and lakes, I trusted being on the road. I believed in the friendliness of small towns and in the essential goodness of people I would meet along the way. If the work I expected to find turned out to be boring and unpleasant, at least the sense of traveling to places unknown would provide nourishment for my soul.

Before I had walked too far, I was picked up by a man named Frank, who was driving a moving van. He told me he owned and ran a freight and moving company and could use some help with jobs he had lined up. Was I was interested? Yes—I accepted his offer.

Frank and I arrived in his hometown of Canton, Missouri, that first day, and he told me that while I was working, I could stay in a local hotel owned by his father. The next day, the alarm clock woke me at 4 a.m., and Frank and his brother, Hank, picked me up. After breakfast and enough coffee to wake us up before the sun arose, we drove to Quincy, Illinois. There, we loaded freight that was waiting for us at a warehouse and delivered it all within the area by noon. We stopped for lunch and then moved people's belongings between houses or apartments until dinner time or later. I washed off the sweat and dirt of the day, ate my supper tiredly, and fell asleep by eight or nine o'clock.

The job was very hard physically, and I was sore the whole time I worked for Frank. Still, I was earning money and getting to see some of the country.

Plus, I didn't mind hard work. While I'd had a good experience the year before when I was employed at the steel mill, I felt no need to find a job with potential for advancement or that required me to use my brains instead of what little brawn I had. I figured a conversation that mostly consisted of orders like, "Hand me that—put it over there" was as cerebral as I needed. I was happy for the chance to be freewheeling and trusted that opportunities would show up as I needed them—and this one had appeared with my first ride.

Working twelve to thirteen hours a day would become routine for the next several weeks as Frank, Hank, and I hauled freight and moved people to Iowa, Kentucky, and Wisconsin, eating and sleeping on the road. Most of the time, I imagine I smelled fairly rank with sweat, but a teenage girl I encountered in Chippewa Falls, Wisconsin, didn't seem to mind. Hank and I moved a small shoe manufacturing business, which the girl's father owned, as well as the family's belongings. As we lifted and carried items, I noticed that the girl kept changing into one cute outfit after another and walking within my line of sight, catching my eye and smiling at me. I was flattered, but there was a lot of hauling to do. Before long, Hank pulled me aside to tell me her parents wanted me to wash up and put on some clean clothes. After I'd spent three days sleeping in the truck and not showering, my appearance was understandably objectionable. I used some soap and water, changed my shirt, and continued moving furniture and boxes. I took the job seriously enough not to stop and flirt with the girl, but it was nice to know that even at my smelliest and grungiest, a pretty young woman was attracted to me.

On Sundays, my off day, I did chores at Frank's house to earn a little extra cash to supplement my $8 a day pay. After several weeks, Frank ran out of jobs for me. He thanked me for working for him and gave me a letter of recommendation that basically said I was a good, hard worker. I appreciated that Frank's father let me sleep for free in his hotel and that Frank had bought me a few meals because all of this meant I had some cash in my pockets as I set out hitchhiking again.

I thanked Frank, said good-bye, and headed west, picking up odd jobs where I could. In many ways, my unsupervised wanderings away from home as a child had prepared me well for life on the road, so I trusted in the unknown and the unfamiliar. I was used to being on my own and didn't need much in the way of food or belongings. Tomorrow seemed to take care of itself.

A Loaf of Bread, a Package of Bologna, and Me

Now and again, I would send my dad and Mary Anne a postcard saying something like, "I'm in Topeka, Kansas, working for a few days. I'm heading west next week." However, I rarely phoned home. It just didn't seem necessary. Years later, after Mary Anne died and my father remarried, my dad would tell the story of my hitchhiking with a note of pride in his voice while admitting with some melancholy that he knew I didn't feel I had a home in those days. I was comfortable on the road; a sense of "home" seemed elusive.

Living close to the edge, dependent on strangers, didn't seem odd or even particularly daring to me. Food could be found everywhere, and I could get by for quite a while on a loaf of white bread, some bologna, and a bottle of milk from a grocery store—a diet that I try not to emulate today. My parents and grandparents had lived through the Great Depression, and neither side of the family was affluent. I suspect I'd internalized the family stories I'd heard about keeping food in one's belly one way or another because I never feared going hungry. During the Depression, to supplement their family income, my dad's parents sold ketchup and potato chips they had made from scratch. My mom's parents had been raised in rural and small-town areas where money was often tight. Though I lived simply, I never felt deprived or thought I lacked for anything.

Back at our house in Mt. Lebanon, I had one suit, and my most prized possessions were probably my transistor radio and a record player on which to play the 45-RPM singles I often bought at the local five-and-dime store. As I listened to songs by the Everly Brothers, Johnny Cash, and Jerry Butler, I daydreamed about high school dances and pretty girls. When it came to money, I saw it as a means to an end. I didn't spend extravagantly or daydream about what I would do if I were wealthy.

No one I knew was materialistic or made lavish purchases. Homes were smaller than they are today, and once a family set up a household, there didn't seem to be a big push to keep filling the house with items bought at a store. My dad made what was considered a pretty good salary, which increased over the years as he rose up the ranks at U.S. Steel, but he didn't need much. He modeled to me a sensible attitude toward money. I don't recall him complaining about how much his take-home pay was or whether others might be making more or grousing about taxes. He spent his money wisely, drove a sensible if stylish Buick Regal, and when he retired years later as one of the top executives at the company, a senior vice president, he made around $75,000, no more than three to four times what the average steelworker did. Today, the ratio would be many times more than that. Like many in his generation, my dad had done without luxuries for enough years that he never developed the taste for conspicuous consumption—and neither did I. Shopping wasn't considered a form of entertainment, and cheap consumer goods from overseas would not flood the market until later decades.

Thinking back, I'm struck by how I, as a middle-class young man in the 1950s and 1960s, wouldn't have considered a necessity certain things that many Americans take for granted today. For instance, I was twenty-seven before I lived in a place with air conditioning—and I lived in some hot, humid places. When hitchhiking, I didn't have a sturdy backpack and frame. I brought along with me a plastic raincoat, which doubled as a ground cloth to sleep on, and my suitcase that held underwear, socks, a few T-shirts, handkerchiefs, jeans, shirts, and a toothbrush and razor. I learned to drink coffee on the road when I needed it to stay awake. Any cup of coffee that was hot would do, and if it was free or cheap, all the better.

As for lodging, why splurge on a nice hotel room when I could sleep out in the open on my plastic raincoat or in a dollar-a-night rooming house? Without steady income, I preferred to save my money and skip the unnecessary luxuries.

Admittedly, I was very cheap. For example, at the end of my junior year in college, I spent a summer in Kansas City, Missouri, lodging at a YMCA. They charged $30 a month for a ground-floor room that had no air conditioning and was off an alley. People staying on the upper floors threw their garbage out the window and urinated down into the alley below, and the summer heat fermented it all, generating an aroma that even the water bugs and cockroaches seemed to want to avoid. Whenever they invaded my room, which was often, I would squash them on the walls with a whack of my shoe and leave them there to show the staff later, hoping to prod them into doing something about the problem. The response was, "Why don't you just pay another $6 a month for an upper-floor room?" While those rooms were much cooler, offering cross breezes, relief from the alley odors, and a smaller population of insects, I didn't want to part with any more money.

In hindsight, I could have spent the extra $6 and made out just fine. The economy was good, there was reason to believe I could pick up odd jobs in the summers, and my college degree in a practical subject was going to make me attractive to employers down the road. Still, I thought spending less was a kind of insurance policy. I felt more comfortable making do with the absolute bare minimum rather than risking a financial shortage. Maybe that extreme frugality gave me some of the courage that propelled me to continue hitchhiking and to trust that wherever I ended up on any given jaunt, I would find work and be okay.

"Governor, do you know of any job openings?"

After leaving the moving company, I found some employment in Marysville, Kansas: I helped people clean up after a tornado had ripped through their town, flinging cars and trucks hundreds of feet as well as tearing huge trees out by their roots. Observing the effects of Mother Nature's destructive power gave me pause. I had always felt at home in the woods, but it was easy to forget how cruel nature can be—in this place, killing and displacing people, reducing their houses to piles of debris. Many of the locals had lost everything they owned, yet they were already talking about rebuilding. I admired their resilience as they picked their way through what was left of their homes to see what they might recover.

From Kansas, I caught rides to Denver, Colorado. There, I went to street festivals in the Mexican neighborhood at night and for the first time experienced Mexican culture and food. The tastes, colors, and music provided simple pleasures to me as I walked around drinking it all in. Living in a suburb of Pittsburgh, I had little experience with ethnic restaurants and neighborhoods. Eating tamales and hearing mariachi bands sing loudly and strum guitars made me yearn to get down to the Southwest and Mexico that summer or the next.

One day while exploring the Mile-High City and looking for a job, I ended up at the state capitol building and decided to take a tour inside. The next thing I knew, I was at the door of the governor's office. He happened to be there at the time, with his door ajar, so I knocked on it, introduced myself, and asked if he knew where I might find work. The governor was very gracious and didn't seem to think there was anything strange about me wandering in and making my request. He told me that the local dude ranches were always looking for workers in summer and suggested I go down to the Pikes Peak area, where it was the height of the tourist season. Dude ranches were popular at the time—people liked to stay for a week or weekend to have a Western experience and play at being a cowboy, riding horses and having sing-alongs around a campfire. Today, I probably wouldn't be able to simply walk into the hall where the governor's office was located. But in 1958, people were far less paranoid about strangers and less concerned with security. I figured if I wanted to learn about opportunities in Colorado, the governor would be a good place to start, so why not ask?

I followed his advice and headed down to the mountains near Colorado Springs, where a dude ranch hired me as a busboy with promises of an upgrade to waiter if a position opened up. The job had a lot to recommend it. It was far less grueling than freight hauling, and the mountainous area I was working in was beautiful. Best of all, my coworkers included girls my age—and there were also some young ladies staying there as guests or living nearby. I did get promoted to waiter, which increased my income a little. And I joined with my peers in vying for the attention of the girls at the ranch, competing with the cowboys whose Marlboro Man allure gave them a bit of an advantage.

My first date of the summer was an inauspicious start to romance on the road. I had agreed to go on a blind date with a girl who was working at the ranch but quickly realized I felt no attraction or chemistry between us. At the end of the evening, we got a ride back to our lodgings in a car with two other couples. Very soon after we parked in the lot, the couple in the backseat with us started making out, and so did the couple in the front seat. My date made it clear she'd like us to do the same, but I wasn't interested. I was looking for a way to escape the uncomfortable situation, but the girl beat me to it: She threw open the door and stormed out. The girl in the front seat turned around and asked, "Carl! What did you do to her?" The girl next to me answered, "Honey, it's not what he *did*—it's what he *didn't* do!" I had to laugh because it was true.

It was more fun when I could pick my own dates. One night, I was returning from a dance in Colorado Springs, where I had enjoyed spending the evening with a girl who was a good dancer. I didn't get back to the ranch until after the curfew, when the gates were locked. The only way to get into the bunkhouse where the restaurant staff slept was to scramble over fencing that penned in the bulls and livestock used for the rodeos. Quietly, carefully, I negotiated the field, taking care not to wake the horses and cows—or worse, the bulls—with my trespassing.

Despite a rough moment or two, working at the dude ranch was one of my better summer jobs. I learned to ride a horse, dated some nice girls, and got into a good fight with a smart-aleck coworker who was determined to give me grief about that night when I was eager to get away from my date.

During my dude ranch stint, I met people whose careers took them from place to place with the seasons. I hadn't known there were people who did this; it seemed adventurous. I realized how hard it must be for them to have a satisfactory family life working the hours they did and observed that no matter how exhausted they were being on their feet all day, they were expected to be polite. The pay wasn't great unless you were at the top of the hierarchy, receiving a cut of everyone's tips. How long could they work the hours they did, lifting and carrying dishes and food hour after hour, retaining a pleasant attitude? I had been okay with my job as a waiter for a few weeks in the summer but was glad to move on. That summer, I gained a lasting appreciation for how hard the work in the service industry is.

"We have a policy of not hiring people who wear bedroom slippers"

As summer came to a close, I headed back to Mt. Lebanon and then to Lehigh to start my engineering studies. I carried a full load of classes with labs, which left little time for sleep or socializing. When classes ended in June, I decided to set out again hitchhiking and maybe try to find work in the oil fields in Colorado or the wheat fields in Nebraska. I'd read *The Grapes of Wrath* and identified with the Joad family's wanderings on the road as they headed westward. Before I could travel, however, I had an operation to remove a bone growth on the top of each of my feet that had been causing me pain whenever I wore shoes. The wounds from the surgical incisions were very tender, so I cut holes in the tops of a pair of bedroom slippers, which I wore everywhere. That left my bandaged feet free from the pressure of regular shoes.

First, I hitchhiked to Fort Morgan, Colorado, where I heard that drilling for oil and gas was being done. When I was just outside the town and standing on the side of the road, a policeman pulled up to tell me it was against the law to hitchhike. He picked me up and took me to the local jail but let me go after a few hours, warning me not to hitchhike again while I was in Colorado. I spent the night in town in a rooming house and, the next morning, hitchhiked to the oil fields, hoping I wouldn't get approached by a police officer again.

At the oil fields, I found the foreman, introduced myself, and asked for a job. He looked down at my feet, then up at me, and said with a straight face, "We have a policy of not hiring people who wear bedroom slippers." I imagine he amused his wife that night over dinner telling her about the kid from the East who showed up in bedroom slippers to ask for a job that required steel-toed boots.

My original plan abandoned, I returned to Fort Morgan and looked for other work that might accommodate my footwear. Sleeping in the park at night to save a few dollars, I continued my search with brief respites to spend a few hours at the local library, where I read the works of some of the Romantic poets—Byron, Shelley, and Keats, as well as Auden and Sir Walter Scott. The dark emotions and the dramatic phrasings of the Romantics fit perfectly with my adolescent mournfulness over my relationship with Pat that had ended a while back:

"Remembrance"

'Tis done! - I saw it in my dreams;
No more with Hope the future beams;
My days of happiness are few:
Chill'd by misfortune's wintry blast,
My dawn of life is overcast;
Love, Hope, and Joy, alike adieu!
Would I could add Remembrance too!
    —Lord George Gordon Byron

Even today, I can still recite some of the poems I memorized that summer.

When I wasn't indulging my adolescent angst over the bitter-sweetness of love, I was considering where to go next on my adventure. I decided to hitchhike from Fort Morgan toward Las Vegas.

The morning I arrived in town, I ran into a woman who managed a small motel. I talked to her about possible jobs, and she gave me some advice and a silver dollar to spend on breakfast. I remained friendly with this generous woman, who told me I could stay in her motel for free whenever she had vacancies. For the next several weeks, I took her up on that offer several times. Two years later, I would return the favor by driving her and a friend to Los Angeles, where I was headed for a fraternity convention. But for now, I was just glad that I had stumbled across a kind person who helped me out simply because she could.

My first job in Las Vegas was working as a busboy in the downtown El Cortez Hotel. For whatever reason, they were okay with my footwear on the job. After a week, I got hired at the Tropicana on the Las Vegas strip. There, I had to belong to the union. I earned wages of $8 per day plus tips and food, as I had at the El Cortez, but the tips were better at the Tropicana. There were some high rollers at the casino tables, from what I could see when walking through to get to the kitchen and restaurant. In one roll of the dice, they might lose $500 or $1,000 and respond by casually lighting up a cigarette and sipping their drink, which made me wonder why parting with that amount of money meant so little to them.

At the Tropicana, I became friends with a waitress who was a little older than I was. She said it was fun spending time with someone her own age—but my interest in taking her out diminished when I learned she was dating a "made man" in the Mafia.

Later, when an opportunity to drive some used cars to an auto auction in Salt Lake City, Utah, came up, I took a break from being a busboy, figuring the job would be interesting and allow me to make some money while seeing more of that area of the country. On one trip through the mountains near Provo, Utah, I was driving a pickup truck and towing another one when suddenly, the driver in front of me hit his brakes and swerved. I slammed on my brakes to avoid ramming into him, and the truck I was pulling behind me started to jackknife. The momentum drew me toward the edge of the road where there was a sheer drop, with no guardrail to stop me. Immediately, I stepped on the gas and straightened the trucks out before they went off the cliff, narrowly missing a car coming from the opposite direction. By luck and good grace, I managed to stay on the road and deliver the trucks and myself to Salt Lake City in one piece.

After that close call, I stayed in Utah for a few days and got a job picking cherries with some migrant families. The first day, I was up in a cherry tree when someone started to shoot at us. Everyone scrambled out of the trees. The foreman thought it sounded like a .22-caliber rifle, and he and some of the crew searched the area to see where the shots were coming from. They never did find the shooter, but later that day, when the foreman said he thought it was safe for us to start picking again, we climbed back into the trees. I figured that since I hadn't gotten hit and neither had anyone else, there was nothing to worry about. Today, I might feel differently about sticking around someplace where people were shooting at me!

Unlike the seasoned workers, I was a slow picker and only made $4 to $5 a day, not much for what was really hard work. Some of the workers tried to show me how to pick faster, but I couldn't seem to get the hang of it. Consequently, I headed back to Las Vegas, worked some more as a busboy, and hit the road again, hoping to see a little more of the country and, once again, go west.

A Captive Audience for an Array of Stories

Sometimes I felt like Alan Ladd in the Western movie *Shane*: someone who stays at a place for a while but always leaves in the end. From one day to the next, I never knew what experiences were waiting for me or how long I would be in one place. I learned how to be resourceful and trust that things would work out somehow without my having to force them.

No matter who picked me up, they usually wanted to talk. Knowing they would never see me again, they would often share intimate details of their lives. A captive audience sitting there in the passenger seat, I learned to listen. In the emotionally starved environment I lived in after my mother died, I had cultivated a habit of being observant and reflective.

I didn't ask too many questions of people and didn't want to seem nosy, but I found that many drivers were quite comfortable delivering a monologue about their loves, lives, kids, disappointments, and, in some cases, misdeeds. I had to wonder if they often talked about these topics with others. Initially, it felt awkward to hear them share such personal stories with me, but soon I became used to it. Years later, when I became a psychologist and analyst, I realized those many hours spent in cars and trucks traveling west through the United States listening to people's tales of broken hearts and lessons learned had well prepared me to listen without judgment as people talk.

In those months, I came to understand a little more about people from different walks of life. An early ride was with an English professor from Northwestern with whom I discussed literature and who seemed impressed by some of the books I had read in my high school honors English class. Near Indianapolis, I was picked up by a man who told me he had been Mickey Mantle's high school baseball coach and could see Mickey's talent back when he was just a kid. It was exciting to be just one step removed from a genuine sports star. One sequence of rides made me realize that I was being exposed to quite a spectrum of people. I first rode with a Catholic priest, who shared with me the joys and heartbreaks of being in the priesthood. The next ride came from a Protestant minister, who shared his story of how he became committed to religious life. The fellow who picked me up after that turned out to be a murderer who had served time. He didn't volunteer anything about his crime, and I didn't probe.

That experience of traveling with a murderer wasn't nearly as scary as my ride with a couple of gamblers coming from Terra Haute, Indiana, however. I was picked up late at night, so I couldn't tell until I got in that the driver, who let me sit in the passenger seat, was extremely drunk. He tried to light a cigarette but couldn't get the lighter to match up with the cigarette in his mouth. As I watched him warily, I smelled urine and noticed he had peed in his pants. I decided that as soon as I saw an exit sign, I'd ask him to drop me off, pretending I knew someone nearby and now wanted to visit them. Before I could say anything, the man got turned around and started driving the wrong way on the deserted highway. Fortunately, we got to an exit fairly quickly, and I got out. As the two drove away, I thought, "That was a close call."

It wouldn't be my only one.

Once, when I was hitchhiking from Los Angeles to San Francisco and about a ninety-minute drive away from the Bay Area, a car with several people in it picked me up after sunset. As I rode with them, I realized they were all members of the Hells Angels motorcycle gang. They talked about bikes, fights, and girls, and then one of them started musing aloud about whether it would be a good idea to "mess me up." His friends weren't encouraging him, but they also didn't intervene. As he continued, I kept my eyes on the road and remained silent, thinking about how quickly I might be able to reach the switchblade in my pocket and defend myself if I needed to. It wasn't a high-quality weapon, and it might jam. If it did, my only defenses would be to keep calm and try to figure a way out of my dilemma. The conversation shifted, but I was on high alert until they let me off when we arrived at the edge of San Francisco. As the car drove away, I took a couple of deep breaths, and my tension began to dissipate. But rather than thinking about just how bad things could have gotten, I pushed aside any lingering fear and set my mind to finding a place where I could stay the night.

I would have a few more adventures that could have landed me in the realm of disaster but didn't. I look back at those summers after high school and during college and am glad that I was able to have those experiences. I was fortunate, and I guess I made some of my own luck, too.

Rock and Roll in Ensenada

That second summer I hitchhiked, I traveled to Ensenada, a town in Baja California, where my fishing skills served me well. Shortly after I got to town, I checked into a cheap rooming house that smelled of disinfectant, spent the night, and got up early to go fishing on a charter boat. There were about a dozen passengers, and I caught over a hundred pounds of bonito and yellowtail tuna. I sold some to people on the boat. Then I went into town to look for a pretty girl I had met the day before, found her at the lawyer's office where she was working, and gave her a fish just because I felt inspired to be generous. She was surprised, and our inability to speak each other's language fluently didn't help me to explain the inexplicable. Finally, I found a restaurant that was willing to feed me for a week in return for my remaining fish. I had money and food for a while, so I began to explore the town.

Outside a souvenir store, I came across a man named Ralph, who was sitting and playing bongo drums. I struck up a conversation and found that he spoke English pretty well and was just a few years older than me. Ralph told me that he owned the store and a local gym, was a competitive weight lifter, and that year had won the title "Mr. Baja California." "I'll show you around while you're here," he promised—and he made good on his word.

I visited Ralph's home, and he introduced me to sites and events I might not have experienced on my own. We went to a local carnival in the Mexican countryside where *pistoleros* showed off their skills. I was impressed by these sharpshooters who could knock a small object off someone's head by using a mirror to shoot over their own shoulders or by firing backward between their legs. After our outings, I'd return at night to walk over to the restaurant to eat the meals they had promised me.

Soon after I arrived in Ensenada, the town hosted what I was told was the first rock and roll concert held in that part of Mexico. Fans traveled from as far away as Tijuana to the well-known coastal city to get a taste of real rock and roll at the Hotel Pacífico. Ralph and I, along with his girlfriend, attended and listened to the bands play far into the night. Even though I couldn't speak Spanish very well, I felt a sense of belonging because the music and the fun were uniting everybody. I knew some of the latest dances—the chicken, the mashed potato, the frug—and danced late into the night before returning to my room a few blocks away.

There were several guys from Tijuana hanging around town, and over the next couple of days, I got to talking with some of them in a smattering of broken English and Spanish. I figured that I would be polite and take a swig of the tequila they offered me, but I remembered promising my grandmother not to drink until I was twenty-one, in exchange for a $20 gold piece she would give me as a reward. Now I knew what tequila tasted like, and I declined to drink any more of it so I could keep my word.

After Ensenada, I headed back up the California coast, figuring I could head north and then go east rather than start to make my way back home the way I had come. I was also hoping to end my summer by visiting a girl, Deborah, whom I had met in Las Vegas and who lived in San Leandro, California, east of San Francisco. We had only chatted for maybe a half hour outside of the Tropicana, where she was staying with her parents, and she seemed nice, so I got her address and told her I would try to visit her in San Leandro before the summer ended. That was the trip where the Hells Angels picked me up, and I was relieved to find a local YMCA shortly after they dropped me off. I fell asleep quickly after a long, tiring day and night. The next morning, I got Deb's number from the telephone operator and dialed it. "I'm sorry," her mother told me, "but Deborah can't come to the phone. She's been grounded." I tried to explain how far I'd come and how I knew her daughter, but my story got me nowhere. "She's grounded, so you can't see her" was all her mother would say.

I couldn't believe I'd come all that way for nothing! I wasn't even all that interested in checking out San Francisco, although I did spend a day there before hitting the road again. I caught rides that took me up through Oregon and Idaho and then headed back east. While in the Chicago area, I visited my great-aunt Gert and great-uncle Joe, did some sightseeing, and attended a Chicago White Sox baseball game. There, I got to see Minnie Miñoso, the "Cuban Comet," who had played for the Cleveland Indians before being traded to the White Sox.

As I was winding up my second summer of hitchhiking before heading back to Lehigh, I wanted to visit Pat, my girlfriend from back in high school. Her family had recently moved to a suburb of Chicago, and she was home for the summer. I had seen Pat only once since she had started attending college in Philadelphia. Our reunion proved to be bittersweet, as I was reminded of what once was and what might have been. Pat had a quiet side and was a deep thinker who could discuss spiritual questions over dinner as easily as another girl might talk about going shopping with her girlfriends. She told me she was majoring in English and philosophy, and I daydreamed that she would end up an author or poet in Greenwich Village. She was the kind of girl who could do anything she set out to do. We were still friends, but we had gone our separate ways.

Lessons from the Road

Perhaps the brief nature of my friendships on the road made me better appreciate the friends I've kept over my lifetime. Even though in some ways I've mostly been a loner, I've been fortunate in maintaining friendships with people from high school, college, and graduate school, and later from my years in business, psychology, and shamanic work. I never spoke much about my adventures to friends or family. I was so used to keeping my own counsel that it never occurred to me to talk about those summers.

In all of my wanderings, I followed the spirit of the moment when deciding where to go—a wonderful, liberating feeling. I learned to appreciate the early evening, the smell of freshly mown hay or grass, strong scents after a rain, the chirping of crickets, and a chorus of night sounds echoing around me as I lay on my plastic raincoat. While I was working at the dude ranch in the Rocky Mountains, I loved to get up early and take in the smell of pine trees and the smoke of a campfire and food cooking. I watched the ever-changing clouds, brilliant white against the intense blue sky, and heard the sound of rivers and creeks rushing by as their waters sparkled in the sunlight. I felt a sense of interconnectedness and peace.

These memories sank deep within me and created a longing to experience them again in some way. Years later in Peru, when I smelled the smoke that rose up from the cooking fires, heard the chatter of night insects and birds, and witnessed the dazzling color and music of Peruvian festivals and dances, it seemed the past was merging with the present in a kaleidoscope of images, sensations, and recollections. I sometimes felt the same as I had during those years I spent on the road—sleeping under the open sky at night, feeling the earth beneath me, and immersing myself in a stream of adventure.

The mingling of past and present still occurs when I visit or read about various places in our country that remind me of places I've been and people I've met. My travels took me to small-town America, truck stops, diners, cafes—and an elegant hotel or two. I recall the beauty of lakes, rivers, oceans, deserts, and mountains. Sometimes, even today, these memories evoke haunting, wistful, or longing feelings within me, making me yearn for a simpler and freer life. But when I step back and reflect, I am living exactly the life I want to be living and am grateful that I have been able to do so.

I occasionally have a recurring dream of being on the road hitchhiking. It's never frightening and always enjoyable. When I wake up realizing that my mind has taken me back to those summers of traveling light, with a sense of freedom and openness to adventure, I know my unconscious is telling me that I have become too caught up in my responsibilities again. I know it's time for a break so I can reconnect with the archetypes of the traveler and adventurer.

All three of my children also spent time on the road as young adults. They never hitchhiked, but among them, they have traveled as far away as Australia and Argentina. To pay for some of their adventures, they took a variety of jobs: for example, bartender, DJ, band leader, and even English teacher (in Europe and Brazil). These experiences gave them perspectives about life that they wouldn't have had otherwise. Despite my not sharing my story of hitchhiking with my kids in great detail, some of its themes seemed to have been passed down to them. Or perhaps their adventurousness and yearning to go exploring has nothing to do with mine.

My travels when I was younger helped me experience my creativity and resilience as I coped with unexpected situations. I think that's true for a lot of people who are willing to take the risk of traveling to unfamiliar places without a specific plan of how to get from here to there without any mishaps. Maybe, too, the adventure of being on the road can satisfy the soul to some degree because it helps us experience that "home" can be a state of mind that we choose to adopt. As I look back, I recognize how rewarding it can be to follow the heart's pull toward travel and discovery before the demands of life begin to place obstacles in our way.

Different cultures have different ways of guiding young people through the transition between childhood and adulthood, helping them graduate from being mostly dependent on others to developing independence and interdependence with family and community members. First jobs, paid or unpaid, and exposure to people whose ways of life contrast with our own are commonly part of transitioning into adulthood in US culture. We hope that our natural risk-taking as adolescents doesn't lead us into situations that are too dangerous, but sometimes we seem to get out of scrapes by sheer luck. As you think about your adolescent years, you might want to look at the risks you took as a teenager, what the consequences were, and what you learned as a result.

Questions for the Reader to Ponder

Independence. Did anyone or anything foster your independence when you were growing up? Would you have appreciated more good guidance as you developed your sense of independence? What would that have looked like? As an adult, do you try to help others develop independence? If so, what childhood lessons guide you as you help others seeking independence?

Going on adventures. Have you ever been "on the road" or its equivalent, where you didn't know from one day to the next where you would be or what you'd be doing? Would you like to go "on the road" now or at some time in your life? If so, where would you like to go? What would you like to do? Whom would you like to meet? How would you support yourself? Could you get by on your own?

Hitting the road. Have you ever hitchhiked or been on a road trip that involved some spontaneous decisions? Or, did you ever prioritize adventure over the security of knowing where you will eat and sleep tomorrow, choosing to live on next to nothing? If so, what did you learn about yourself as a result?

Being true to your values. Have you ever been in a job situation where you felt pressured to betray your values? What did you do? Knowing now what you didn't know then, would you do anything different?

Jobs. What were your first two or three jobs? What did you like and not like about them? What did they teach you about life? What did they teach you about yourself?

CHAPTER FIVE

Burning Out the Mystic

I struggled to stay awake during long classes at Lehigh and memorize terms that I knew would be on exams lasting as long as four hours each. My brain was stuffed with formulas and facts about brittle fracture, tensile strength, and metallic phase transformation, leaving no space for the metaphorical meanings of these processes.

My early experiences in nature had shown me there was more to reality than what was visible in the ordinary world. My very active imagination as a child led me to create vivid daydreams, often with myself in the role of an adventurer—and some of these daydreams carried into adulthood. I even lived some of these adventures during my time on the road. But by the time I was ready for college, I believed my experiences of oneness in nature and my interest in the liberal arts would not serve me well in everyday life.

The culture I grew up in regarded daydreaming and mystical experiences with suspicion or dismissed them outright. People known to be imaginative were considered naïve, unrealistic, and doomed to failure. My parents and grandparents highly valued a practical education, and I absorbed those values. Because they seemed to work for the people around me, I didn't consciously question them.

My decision to major in metallurgical engineering at Lehigh fit with my family's attitudes about money and financial stability. I thought the rational, scientific realm of engineering would "burn out" any impractical, mythopoetic tendencies that might still be lingering within me and causing some internal conflict. I needed to make room for all the knowledge and ambition that would help me achieve success and secure my future, meaning a solid middle-class life. Becoming a dreamer, giving into my yearning to explore life's mysteries, might get in my way, so I hoped those longings would conveniently evaporate.

Metallurgical engineering involves working with the properties of metals and learning the technology of their production and refinement. The Pittsburgh area was the center of steel production in the US at a time of tremendous investment in infrastructure, manufacturing, and the automobile culture that allowed people to live in the suburbs and commute to work and social activities. At the time, I didn't realize that metallurgy has an age-old connection to the ancient art of alchemy and its practitioners who aimed to purify and transform base metals into gold. Moreover, alchemy is symbolic of the process of transforming one's base, earthly nature to become a more exalted, spiritual being. In Jungian psychology, individuation is the process of discovering parts of the self that have become split off from each other and transforming and reintegrating them so that you're less driven by unconscious impulses and you have greater self-awareness. I wanted Carl the Poet to give way to Carl the Successful Businessman and didn't see how I could express both of these aspects of myself. I had no idea my chosen profession was rooted in the mystical and wouldn't learn about that until much later in life.

Pajamas in Class

Being hardworking and productive came naturally to me, but you might say I went into overdrive my freshman year at Lehigh, taking twenty-one credit hours, spending hours doing lab work, and attending military drills every week as part of the Army Reserve Officers' Training Corps (ROTC). ROTC was required of every student because Lehigh was a land-grant college, but I would have taken the class anyway. My plan was to go into advanced ROTC after my sophomore year and graduate as a second lieutenant in the army. Had I done so, I would probably have been shipped to Vietnam. Many of my classmates went, and some were killed. At the time, Vietnam wasn't much on my radar. War was an abstract concept for me. I just wanted to serve my country for a while postcollege before deciding whether to stay in the military or follow in my dad's footsteps and go into business.

In the late 1950s and early 1960s, officially, the US military presence in Southeast Asia was advisory. The number of troops serving there would remain limited for the years I was at Lehigh but would increase shortly after I graduated. My plans for advanced ROTC changed at the end of my sophomore year when I failed my physical—being deaf in one ear and having a bad knee made it impossible for me to continue along the path of becoming an officer. Technically, I could have been drafted at some point, but that was not at the forefront of my mind as I went about my days at Lehigh.

Right after my brother, Kirk, graduated from college, he enlisted in the army and was shipped to Vietnam. Kirk ended up becoming a sergeant in an intelligence unit, earning a Bronze Star and serving three tours of duty. I was proud of him. That said, I didn't truly appreciate the danger he was in, even when I heard about other soldiers being killed. I compartmentalized any fears I had and didn't imagine anything bad could happen to someone close to me. Fortunately, Kirk did survive the war without major physical injuries.

I was so focused on my studies that I didn't put much thought into what was going on in Southeast Asia—or even what was happening domestically. I was elected to the student council freshman year, and at a meeting I attended as a council member, someone raised the topic of "HUAC" (the House Un-American Activities Committee). Naively, I asked what "HUAC" was. A student reporter for *The Brown and White*, Lehigh's school newspaper, saw this as evidence that I was ridiculously out of touch. He lambasted me in print—perhaps rightly so, but it was embarrassing and frustrating to be criticized in this way. I felt qualified for my role on the student council because I knew what many of the students' concerns were due to my knocking on doors and listening to what they hoped I would address as their representative. But when it came to national or international news, I was fairly uninformed: I didn't read the newspaper past the sports and comics sections. I didn't see a need to at that stage in my life.

Starting my freshman year at Lehigh, I was in class or studying most of my waking hours. Sometimes, I would even go to my 8 a.m. classes in my pajamas. If I had a break between classes, I might lie down on a lab table and grab a catnap to try to keep up with the demands of my course load. On a Friday or Saturday night, I might go out on a date with a girl—typically, to a dance. Or, I might play a game of Ping-Pong with someone or head over to the university's gym to work out. Team sports were out: I couldn't commit the time that would be needed for games, meets, or regular practices.

My engineering course work was difficult, but I applied myself until I passed all the required subjects. I liked aspects of metallurgy but had no real passion for it. I was simply readying myself for adulthood, closing the door on adventure and becoming serious about setting the foundations for the life I wanted to build—or assumed I wanted to build.

Two-thirds of the engineering students could not keep up the pace and dropped out of the program. I pushed myself and had the good luck to get through those years without becoming exhausted or overwhelmed despite putting all my energy into school and having little downtime.

Damn Heavy for an Angel

Fortunately for me, I was able to balance my intense levels of studying with at least some degree of socializing. In 1959, I decided to join a fraternity as it seemed like a good way to generate a social life. Rush was held in the spring of our freshman year, and I became a pledge at Beta Theta Pi, with my pledge period continuing into the late fall of 1959 and ending with Hell Week, as they called it. Like the other pledges, I learned the fraternity's history, lore, and songs. The exact start of Hell Week was kept secret from us, probably to build up anticipation and excitement about what we would be asked to do to prove we were worthy of becoming Betas.

Hell Week subjected students like me to various physical challenges we couldn't refuse if we wanted to be accepted into the fraternity. No drinking was involved, but we pledges were verbally harassed and expected to do vigorous calisthenics at all hours of the day and night, including running up and down a nearby mountain. We had to carry rocks wrapped in sheets, which we called "our angels," everywhere, including our classes. We even slept with them. Each day, we had to find a bigger rock, with the brothers weighing them daily and replacing them if they weren't heavy enough. By the end of Hell Week, some of us were lugging around huge rocks that weighed forty to fifty pounds.

One of our assignments during Hell Week might have been a bit easier for me than some of the other pledges given that I had spent two summers hitchhiking around the country. After a surprise middle-of-the-night wake-up call, we were assigned to steal an object from a couple of Beta fraternity houses on other campuses. I was to get myself to the chapter houses at the University of Pennsylvania in Philadelphia and Columbia University in New York City via public transportation or hitchhiking, stay overnight, and then return with something I'd snuck out of the house. The brothers at the Beta house at Penn may have suspected that when the stop sign they had in the meeting room of their fraternity house disappeared along with me in the middle of the night, it had something to do with a Hell Week challenge.

At the end of Hell Week, when the decisions for who could join and who couldn't were made, I did get a little nervous about whether or not I would be accepted into the brotherhood. I was in a room waiting to learn my fate when I heard voices outside my room talking about me. One of them belonged to someone who supposedly was a representative of our national fraternity. Another more familiar voice said, "Carl Greer? Ehh, he's kind of a social nebbish." But shortly after that, the brother whose voice I'd recognized opened the door to the room I was in, handed me a can of beer, and congratulated me for becoming a member of Beta Theta Pi. In relief, I took one swallow, just as I had the tequila down in Mexico, but stopped there. I was still thinking of that $20 gold piece from my grandmother and my promise to her. Later, I learned that the conversations in the hallway were staged for all the pledges—there wasn't a national representative involved in the decision making process, as we had been told. The brothers had said that just to make us sweat a little. The so-called national representative was probably a former Beta Theta Pi brother from our chapter or another one.

When I was a pledge and after I became a member of the fraternity, I experienced some good-natured teasing about my leather jacket, which was like those worn by many of the young men at my high school. In contrast, tweed sports jackets were the style among some of my fellow Betas who had gone to prep schools. Also, my fraternity brothers nicknamed me Giggles because I have kind of a funny laugh. Many of the brothers had nicknames—Shev, Gooch, AT, Boomer—so I didn't mind.

Once accepted into the fraternity, I made many good friends. I came to serve in several leadership positions, including being president my junior and senior years, and took the responsibility seriously. One night, I had returned from a trip to a local steel manufacturing plant to find the Beta house almost empty. "Where is everyone?" I asked.

"They're in the basement," I was told. It turned out that some of my fraternity brothers had rented a pornographic movie and had invited a number of guys from other fraternities, mostly jocks, to come over and watch it.

I didn't think that kind of activity was in keeping with the character of the fraternity, but I felt conflicted. I didn't want to come across as preachy or moralistic, but I *was* the president. After wrestling with what to do, I made up my mind and went down to the basement. The guys had tacked up a white sheet on the wall as a makeshift screen and were about to start the projector. I stood in front of them and said, "Sorry, you can't watch this movie here."

I started to take down the sheet. One of my fraternity brothers, who had brought the movie, got up and grabbed the other end of the sheet to keep me from pulling it down. He was a large football player, but I wasn't about to back down.

Before things could escalate, the former president of the fraternity got to his feet and said, "If Carl says we can't watch it here, then we can't. Let's go—we'll watch it somewhere else." I'm not sure what made him do it, but his words defused the conflict and changed the energy in the room. The group followed him out without saying another word. I'm glad I didn't have to get into a fight over my taking a stand. The next day, my fraternity brothers and I said what we needed to say to each other, and there were no pornographic movies in the Beta house during my time at Lehigh.

Fraternities often get a bum rap, and sometimes, deservedly. But being a Beta was formative for me, and the experience with the movie was an aberration. My brothers and I shared a commitment to be as successful as we could in academics and athletics and encouraged each other to get involved in university activities and student government. And we had each other's backs: We sang, worked, and hung out together.

A Time of Transition

Fraternity life offered me a social outlet, but I also dated several girls during those college years, starting with Ana. She was a Portuguese girl I met at a high school dance I wandered into during my freshman orientation week when exploring nearby Bethlehem. I heard music, walked in, saw her dancing what looked like the cha-cha, introduced myself, and asked her the name of the dance. "It's the calypso," she said, and when I asked her to teach me the steps, she obliged. I still remember some of the songs they played that night—"Donna," "La Bamba," "Angel Baby," and "In the Still of the Night." I ended up going to her home in Bethlehem over Thanksgiving break and met her grandparents, who were raising her.

One of our dates was particularly memorable: It was nighttime, and we were parked along what I thought was a deserted side road near Bethlehem, which was actually a private road leading up to someone's estate. I was startled by a flashlight being shined in my face through the driver's side window. When I turned, squinting to see its source, I saw a police officer in uniform and a gun pointed at me. Ana and I froze as the officer ordered us to get out of the car. He seemed nervous as he looked us over and then told us to get back in the car and follow him to the police station. There, the police chief recognized me from the gym where we both worked out and Ana because he knew her family (who lived in town). The chief asked the officer to leave, chatted with us for a few minutes, and let us go with a warning not to park on private property. I was impressed with how cool and collected Ana was during the whole experience. She had moxie! But I didn't have the time to consider a serious relationship and eventually, Ana and I drifted apart.

After my sophomore year, I began my break in classes by taking an 8-to-4 job in the metallurgical engineering department at Duquesne Works outside of Pittsburgh. I believed my job there would help me acclimate to the adult world of business. It did, but I had a few lessons to learn along the way. At the end of my shift one day, on a dare, I carried a female coworker out of the plant. She and I both thought it was funny; the plant management didn't, and I was written up for a safety violation. Embarrassed, I realized I had to turn up the volume on my maturity if I was going to succeed in a professional workplace.

Aside from that impulsive moment with my coworker, I stuck to the rules and acted as professionally as I could for the rest of the time the job lasted. I would earn enough money that summer to buy a used '53 Chevy, for which I paid about $300. Now I had a vehicle, another mark of becoming a stable, responsible adult.

During a ten-day plant shutdown in July, I went to visit my grandparents in Paris, Kentucky. My grandfather was now suffering from advanced Parkinson's disease, and my grandmother was his sole caretaker. She was almost eighty years old and often had to carry him from place to place. Even though he was very frail and shrunken by that time, he was still hard to maneuver. My family helped when we visited but weren't there much. It made me sad to see that the stress of caretaking for the last few years seemed to be taking its toll on Nana. She was cross with Grandad, and the realization that their relationship had changed was a reminder to me of the impermanence of things. Grandad couldn't talk as he stood in the driveway with Nana to say good-bye at the end of my visit. He was crying, and I drove away with a heavy heart, aware that was likely to be the last time I saw him—and it was.

As the months flew by, my old life was giving way to a time of transition. I looked forward to what I hoped would be the prize at the end of all my hard work at preparing for the future: a good life as a businessman and, I assumed, a husband and father. The "happily ever after" story I aspired to bring to fruition was not one I planned in any great detail, however. I've always sort of muddled through, taking advantage of opportunities that presented themselves. I didn't try to envision a future any different from the one that was expected of me.

Where would my mythopoetic self fit in? It was hard to imagine a place for it, so I hoped that my longing for mystery and that extraordinary sense of connectedness I felt in nature would be satisfied by the occasional fishing trip or by spending time outside. Being on a lake listening to the birds and the sound of the water lapping against the shore, walking in the woods, or just sitting, reading, on a park bench did feed my soul here and there—enough to keep me from experiencing any angst about the choices I was making. My path was set for me, and it felt right—or right enough—for now.

During my junior year, I started to date Jerri, a girl I knew from high school. She had finished up her degree from Stephens College in Columbia, Missouri, and had started working for TWA in Kansas City. Before my senior year, I decided to spend most of the summer in Kansas City to be with her. It occurred to me that before the fall, I could earn some credits toward my degree so I would end up with a lighter load as a senior. Plus, I could take on a job or two to pay my costs including, as I mentioned before, renting a room on the cheapest floor in the YMCA.

My engineering program left room for three elective courses, and I took two of them, accounting and government, at the University of Kansas City that summer. Both were very practical. Only psychology, my third elective, which I took at Lehigh my freshman year, fed my mythopoetic self to any degree. Even so, the course was heavy on statistics and information about stimulus and response research.

While I lived in Kansas City, I was able to spend a lot of time with Jerri. Kirk, who was soon to start his senior year of high school, had followed me west and was working as a short-order cook on the Kansas side of town. He and I saw each other several times, and he stayed with me at the Y a night or two, but mostly he had his own arrangements—which were less bug-infested.

I began doing whatever jobs I could pick up. For a while, I worked at a cemetery doing grounds maintenance during some sweltering days, but I was used to sweat and physical labor, so I had no complaints. My ice cream truck job was far more pleasant. I sold popsicles, drumsticks, ice cream sandwiches, and other frozen treats in the city, some of its suburbs, and a few small towns nearby. When it was hot and muggy, which it usually was, I had plenty of customers. It was pleasant work, and I enjoyed the social aspect of it.

When my cookie tin of cash disappeared from the truck one night, I was angry. Never having been robbed, I wasn't willing to accept the loss and the unlikelihood of recovering the money. I spent the next day walking around the high-crime neighborhood where I'd been when my money was stolen. I asked a number of people on the streets and in stores and restaurants if they could help me identify who had taken my cookie tin. I imagine some of them were amused by my determination to find the thief or thieves, given that it was the sort of neighborhood where petty thefts were common. Everyone I talked to was polite, but the money and the tin never made their way back to me. I realized by the end of the day my inquiries weren't getting me anywhere, so I gave up, resigned myself to my loss, and dipped into my savings to invest in inventory so I could start selling again.

Comfortable Enough

After that summer, Floyd Hall, a senior vice president at TWA, was hired by Eastern Airlines to be its president, and Jerri, as his secretary, was asked to follow him to Eastern's offices in Rockefeller Center in Manhattan. It was an excellent opportunity for her, so she readily agreed. By this time, I was a senior at Lehigh, and Jerri was living close enough for us to get together regularly. That fall, I gave her my fraternity pin, a tradition that signaled we were serious about each other. Later in the year, I proposed—and she accepted. Then, I started thinking about what my next step would be when it came to studying and working.

That mythopoetic self within me began to reawaken as I talked to one of the Lehigh professors who was a psychoanalyst. Becoming an engineer didn't appeal to me beyond being a means to an end, although I appreciated that it provided me with some mental discipline and a good foundation for a career in business. I wanted to be successful and felt I was in training for a good life that would include family and security, so I had not minded devoting four years to a discipline that did not excite me. But the potential for something more enjoyable led me to follow that professor's encouragement and apply not just to graduate schools in business but also in psychology. Both Columbia University in New York City and the University of Minnesota accepted me into their psychology programs, and Columbia also accepted me into its MBA program.

On the brink of a big decision, I looked deeper into the profession of psychology. I had met some people in the field who seemed to have more than their share of psychological issues, and I didn't want to become like them—I didn't want to become any crazier than I already was! Also, psychology as a discipline seemed to be a mix of approaches and theories that few could agree on, with several new and revolutionary ideas being introduced. Critic Hans Eysenck was claiming that psychotherapy had no documented effect and psychoanalysis had negative effects, while Thomas Szasz was promoting his belief that mental illness should not be treated like a biological one.

The field was intriguing, but the prospect of choosing among the many approaches or setting up research studies wasn't appealing.

Besides, I planned to get married in June right after graduation and my twenty-second birthday, so now I had to think about supporting a family, and psychologists didn't seem to earn a lot of money or have much financial security. With practicality at the top of my list, I finished my degree in engineering and planned to follow in my father's and grandfather's footsteps by getting a good job in the steel industry. I'd felt comfortable working during the summer at Homestead Works and Duquesne Works and believed I could succeed in business.

I received job offers from several steel companies—and almost moved to Chicago to work for Inland Steel in its Inland training group. It was a prestigious management training program and would almost certainly lead to a good position with the firm, so I was tempted to accept. Then I reasoned there might be even more potential for me down the road if I earned my MBA. I declined the job, deciding instead to attend the Graduate School of Business at Columbia University in New York City.

On Monday, June 11, 1962, I graduated from college. The next day, I celebrated my birthday, and on Saturday, I married Jerri. That evening, we flew to New York City—my first flight ever—and spent the night in a hotel near the airport. Sunday, we traveled to the resort of Caneel Bay on the Island of St. John, where we honeymooned. In retrospect, a whirlwind of major life experiences had occurred within the space of less than a week. After that would come yet another change: moving into Jerri's place in Manhattan.

Jerri was living in a cramped studio apartment in a complex called Tudor City near the UN. The extra-small kitchen appliances were lined up along one wall, and the bathroom was tiny. We had a Murphy bed, a practical contraption that folded into the wall during the day, and for extra cooking space, we set up a hot plate in the bathroom. I settled into our new home, hoping soon we could find a bigger place.

"I just don't like him"

After working hard in college and in my various summer jobs, knowing I had committed to a rigorous MBA program, I felt drawn to an eight-week-long summer job advertised in the newspaper that would involve a very different role for me. The Federation of Jewish

Philanthropies of New York needed camp counselors to work with some kids from disadvantaged backgrounds. They hired me, and I was put in charge of a chartered bus that transported a group of young teenagers of various races from a poor neighborhood in Canarsie, Brooklyn, to a ferry that took them to a summer camp on Staten Island. Sometimes, we would also take them to museums and other cultural sites in New York City.

Besides having the responsibility of keeping order on the bus, I was in charge of about fifteen teenage boys. The old school buses we used fit three kids to a seat, and there were no seat belts, which meant that the kids could move around and become rambunctious. On one of our first trips, a boy in my group suddenly pulled out a small knife and stabbed the kid sitting next to him. I separated them, put a bandage on the superficial wound, and asked the boy who owned the knife why he had done it. "I just don't like him," he answered. I wondered briefly about the psychology behind his response, but I didn't try to lecture or advise him, in part because back then, I didn't know how to. Instead, I told him simply, "Don't do it again." And he didn't. After that, he seemed to respect me for having made the rules clear—we don't stab people!

I was also consistent about setting firm limits and enforcing rules, which I was coming to realize many of these kids must not have experienced at home. After a couple of incidents with the kids on the Staten Island ferry, I got tired of them acting up, refusing to listen, and disturbing the other passengers. On the next trip, before they got off the bus, I stood in front of them and announced:

"When I do this"—I snapped my fingers—"I expect you to be quiet and listen to me. When you get off the bus, I want you to walk, not run, on the ferry and respect the other passengers. If you don't, I'm going to roll up the windows and no one gets off the bus for anything—food, water, or bathroom breaks."

At first, the kids didn't believe me, but the next time they acted up, I followed through on my threat. It was broiling outside, and it had been a long bus ride. After a short time sitting in a sweltering bus, they quickly learned to behave. It may seem harsh, but at the time, it was the only strategy I could think of to get them under control and prevent any serious problems—and it worked.

Some of the camp counselors couldn't handle the pressure of trying to control kids who lacked self-discipline. They would try to reason with their charges using a lot of words, which rarely worked. Frustrated, the counselors would quit after a day or two. On the other hand, one woman leader was able to impose her authority instantly in a firm, but never harsh, way. Only five feet tall, Miriam had been raised in an Israeli kibbutz and knew how to command respect from kids.

She and I both understood it was important to maintain order and corral the kids or they were liable to cause damage to themselves and others. Many of them had never been to a museum or any other cultural site and didn't know what to make of them. In one case, a couple of boys had stuffed rocks in their jeans pockets and threw the stones at the museum displays' plate glass. I grabbed each boy by the scruff of the neck until he stopped. It was the most direct way I could think of to teach them what was acceptable and what wasn't. When their parents found out and complained to me about how I'd handled their children's behavior, I said, "If your boys damage any property, which they were about to do when I stopped them, they could get arrested. I can let them do what they like, or I can handle things and prevent this from happening. It's your choice." After that, there were no more complaints.

I was young and didn't exactly look imposing, but I was able to assert my authority by setting limits and sticking to them, even if that meant restraining the kids when they wanted to run around in a public area. I also had a lot of fun with them, and that probably made it easier for them to respect me when I set down the rules.

It helped a lot that I genuinely liked the kids and enjoyed being with them. I think they picked up on that and appreciated my attitude. Within a short time after I began supervising them, their behavior improved. We joked with each other and sang the latest rock-and-roll songs as we rode back and forth on the bus.

I remember one young girl on the bus who was often quite a hellion—but as she started singing, I became transfixed. She had the sweetest voice and seemed to transform in front of our eyes when she began to sing a popular song many of us knew: "Wonderful World." Observing her as the other kids chimed in, I came to recognize the power of music to change people and bring a group together. Although I wasn't a musician, I had always felt energized by different types of music from bluegrass to the blues, Celtic music, and early rock-and-roll singers and bands. Music allowed me to connect with a more soulful part of myself—and encouraging sing-alongs was a great way to connect with the kids. I remember the playful "Alley Oop" by the Hollywood Argyles was one of our favorites.

I liked working with the kids when we were taking a side trip or at the camp itself, where they did arts and crafts, went on nature walks, and participated in sports. I taught several of the boys I was supervising how to play softball and how to swim, which were new experiences for many. One young boy was deathly afraid of the water, and I spent several weeks helping him to overcome his fear. I was pleased when he was finally able to put his head in the water and swim a bit on his own. Unfortunately, a few days before the end of our camp, when I wasn't around, some kids splashed water in his face and scared him. This incident seemed to completely reverse all the work he and I had done together over the summer. I've often thought about him since, wondering if he recovered some of the skills he learned and regained his confidence in the water. It reminded me that training and lessons aren't over until they're over— and unforeseen events can counteract them.

Many years later, when considering how I might serve my community, I thought back to those kids I had worked with the summer before I started at Columbia Business School and how much they grew as they had fun at camp and visited places so different from their own neighborhoods. Today, I fund charities that serve kids like them, as I know how much just a few weeks' respite from their everyday lives doing fun activities can mean to kids with few recreational opportunities.

Be Careful Whom You Foot Sweep

That summer, I was at a barbershop in Brooklyn to get my hair cut when suddenly, I heard a thumping noise below us. I asked about it, and the barber told me that a man held judo classes in the basement. I decided to check it out.

The basement had been converted into a practice area with padded mats where I could see a judo instructor was teaching a student. The two men were executing a series of choreographed routines, which I later learned are called *katas,* and were also engaging in *randori,* or free fighting, where they grappled and threw each other.

I was intrigued, and when they took a break, I asked the instructor if he would teach me. He agreed, and for a time, I took individual lessons with him. Then the instructor invited me to his evening class for a lesson. It turned out I was not just "the new guy" but the only white guy in the group and had much less training than many of them. Even so, the men all accepted me and made me feel welcome.

After a particularly vigorous randori, one of my classmates said, "You fought well." I felt proud to have held my own with more experienced students and soon was back for more. I wanted to learn how to fight and have the confidence of knowing I could defend myself if I needed to.

It wasn't long before I decided to continue studying judo at the McBurney YMCA in Manhattan, closer to where I lived and would be studying. While my course load at Columbia was heavy, I was able to work judo training into my schedule.

I also ended up studying martial arts at The Buddhist Academy on the Upper West Side of Manhattan. One day, I was fighting an instructor who had won quite a few championships. I tried several times to knock his feet out from under him, using a move called a foot sweep, and succeeded only in bruising his shins. This annoyed him so much that when he threw me to the mat, he maneuvered me into a painful arm bar—a position that locks and stresses a joint (in this case, my elbow). I tried to break free but couldn't, so I slapped the mat in the universal signal for "Stop." Apparently, my opponent had decided to teach me a lesson for having kicked him. Instead of following protocol and stopping, he exerted more pressure and hyperextended my elbow. That incident showed me that despite the etiquette and rules associated with judo, it was not always a gentlemen's art. You had to expect anything because not everybody was going to play by the rules.

I began developing higher levels of skill and rising up the ranks. Mastery can take years, but I was young and determined. For a while, I worked out at a dojo in Queens run by Hank Kraft, a third-degree black belt who had studied at the Kodokan in Tokyo, the epitome of Japanese training schools, while he was stationed with the US military there. I was twenty-three at the time and often sparred with a nineteen-year-old named Ricardo. We had more enthusiasm than skill. One day, we were banging each other off the walls of the room when a thirty-two-year-old student in our class entered. I thought, "Gee, this nineteen-year-old is making me work hard. I wish I had started judo earlier. I can't imagine how tired I'll be when I'm old, like that guy over there." My perspective has radically changed about how "old" thirty-two is! I also came to learn that age is not the deciding factor in whether your opponent will be able to dominate. Sometimes, a forty-year-old's skill, strategy, and conditioning are such that a younger man is no match for him.

I spent countless hours training in martial arts because it had many appealing aspects for me. It helped me relieve stress, which I had plenty of when I was studying at Columbia—and later, too, when I was teaching and then working in business. But some of the best facets of martial arts I wouldn't fully appreciate for many years. In time, I would begin thinking more deeply about balance, flexibility, and using my energy effectively—lessons I learned in martial arts that would serve me well as a businessman and as a Jungian analyst. At this point in my life, however, martial arts were enjoyable, took my mind off the pressures of school and work, and built my confidence in being able to handle whatever life might throw my way.

My summers spent on the road gave me a sense of adventure and helped me become more aware of who I was and what I was capable of achieving. As I crossed the threshold into adulthood, my responsibilities increased.

For many people, the desire to be responsible and achieve goals diminishes their sense of playfulness and curiosity, repressing their mythopoetic self. Thinking about your own transition to adulthood, whether it was marked by college, marriage and parenting, or beginning to work full time, you might want to reflect on the choices you made back then—and whether you are stuck in a story you were living when you first became an adult, one that may have become confining for you.

Questions for the Reader to Ponder

Becoming an authority figure. When was the first time you realized that you had become an authority figure? What, if anything, was challenging about this new role for you? How did you handle the challenge? When do you enjoy being a leader, teacher, or authority figure? When do you not enjoy it? If you're more of a follower than a leader or authority figure, would you like to step into a leadership role more often? Why or why not? And if you'd like to step into that role, how can you make that happen in some area of your life?

Poetry and myth. What are some poems or myths that you especially appreciate? Why do they appeal to you? Is there a poem or a mythological and archetypal theme, such as being a warrior able to defend yourself and others, that especially speaks to you today? Is there a poem or theme that you felt described your values and what you wanted to do in your life years ago but that no longer does? What changed that this poem or theme no longer speaks to you as it once did?

Decision making. When have you made decisions that had a significant impact on your life? What helped you to make those decisions? If you made what turned out to be the wrong decision or decisions, were you able to correct course—and, if so, how?

CHAPTER SIX

Getting Established in the Big City

Finishing up a White Castle burger as I walked home from the Queens subway station, I wondered what Jerri was making for dinner. A long day of classes had left me famished, so I'd bought a snack to tide me over. On other days like this, I purchased a Sabrett hot dog on the street or even an éclair from the nearby bakery. I was young, active, and doing martial arts most days, and could get away with eating heavy comfort foods without fear of gaining weight.

It was the fall of my first year at Columbia, and Jerri and I had moved from our place in Tudor City to the top floor of a house in Forest Hill Gardens, Queens, renting from the family that lived on the other two floors. I was getting used to taking the subway most places, and the only time I became disoriented below ground was after boxing with a fellow Columbia student. During our sparring, my opponent hit me hard in the head. I thought I was okay but obviously wasn't: I missed my stop and was well on my way to Long Island before I realized I had to double back.

Boxing appealed to me for some of the same reasons other martial arts did. I wanted to feel I could handle myself in any fight. However, judo was more interesting to me because of the overall philosophy of being in control of your strength and using it wisely, so in those years when I was at Columbia, I spent a lot of time developing my skills at various dojos. I liked the idea of being prepared for a Charles Atlas bully-on-the-beach moment, illustrated in comic books and magazines in those days as part of an ad for bodybuilding. That moment of standing up to a bully never came, but martial arts kept me fit, satisfied my yearning to make progress through effort, and, as I said, helped me alleviate some of the stress of long hours studying and working.

I Only Knew What I Knew

After that first summer in New York, I had begun to work on my MBA at Columbia as planned, but a year in, I switched over to a PhD program, believing it would give me more options when I got out of school. I was earning good grades, which helped me to win several fellowships, so my tuition was paid for.

In 1964, I was asked to teach classes for MBA and PhD students that I had taken only a year or two before. Many of the business school students attending my classes were a few years older than I—and had business experience far beyond my summers at a couple of steel plants. I imagined some of my students might be thinking, "How is this kid, who has never worked in business, going to be able to teach me?" I tried to be well prepared at all times and present the material in the most interesting way I could. My martial arts training had developed my self-confidence, and time that I'd spent on the road helped me set limits with my students. Most respected me and my authority, but I recall one guy I had in class who kept talking while I was lecturing. After this happened a couple of times, I stopped midlecture, walked over to where he was sitting, and said, "If you continue to interrupt me, I'm going to ask you to take your desk, put it into the corner, and face the wall for the rest of the hour. If you talk again after that, I'm going to drop you from the class."

He didn't talk over me again.

Teaching and studying business simultaneously was challenging, but I found the academic environment stimulating, and business was far more interesting to me as a field of study than engineering had been, so I was glad I had made the change. Interacting with students was rewarding. Plus, there was some variety in the courses I taught: security analysis, finance, management, and managerial economics.

Most of my students in the business school were men, but there were a few women. I did get a chance to teach more women when I took a side job at the Tobé-Coburn School for Fashion Careers in NYC. The school trained young women who wanted careers in the fashion industry, and most of the students had little interest in the topics of the required economics course I taught. But a few surprised me by developing an excellent grasp of economic principles despite having only a high school education plus a few college-level courses. In fact, this handful of students seemed as quick to catch on as my students at Columbia, who had much more exposure to courses in economics. It's interesting to wonder what these women might have done with their careers had they not been culturally conditioned to focus on a field of business that was deemed more suitable for their gender.

During my time at Columbia, I knew little about issues such as sexism or racism, but I was developing a broader worldview, paying more attention to the news, and becoming better informed. I was out in the world now, and I felt an obligation to expand my knowledge and understanding. Still, there was much I had to learn that I'd had little exposure to, and I didn't grapple with concepts like social justice and economic inequity the way I do today.

At one point during this era, the students at Columbia, like their peers on other college campuses, took over the administration building and refused to leave before demands they issued were met by school administrators. As I recall, they insisted that students should have more influence over the courses they were offered and that grades should be banned. I wondered how many Columbia students in their late teens and early twenties were qualified to decide what they needed to know to ensure a solid educational foundation for their futures. And grades seemed an important measurement tool to help them understand where they stood in comparison to others in the same program—or in programs at other schools. Another demand was for attendance in class not to be mandatory—but how were they going to learn what they needed to know if they skipped lectures?

My thinking was rooted in practicality—and I had trouble understanding their perspectives. Once when I was wearing my sports coat and tie and walking to my classroom to begin teaching, I stopped for a moment to listen to a long-haired fellow, who was wearing jeans and a T-shirt, speaking at a demonstration outside the library at Columbia. Through his megaphone, he was urging people to lobby the government to spend more money to help certain groups of people. I asked him if he had a savings account. When he answered "yes," I asked, "If you feel so strongly, why don't you just donate your own money to charities you believe in? Why should the government raise our taxes when the private sector and we, as individuals, can be the ones to help?" What I had to say seemed to have no effect on him, and I had to get to class, so I moved on. My conservative values clashed with the counterculture of the time.

I hadn't experienced discrimination or looked around at my peers and thought, "The system we are a part of is unfair," so I didn't understand what he was trying to get across. I understand it better today. Some groups will not get reliable help through the private sector and need government help: the disabled, displaced workers, and educationally deprived groups, for example.

At the time, I was a free-market capitalist and felt that the social responsibility of business was to maximize profits to their shareholders and then let the shareholders decide what to do with dividends they received from the company or with money they got from selling their shares. I have since rethought the role of business and government, together and individually, in addressing societal problems. These days, I think businesses should play a bigger role than they have previously. For example, they could encourage their employees to do pro bono work. They could also finance some initiatives in their communities that help in areas such as education, employment, and job training. This way, low-income people would not have to be as dependent on the government. Many for-profit companies have organizational structures that could be used for creating and managing programs to help the disadvantaged. Additionally, if nonprofits and businesses work together, forging partnerships, they could make a real impact in communities where these organizations are based. The programs could involve such things as teaching computer and economic literacy and workplace skills. If businesses engaged in more of these activities, they would ultimately benefit. The capitalistic system that so many businesspeople believe in would be strengthened because when people are able to thrive, they have more buying power.

In later years, after I had more life experience, I could look back and see how little I knew about the challenges people around me were facing. Even working with the underprivileged kids that summer before starting at Columbia hadn't triggered in me a sense of obligation to serve others in the community—beyond giving money and, when the occasion presented itself, volunteering to help out, such as through a church. At that time, most of my peers were of my social class and assumed, as I did, that the American dream worked for everyone willing to play by the rules. I wasn't being exposed very much to ideas that might have challenged my thinking. I didn't question societal structures and assumed that anyone could make the most of the many opportunities I figured were available to everyone. My focus was on building a life for myself, and I didn't spend much time thinking about what struggles people I didn't know might be having.

"They only dust for fingerprints on TV"

Jerri and I would enjoy more vacations to Caneel Bay as a result of the perks of her job. We benefitted from the Eastern Airlines/RockResorts partnership: Laurance Rockefeller was an early investor in Eastern Airlines and a major stockholder, and he also established some resorts in exotic locations. Eastern offered its employees like Jerri free air transportation or lodging, or both, which helped us take trips we otherwise could not have afforded.

Jerri and I agreed we wanted to have a family someday. For now, we wanted to take advantage of the flexibility in our schedules to explore the world and slow down the pace of our lives with vacations when we could. We were lucky to get to see as much of the world as we did and be able to spend downtime in so many natural, beautiful places. My hunger for nature time was often satisfied when we took time off to travel—and I also enjoyed being exposed to a variety of cultures and ways of life.

Just like when I had hitchhiked, I discovered that people often defy the stereotypes about them. For example, I had heard stories about how the French were haughty and didn't like Americans, but Jerri and I had a very different experience of the French people. Once, we were on an open-air bus in Paris trying to find our destination and asked the passengers sitting near us for help. When we got off the bus, we started walking in the wrong direction and suddenly heard a number of people on the bus calling out to us to turn around and walk the other way. I was learning to trust my own experiences instead of relying on what I had heard or read.

After two years of living in Queens, Jerri and I were eager to become homeowners and build our "nest." Both of us were from backgrounds where material items weren't highly valued; our parents, who had lived through the Depression, were frugal, and we had picked up their habits. Nevertheless, while Jerri's modest income and the small amount I earned from teaching allowed us to get by, it was difficult for us to save money for a down payment on an apartment. We borrowed $5,000 from a friend to buy a two-bedroom apartment in a co-op called Hudson View Gardens on the Upper West Side of Manhattan near the Hudson River and the Cloisters. My friend was a missionary, but he had more money than we did, and I paid him more in interest than he could earn putting his money in a savings account.

The apartment we chose to buy, built in the 1920s, was in good shape, but Jerri and I wanted to make it our own. I laid tile we had picked out for the kitchen floor; sanded, stained, and shellacked the counters; polished the parquet floors, and put up shelving. Jerri worked alongside me on many of the projects, and together we found furniture and fixtures that we liked.

A few weeks after moving in, we still had many of our wedding gifts in boxes because there was much to do to arrange our space as we wanted—but some of those gifts disappeared one night as we slept. It hadn't occurred to Jerri and me, who had grown up in the quiet suburbs of Pittsburgh, that buying a first-floor co-op would mean having to keep the windows locked. It seems a cat burglar crept in through the unlocked windows that we had opened so that a cool breeze might lift the summer heat. We could see dirty handprints on the walls of our bedroom. Realizing what had happened, we called the police and soon, an officer arrived to take our report. I pointed out the handprints on the wall, thinking they could be used to catch the thief. The officer said, "It's not like on TV. I won't be taking and running prints." What was a big deal to Jerri and me was a rather ordinary event to a New York City cop. For him, catching the culprit was a low priority.

I also encountered the police when more than once, I found our blue VW bug on the sidewalk and had to explain why it was parked there. Some local pranksters were clearly amused that they could lift the lightweight, compact vehicle, and the joke grew stale for me after the first time, but I didn't trade in the car. After all, it was only two years old, and I had gotten it for a pretty good price—$1,000. Plus, it was very practical for getting around New York City, where parking spaces could be scarce and often, tight. The Volkswagen "Beetle," or "bug," has come to be associated with the counterculture of the 1960s, but for me, it was just a car that worked well with my life in New York City. Buying the two-year-old VW was one of my early investment decisions. The alternative had been to purchase a ten-year-old Mercedes-Benz sedan in impeccable condition for the same price. I felt the Volkswagen would be a more economical choice, and I liked that it had lower mileage even though I loved the Mercedes more. Practicality went up against sentiment, and practicality won—as it typically did at this time in my life.

Driving in busy New York City traffic wasn't easy, so while we had the VW, Jerri and I continued to rely on the bus or subway to get around during the week. Having the car gave us more flexibility, however, particularly on the weekends.

"Why not a half dozen?"

In those years in New York, I felt I was training in more than one area of my life. In addition to practicing martial arts, I was learning about business and the craft of teaching. I felt comfortable being a student striving to develop mastery. Simultaneously, I was stepping into the role of teacher and authority figure.

In a sense, I was also training to be a family breadwinner, or "head of household." I went along with a cultural current for men that swept me along: You get married, establish yourself in your career, and enjoy some years with your wife before kids come along. I wanted to start a family fairly soon. The recommendation at the time was to have children as early as possible to avoid any birth defects. I remember asking my doctor about an athlete's foot medication I was taking and deciding not to use it since I was told there was a chance it would affect Jerri's and my ability to have a healthy baby. Other than looking into that concern, I didn't feel I had to prepare for parenting. There were no classes for expectant fathers—at least, not that I knew of. And as wives gave birth, husbands sat in waiting rooms until they were called. "Planning" a family, to me, was figuring out where we would live and what type of lifestyle we would have. I wanted a half dozen kids, but of course, that vision didn't account for how Jerri would manage all of them as their primary caretaker! Mine was a romantic notion born from liking kids and the idea of a big, happy family, and I didn't think through the particulars.

I was confident I could be a good provider without Jerri bringing in an income. Her career seemed satisfying and meaningful to her, but like many middle-class women in that era, she didn't see it lasting after we had children, when she would switch her focus to taking care of the kids and our family home. Our roles were set out for us, and we didn't question them—there didn't seem any reason to.

My general outlook was that the world and my life seemed full of possibilities as long as I was willing to put in the time and effort toward reaching my goals, and every day, I was working hard to do that. Whatever problems there were in the world, they seemed far away from me and the life I was building for myself and Jerri.

Even so, sometimes when I rode the bus to our home in Washington Heights, I would look at the arms of some of the straphangers and see tattoos from concentration camps in Europe. I thought about these Jewish New Yorkers who had survived the worst and emerged to start a new life in America. What they had gone through was unimaginable. Looking at them made me wonder how anyone could have treated them so inhumanely—and I thought about how extraordinary it was that they could now simply go about their everyday lives in the most ordinary way. Their strength and courage really struck me and made me think about my good fortune to be born into the circumstances I was born into.

I also thought about the need for vigilance to keep horrific events like World War II and the Holocaust from happening again. Jerri and I made friends with people at Columbia and Eastern Airlines, and one couple we got to know through Jerri's job was a woman who worked with her and the woman's husband, who was a carpenter. At one point in our conversations with them, it came out that the husband had been a member of the Hitler youth. I knew this man was a churchgoer, and he seemed like a nice fellow, but the revelation was shocking. How many of the bigoted and racist beliefs of the Nazis had he held—and did he still hold any? Being so close to someone who supported evil acts was sobering. I hadn't thought about how people we think of as monsters might look quite ordinary. I would like to believe this particular man completely rejected the teachings of his childhood. In time, our social circle changed, so I never found out if that was the case.

IBM, FedEx, and a Decision

The path I was on seemed promising, and already, I had solid evidence that I was progressing in establishing a solid home base. I had a wife, a home we could call our own, and a firm foundation for a career that would support us and children. And when our daughter, Caryn, was born in 1966, I felt even more determined to be a reliable provider for my family. In that same year, I received my PhD and became an assistant professor of finance and banking. I was also doing some consulting, and by teaching an extra load, I earned an eight-month-long sabbatical by the time Caryn was walking.

Toward the end of my stint teaching at Columbia, FedEx was just starting up, and Floyd Hall, Jerri's boss at Eastern, asked me to head up the rival service he was thinking of creating. I said no; I wanted to continue my work as an assistant professor. Around the same time, one of my students introduced me to her father, Harold Martin, who was president of Martin Oil Service, which owned gas stations and other businesses. Harold had developed cancer, was looking to groom a successor, and offered me a job. Again, I couldn't see myself leaving my teaching life, so I turned him down. Later, as my upcoming sabbatical approached, I accepted a job offer from IBM to teach for eight months in its executive development program. I planned to gain some good experience and then return to my teaching career at Columbia.

Prior to my starting at IBM, Harold Martin contacted me again and asked if I would reconsider coming to work with him in Chicago. I thought about it. I would get more real-world business experience working with Martin than I would teaching in a training program at IBM. I talked it through with Jerri and decided that if IBM would release me from my commitment, I would go to work for Harold Martin as his retail-marketing manager. IBM was very gracious and told me, "Do what you think is best for you." I figured that if I decided I didn't like the job at Martin Oil, I could always go back to Columbia.

Twenty-seven by now, with a baby daughter, a wife, and a PhD after my name, I could see the potential at Martin Oil. I felt I had a chance to become the heir apparent. I met several of the other executives, who were in their forties and fifties, and could see that while there were many skilled and knowledgeable men working for him, Harold had some reason for looking outside of his pool of talent for someone to take his place. I believe he had faith that should he not survive his cancer, Martin Oil could and would thrive if he were to set me up to take over. Harold didn't give me specifics about just how ill he was, but I picked up on his urgency.

Jerri and I started packing and preparing to move to the Chicago area right after I was released from my IBM commitment (and still being paid by Columbia University for my sabbatical). Melinda, Harold Martin's daughter and the student of mine who had recommended me to her father, helped Jerri and me find a townhouse rental in a suburb close to Martin Oil's offices. Then Jerri and I sold our apartment in the co-op for around $10,000, double what we had paid for it just a few years before, yielding a good profit and allowing me to pay back our friend who had lent us our purchase price.

My life as a businessman had begun.

Becoming a spouse and a parent are both big milestones in most people's lives. When creating family, we find ourselves thinking about our resources—money, time, and attention—and how to not short-change ourselves and those we care about. If we don't reflect on what we are doing as we set up a household and begin a family, we are likely to end up living according to familiar patterns from childhood without consciously considering alternatives.

As you think about your family and household, you might want to look at how you balance different people's needs, including your own, and why you made the choices you did.

Questions for the Reader to Ponder

Establishing a household. As you think about your first permanent living quarters after leaving your family home, what are your feelings and thoughts? What words or themes come to mind? What did you do to establish a home that made you feel secure and even relaxed and nurtured? If you lived with others, did you work together harmoniously as you set up your household or did you have conflicts? What did you learn from the experience?

Spending money. How do you and others in your household make decisions about spending money? For example, when making big purchases, do you and your partner (if you have one) usually check in with each other beforehand? Do you feel guilty or anxious spending money on yourself? If so, why is that? Do you ever end up in conflicts with family about the financial choices you have made that affect them?

Teaching. We all teach in different ways, whether we're teaching an employee or a child and whether we are teaching a specific skill or imparting knowledge. Do you believe you're a good teacher? Why or why not? Would you like to be a better teacher? If so, why? As you think about those who have guided, taught, or mentored you, what made them such effective teachers and supporters of you? If you were disappointed with someone who could have played this role but didn't (or did but played it badly), what did you want them to do for you that they didn't do? Was there an upside to them not giving you more guidance and support?

CHAPTER SEVEN

Donning the Necktie

With Caryn in her baby seat and Jerri and me in the front of our VW bug, I drove westward while a moving van transported the contents of our apartment. The winds were fierce as I drove on the Pennsylvania Turnpike, so keeping the car steady wasn't easy. Looking back, it's an apt metaphor for my driving forward on the road to a new experience and recognizing that there were forces beyond my control that I would have to manage if I were going to remain steady and be successful in my new venture.

When I arrived in Chicago in the fall of 1967, Martin Oil Service owned about 100 service stations across thirteen states and the District of Columbia. It also owned five terminals for holding gasoline and diesel oil, some car washes, and two barges on the inland waterways—the Mississippi and other rivers. With my background in metallurgical engineering and my PhD in business administration, I felt I could contribute to the company's success. Although I didn't realize it initially, my time on the road had taught me to relate to a variety of people, which would be helpful given that on the job, I would encounter executives, service station owners and attendants, engineers, truckers, and more.

I had made it a condition of my employment that I would be allowed to run things my own way without Harold or anyone else micromanaging my decisions. "If the results aren't good," I told him, "then let me go." I also asked for equity in the company and profit sharing. I could see the potential for not just earning a salary but growing my wealth as I helped grow the company. Over time, I ended up acquiring additional stock until eventually, the Martin family and I each owned approximately 50 percent of the companies I ran. Martin Oil Service was worth about $10 million when I started, and our respective interests would grow to many times that in the decades to come.

Back when we were first settling into our new home, Jerri and I started to make friends and explore our new city and its surrounding areas. I was looking forward to spending our first holiday season in the Chicago area and taking Caryn to see Santa Claus and the Christmas displays downtown at Marshall Fields. I had fond memories of my dad doing this for Kirk and me when we were kids living in Gary.

For Jerri and me, the summer of 1967, dubbed the "Summer of Love" by the media and cultural commentators, had been a summer of planning for the future, with me focused on entering the business world and Jerri focused on the domain of family and home. Antiwar protests and the hippies' "happenings" just weren't a part of our lives. The contrasts between the counterculture and business culture were sharp, but you could say that the contrasts between that era and now are even sharper. America was on the verge of rapid changes in how people lived, worked, and thought, and in time, these changes would affect the way I saw the world.

"Fill 'er up with regular"

In the late 1960s, management jobs in business were mainly held by men rather than women. I believe that the oil and gas business may have been even more male-dominated than some other industries.

When I began working at Martin, OPEC, the Organization of Petroleum Exporting Countries, was only seven years old, and prices for oil seemed fairly stable. Gasoline sold for around thirty or thirty-one cents a gallon, the equivalent of $2.25 or $2.30 today. Prices had only risen about a half penny per gallon per year for a decade. I couldn't see any reason that would change. These days, gas prices can fluctuate greatly depending on international politics.

In 1967, lead was regularly added to most gasoline to prevent the engine from uncontrolled combustion (knocking), raise the octane level to increase gas mileage, and protect the valves from deteriorating. This would be the case up until the 1970s, but greater awareness of the environmental effects of lead changed the gasoline business. Leaded gas began to be phased out and by the 1990s, no one at the pump had to request leaded "regular" gasoline versus "unleaded." In the '60s and '70s, it was common for people to not think about the impact of the chemicals we were putting into the ground, water, and atmosphere. We were all a part of a car culture that has shifted over the years as people started to question their impact on the environment and the need for so many people to burn fossil fuels to get from here to there. In the oil and gas business back then, alternative fuels or ways of powering cars felt futuristic—not something we would be dealing with anytime soon.

Many of the typical cars in the late 1960s were big and luxurious, and new highways, built in the 1950s under President Eisenhower, stretched out across the country. Car ownership was at its peak of one passenger car for every two Americans, but owning and running filling stations or gas stations was not as stable and lucrative a business as others were. There were several factors that made it difficult.

First and foremost, our profit margins were slim compared to other businesses. There wasn't much of a markup on gasoline, and selling it was our main business. In good times, we would only make a few cents per gallon.

Some consumers believed that major gas station chains offered higher quality gas, but in reality, the difference in quality between major chains and independent ones like Martin Oil was negligible. Price wars occurred, but they took their toll on every seller's bottom line. We didn't have the kind of cushion that bigger companies had, so price wars could really hurt us.

Right away, I recognized that if we were to lower our prices too aggressively, it could erase our profit margins completely. What we needed was to cut superfluous expenses and find the most effective ways to market our gasoline.

We also had to start thinking about ways to diversify beyond just selling gasoline and car-related products such as motor oil and windshield wiper fluid. Other sources of revenue with better margins could protect our cash flow should we face some unforeseen disaster.

Martin Oil gas stations were known for volume. In fact, we sold more gallons of gasoline per station than almost any other company. I thought it was important to keep that distinction. Harold Martin was highly regarded as an innovative marketer, and as the new retail-marketing manager, I wanted to continue that tradition.

"Who's the new guy? And who does he think he is?"

In those early days, perhaps my biggest battle was to not let any of the older executives, some of whom regarded me with skepticism and resentment, rattle me. I was not only younger than all of them and new to the oil business but also an outsider who had been brought in by the owner. I had to stake out my territory and defend it. Harold Martin and Executive Vice President Ron Peterson, who reported to Harold and was my boss, both expressed great confidence in me. Ron, an experienced oilman, was also an outsider who had been hired just a year before I arrived, so I felt a kinship with him. He would teach me a lot about the business and prove to be a valuable ally and friend.

In my first year at the company, Harold would often call me and keep me on the phone for three or four hours straight. He was spending a lot of time at his home north of Chicago and rarely came down to the office because his battle with cancer demanded his attention. I am sure he was often very tired from his treatments. At the end of each conversation, to reassure him that I had listened carefully and would take care of everything he asked of me, I would summarize by saying, "Mr. Martin, here is the list of things I've heard you say you want me to do." I would read off the list and ask if he had anything he wanted to add before we finished our call. Although I wasn't consciously aware of it at the time, I see now that he must have sensed how short his time was. He seemed determined to share with me not just what we needed to get done but all the insights and guidance he could.

My ideas seemed to go over well with Harold, but when it came to the other executives, I picked up that some had an attitude of "Sure, give him plenty of rope. He'll end up hanging himself like other new guys have." I learned that several optimistic, innovative newcomers had come and gone over the years and a jaded sensibility had taken hold among many executives. It showed in subtle ways.

That first winter I was at Martin, I was brushing snow and ice off my Chevy Caprice—my company car—with a broom. A man involved in maintenance at our stations criticized me in front of others, warning me that I might scratch the finish. Now, he could have been right, but his condescending tone irritated me. I asked him to come to my office, closed my door, and said to him, "I'll just say this once. If you talk to me like that again publicly, we'll have big problems. If you have something to say, come and talk to me privately."

My early experiences in speaking up for myself were proving useful, and having conversations like that one defused any confrontations fairly quickly. Some of the executives were not used to someone standing up to them. With Harold Martin seldom around, they saw the office as their own fiefdom. They assumed that Harold understood how important they were and figured that if the time came for him to step away, he would hand over the reins to them—which didn't turn out to be the case at all.

By March of 1968, my rise in the company was meteoric: I was promoted from retail-marketing manager to executive vice president. Everyone in the company reported to me, even the older men who had been there for years. That did not sit well with some of them. Although Harold Martin often called me directly, I reported to Ron. My promotion showed I had avoided becoming entangled in that loose rope I had been given.

It was clear I was here to stay.

Harold had been a legendary marketer and an extremely successful businessman. When I arrived in the last phase of his life, he didn't always have the energy to check up on the executives who reported to him. Many had become used to being yes men—coasting along and not taking decisive action to push past obstacles, solve problems, or seal deals that had become stalled. I had seen and heard that Harold, who must have been under a lot of stress dealing with his cancer, would shout at those who reported to him if they did not produce the results he wanted or if they displeased him in some other way, but after that, things would blow over and little, if anything, would change.

In contrast to Harold's style, I seldom reacted emotionally, even when some of the men I worked with would get annoyed with me after I confronted them about missed deadlines or lack of progress toward a goal. One of the executives, Bob Bushek, Harold's brother-in-law, took offense when I pointed out that he hadn't followed through on a promise to get something done by a certain date. He got so angry at me that he challenged me to a fight in his office. Bob was an amateur baseball player and in good shape, a tough guy and older than I was. I walked over to him, looked him in the eye, and said, "Bob, you're nuts." I laughed. We looked at each other for a few moments—then he laughed, too. This shifted the energy of the confrontation, and we continued our conversation.

Being fit and having trained in martial arts contributed to my confidence in this situation. I took Bob seriously but didn't feel it would serve him, me, or our future relationship to get into a fight with him. I knew it would be a waste of energy to confront him verbally to get him to back down. I had internalized a martial arts principle known as *ma*: keeping the proper distance from an opponent. In judo, being too close or too far away physically while fighting would make me less effective. Similarly, being too close or too distant emotionally in a work situation would make it difficult for me to achieve my objectives. I didn't get upset and into a fight with Bob, physically or verbally. I also didn't walk away and cross my fingers that his anger would dissipate in my absence. I kept a productive conversation going despite his volatility. He realized he would have to calm down to get his ideas heard.

The Thanksgiving of 1968, Harold called me around 9:30 in the morning, and I remained on the phone with him pretty much all day. It sticks out in my mind because I was torn. I knew Jerri wasn't going to be happy having to spend the holiday with very little of my attention, but she accepted the situation. I could feel that for Harold, time was of the essence, so his call just couldn't wait. Sadly, Harold Martin passed away that December from pneumonia after cancer treatments had severely depleted his immunity. It was a shock, and I thought about how his family must have gone through that holiday season in a daze. I would have many more holidays with Jerri and Caryn—losing one Thanksgiving to work obligations was nothing to complain about given the big picture. Now, I was glad Harold had kept me on the phone for so long that holiday morning, continuing to teach me and share his experiences with me. And I was happy that he felt he had someone who understood his vision for the company and respected it. I hoped that he died with the peace of knowing I was committed to being a good steward of all that he had built up, a foundation of security for his family.

At the end of December, the board of directors (Harold's wife and daughters) made their decision: Ron Peterson was chosen to be chairman of the board, and I became president of Martin Oil.

Several executives, including Harold Martin's brother-in-law, were less than pleased with the decision. But from the start, it had been clear to many that Harold was preparing me to step into a higher position. The executives who worked with me had to accept the reality that I was the boss. I was busy learning and strategizing but also had to spend some time dealing with bruised egos. If other executives went through the Kübler-Ross stages of denial, anger, bargaining, depression, and acceptance as they thought about me having been promoted over them, they mostly kept their drama hidden. By the time of Harold's death, I had been essentially running the company for nine months, so the executives were familiar with me, my vision, and my work style, and they adjusted.

Overall, the transition was less rocky than it might have been. It probably helped that I was trying to be sensitive to the discomfort around Harold's will. He left money to his daughters, his wife, and certain employees and left out others, perhaps unwittingly. I suggested to the Martin family that some valuable employees who had been excluded receive some money after Harold's death. It all worked out without our losing any crucial executives or staff members—which was important to me. I didn't want the founder's death to mean the end of his company, as is too often the case in these types of situations. I'm very glad that despite that difficult chapter of Martin Oil's history, it took us into a prosperous future free of infighting.

The Rough-and-Tumble Side of Town

By the time I became the executive vice president of Martin Oil, Jerri and I had joined a local church and were setting down roots in the community. With all that was going on for us, we were only tangentially aware of the melee between police and protestors in August of 1968 during the Democratic National Convention. I was more affected by the civil unrest after the assassination of Martin Luther King Jr., about five months earlier. Many of our stations were in the areas affected by the riots, so I had to be very involved in making sure everyone was safe. At one of our stations in a mostly African American neighborhood near Sacramento and Taylor, the manager, who was African American, grabbed his gun and went out of the station to rescue a white man trapped in his car. This fellow's life was being threatened by angry rioters who surrounded and attacked his vehicle. I could understand the level of pain and anguish expressed outwardly at the loss of Dr. King, but I was worried for my employees and our customers. I had never experienced having to take responsibility for keeping people safe from random violence, which was spreading through Chicago. On certain streets, chaos could erupt like a brush fire. Several people died, hundreds were arrested, and it was a frightening few days as we watched the news coverage of the violence.

In the next few years, Chicago settled down, and Jerri and I welcomed our son, Michael, into the family in 1970. Janet, our youngest daughter, followed in 1973. Jerri and I hired sitters occasionally so we could have date nights, usually going to nearby restaurants on the South Side of Chicago but occasionally to an event downtown.

One thing I was learning about my new city was that many perceived the South Side to be working-class, down-to-earth, or rough around the edges compared to the communities on the North Shore. I was sometimes aware of the subtle stigmatization of people on the South Side by those in the northern suburbs such as Kenilworth and Winnetka and on Chicago's "Gold Coast" at the city's north end.

Once, we had some bankers come down to the South Side to meet with a team at Martin Oil, and when lunchtime came, just for fun, I brought them to a place called Willie's Wee-Nee Wagon. We bought hot dogs and ate them while sitting outside at a picnic table. No one seemed too worried about spilling mustard on their suit, but it was probably not the kind of business lunch they were used to having in the Loop! I could have sprung for a meal that involved tables and chairs indoors, but part of me enjoyed reinforcing the South Side stereotype with my choice of a lunch spot.

Another time I seemed to have raised eyebrows with my attire was when I competed in the Illinois State Platform Tennis Tournament with Bill Roberts as my partner. Bill worked with me at Martin for some years as head of our finance department and is a good friend. At the end of the first day, we were still in the tournament (although in the back draw), having won all but one of our matches. Seated at a banquet being held on the North Shore, we listened as the master of ceremonies began naming the many places around the state from which teams had come. "We even have a team from the South Side!" he exclaimed—as if Bill and I were from some sort of exotic and untamed place. I chuckled at the murmur of the crowd. The next day, Bill and I were playing in the finals of the consolation round. Growing increasingly warm as the cold and cloudy Chicago day became sunnier, we removed layers of clothes to stay cool. I ended up playing in my long underwear. In contrast, our opponents from the North Shore continued to look quite dapper in their sweaters. I was comfortable in the clothes I was wearing. The down-to-earth, South Side ways suited me—as did deliberately reinforcing the stereotype.

I was glad I had listened to my instincts: My job was a good fit. As president of Martin Oil, I was dedicated to improving our profit margin and overcoming a variety of difficulties that required my attention if we were going to sustain our success.

When coming into a new situation as an outsider, you have to learn the rules of the culture before trying to change them. As you look back at times in your own life where you were out of sync with a new situation, you might want to reflect on the choices you made and how well they worked for you.

Questions for the Reader to Ponder

Finding your own way of doing things. As you think about your career, your family, or any endeavor that matters to you, do you wrestle with doing things differently from what others might expect or desire? If so, why? If you tend to conform to how others do things, why do you think that is? What, if any, consequences do you fear you would experience if you did things differently from how others do them? Can you see any ways in which your fear and inflexibility prevent you from achieving your goals and sustaining the best aspects of your career, family life, or important endeavor? If you tend to be a maverick, how does that work for you, and what are the downfalls, if any?

Being the outsider coming in. Have you ever felt that you were an outsider having to fit in and not sure how to do that and be accepted? What, if anything, did you try to do to make that happen? How did it work out for you? In retrospect, what, if anything, could you have done differently to make the transition work?

How people perceive you. What do you do when you feel you're being perceived in a negative way or as a threat? Do you conform, become angry, assert yourself, try to change others' perceptions, or something else? Does your response to this type of situation work for you? If not, how would you like to react differently when people are not accepting of you?

CHAPTER EIGHT

Working with All the Moving Parts

"You expect less from Martin, but you get more!"

That was one of our slogans delivered in a chipper voice through radios in cars and homes throughout Chicago. It resonated for our customers who, for the most part, were working class and could relate to the idea of a scrappy little guy that people tend to underestimate. Our advertising reflected a "can-do" attitude that appealed to me, too.

Coming into Martin Oil with little experience in business, I expected to face a bit of a learning curve and perhaps some challenges in winning over men ranked above me who might see me as just an academic. Even so, I felt confident as I eagerly dove into learning about Martin and what was working and what wasn't. Quickly, I realized I would have to make some bold moves that could raise some eyebrows among the other executives. I hadn't intended to make big changes right away, but I could see that the low-margin business was not as stable as it could be or as I wanted it to be. I was determined to strengthen it so everyone at Martin could prosper into the future.

Initially, my focus was on promotions at our stations. As I said, I wanted to keep the core of the Martin Oil brand: We were one of the largest independent gas station chains but tiny compared to Shell, Texaco, Mobil, and some others. We couldn't lose money on selling gasoline during a price war with other stations and make it up somewhere along the supply chain because we couldn't control it the way larger companies could. I knew we would have to develop creative marketing strategies to be successful and less vulnerable to being undercut and even pushed out of business.

Our "little guy" customers tended to live in neighborhoods where family budgets could be very tight. Martin Oil's high volume of gasoline sales was due in part to our reputation for giving away more free household items than most other gas stations did. I decided we would continue to build on those promotions that were popular with our core customers.

"How come I never get the ace of clubs?"

Here's how premium giveaways worked: A customer could drive into one of our stations, fill up his tank, and bring home free glassware, laundry soap, or paper towels—the items we offered to customers buying gas were very practical. Another popular promotion was giving away savings stamps with purchases. Customers would affix the stamps to the pages of booklets that, when filled, could be exchanged for cash or household items found in our premium catalogue. This promotion worked like S&H Green Stamps, which were very popular in those days. We added new incentives to stir up even more interest: Scratch off a section on the front of the book, and if you revealed two stars, it would double the book's value. Three, and you tripled it.

However, when I looked closely at the numbers soon after my arrival, I realized that our program for exchanging stamp booklets for catalogue premiums was uneconomical. The cost for the many employees managing this aspect of our stamp program wasn't justified by the modest benefits. I began shutting down the program, reassigning those working in it. We had plenty of other promotions that were popular, drove higher sales, and were more cost effective than the stamp booklets.

We also gave out scratch-off game cards with purchases. One game let the customer guess the winners and losers of NFL games. If they picked the teams that ended up winning, they could exchange their card for a cash prize. There were also bingo and poker games— customers kept buying from us when they were just one winning number or playing card away from their prize. They would come in again to get another card and scratch the edge of a coin against it, hoping it would reveal a number or image that they didn't realize was rare. The missing number or playing card image was printed on just enough game cards to have some winners but not so many that the promotion's cost would be too high to justify it.

I had to rely on the printer to keep close track of how many winning cards were printed, and one day, shortly after I began working as the retail-marketing manager, a concerned district manager phoned me. He said that at our Queens and Brooklyn stations, an unusually high number of winners were coming in to collect their prizes. After talking to the printer, I realized too many winning cards were out there. How many had been given out and how many were still in stacks at our two New York stations, I didn't know, but the news was sobering. There was a distinct possibility that if we made cash payments to all the winners, Martin Oil could experience a serious financial hit. And if we were sued for not honoring all the winning cards, that would be disastrous, too.

Immediately, I started making calls, stopping the Magic Bingo game in the two stations we knew were affected and checking that none of our other stations had the same problem. It was a nerve-racking few days as we worked to be sure we had taken back all of the cards. By early the next week, it was clear the crisis had been contained. The foul-up had been a costly wake-up call. Afterward, I set up procedures to ensure there would be no more printing errors on the game cards.

I also was learning about the various inks used to create the cards and scratch-off boxes. This lesson came after one of our employees was found to be using an ultraviolet light to read through the heavy scratch-off ink, hoping to discern which cards were winners so he could hand them out to family and friends or sell them.

Cheating and theft could happen in many ways. We caught one of our employees pressing a stethoscope to an oilcan he had shaken: He was hoping to hear a token fall to the bottom of the can, which would indicate that this can was a "winner." Other employees stole money from the registers or items from the stations, so keeping on top of our accounting procedures and inventory management was important. Managers and vendors might be in on the thefts, too. Sometimes we used lie detectors to determine whether someone was lying about having stolen from us or cheated us in some way. Despite knowing that we checked our figures, a few employees, including some managers, still took the risk of stealing or cheating. Clearly, some people didn't think long term and didn't appreciate that it would only be a matter of time until they were caught—and they were.

Customers sometimes stole from us, too, by driving off in their cars before paying. We didn't often catch them and didn't have cameras to identify license plates, as is the case today.

For the most part, our employees, vendors, and customers were honest. Nonetheless, we had to be vigilant so we could keep shortages to a minimum. Limiting our losses was a big part of the job for our station managers. Today, we would probably have even more technologies that would help us stay on top of our accounting and inventory management.

Rolling Up My Sleeves

I felt that to be successful as a businessman, I would have to work late many evenings and even some weekends. Jerri and I both accepted that.

Although it could be a bit of a strain on Jerri with young kids, I often traveled a few days a week when I visited stations and some of our other operations, which were growing in number. There was nothing to replace meeting face-to-face with people and being at a location to see for myself what was working and what wasn't. I would call home at night to talk, but otherwise, Jerri was on her own. I was often out of touch. She was a stay-at-home mother in those early years and had established friendships in our community, which kept her from being too isolated when I was at work or traveling.

A benefit of being not as connected on communication devices back then as managers are now is that I had time to reflect on my operations. That made it easier to come up with new ideas as opposed to feeling I had to constantly respond to queries from my team and others. Once I got into my car or was seated on an airplane—or found myself anywhere that there wasn't a landline phone—I was free of distractions. No one could contact me. Of course, being able to stay in touch during a challenging and fast-paced business negotiation or when on a deadline is helpful. Even so, as a society, we are struggling to manage the downside of constant communication that makes it hard to have uninterrupted time to reflect or ponder.

Believing in the value of hands-on experience, I had most new management hires at Martin work in a station for a month or two to learn any nuances about the operations they would be involved with. I wanted them to wait on customers who came in for a fill-up and oil change and observe the people and processes, like inventory control, to get a feel for what was behind the numbers on a piece of paper. I hoped my managers might pick up on something that could better inform the decisions they would be making. Being in a physical space with other people can make it easier to notice information that someone might miss by just checking in remotely. The pace of the work, the habits of the customers, the effectiveness of displays for enticing people to spend more—all are details of an operation that are easier to spot when you are there for a period of time.

Some of my new hires were embarrassed to be seen working in a gas station because it was out of sync with their self-image as a rising executive. One of them, who had come to us from a Big 8 public accounting firm, had been "born to the manor," so to speak, and lived in a tony downtown apartment. He told me that following my instructions, he dressed in a Martin Oil uniform to spend time working at a station. Apparently, a neighbor of his entered the garage of his building where he was just about to get into his car. He laughed as he told me what he did next: To avoid being seen, he quickly ducked behind a pillar.

When I first came to Martin, we all wore suit coats and ties—the norm in business back then. Even so, we dressed more informally than some professionals in the Loop did—the lawyers, for example, or the bankers and accountants who met with clients in high-rise office buildings. Ties started to be abandoned, and as offices everywhere adopted "casual Fridays," we started dressing more casually as well.

However, I continued to wear a metaphorical necktie. I was no longer the free-spirited kid I had been just a decade before. I was responsible for the well-being of my family and a company with more than a thousand employees. I was happy with my choices, but Mythopoetic Carl—my spiritual side—was rarely to be seen.

Beyond Just Selling Gasoline

Promotions and advertising were a smaller part of my job after becoming president. A priority for me was making sure we had safe working conditions and fair pay for our employees. Also, I wanted the company to grow over time to benefit everyone, including the owners.

At the beginning of my work for Martin Oil, global interconnectedness and disruptive technology weren't big factors the way they are in businesses today. Unbeknownst to me, both would start to affect the company in the 1970s and influence it even more in the decades to come. While the biggest and swiftest changes would not come until the early to middle part of the decade, as the new president, I recognized that we had to keep trying out new ideas to stay on top in the volume-sold game and keep an eye on our revenue streams.

To reduce costs and increase profitability, I looked closely at the use of credit cards to pay for purchases. When I started, we had a Martin Oil credit card, which I quickly discontinued because it was more cost effective for us if our customers paid in cash. We continued to allow them to use major credit cards, which required us to pay fees to the credit card companies, but we incentivized cash purchases with discounts on the price per gallon.

One of the ways I saw that Martin Oil could expand was to make deals with owners of already established convenience stores. We negotiated for the right to install underground tanks and pumps in front of their stores in exchange for sharing the profits with them. As the number of our own stations increased (including stations that had profitable stores integrated into them), we developed our truck stop business, too.

We also ventured into banking, oil and gas exploration, and later, steel warehousing as well as real estate. Over time, we invested in farms, office buildings, shopping centers, apartment houses, and movie theaters. I had to oversee multiple businesses and initiate and close many deals. Nearly all of them were successful, so on the whole, our diversification plan worked very well. Ultimately, of all our businesses, it would be our oil and gas exploration efforts that would yield us our biggest profits.

"Put our attendants in purple tights?"

I drew satisfaction from seeing a good return on our investments and observing an increase in the numbers that measured our performance. The tangible evidence of improvement and increased profits provided me with a sense of accomplishment and success. There were plenty of metrics to use as measuring sticks for how well we were doing: number of gallons of gas sold per station, number of barrels of oil produced, and so on. Improving our numbers kept me excited.

Even as president, I continued to find the promotions side of the business enjoyable and fun—in part because we weren't afraid to use humor to build our brand. Our short-lived slogan "You expect less from Martin, but you get more" was meant to be a wry response to Standard Oil's "You expect more from Standard, and you get it." Standard Oil sued us for copyright infringement, but our ads didn't run for long, so they dropped the suit.

We might run a promotion on a weekend and have a person in a clown or gorilla suit passing out coupons for a household item premium if you filled up with fifteen gallons, good for the weekend only. The costumes were a classic attention-getter I still sometimes see used today by companies trying to drum up business. Some might think it's corny, but it worked for us.

We also gave away purple martin birdhouses: Purple Martin Ethyl was our premium gasoline brand, so the idea was to get people to associate Martin Oil with the Purple Martin. Those ads also featured a jingle—an advertising message set to song—that we hoped would help people to remember our name. Jingles were popular at the time: The catchy melody and simple words would stick in customers' minds and make them think of us when their gas tank was running low, or so the theory went.

One of our zaniest advertising campaigns featured an announcer saying something like, "Here at Martin Oil gas stations, we have the best service, the best giveaways, the best prices—what do we have to do to get you to fill up at our station? Put our attendants in purple tights? . . . Okay, we'll do it!" Then, the listener heard one of our actual gas station managers say in a thick Southern accent, "Uh-oh, uh-oh, I ain't wearin' them tights!"

Then there was the ad featuring the Martin Tooth Fairy and another where we had someone play a reporter who wanted people to know that a giant chicken was threatening the city of Chicago. He said that if you drove into a Martin Oil gas station, you could get a free booklet on how to avert giant chicken attacks and urged listeners to please help us to save Chicago from this terrible threat of a giant chicken by driving in today and picking up the booklet. All of these ads served to get people talking about Martin and increased our sales.

We bought a lot of time on local radio stations over the years, so back when I was in charge of promotions, I'd meet with radio station advertising salesmen. I couldn't put away liquor the way some of them did (and wouldn't want to). I drank socially but in moderation—and ordered iced tea or water during the day. Some of these men would drink three or four cocktails at lunch yet walk out of the restaurant, cigarette in hand, seemingly as sober as could be. I don't know how they did it. I would have fallen asleep before we got the check.

When it came to strategizing about how and when to advertise, sometimes I would run ads in local newspapers or magazines and sometimes on the radio or TV. That required evaluating how many people any particular ad would reach and whether my ideal audience (blue-collar communities where most of our stations were located) would be exposed to the ad and take action because of it. For example, would they be more likely to tune into the radio during afternoon drive time when the cost per ad was higher, or at ten o'clock at night, when ads were cheaper? Would an ad cause them to buy more gasoline from us than they would have otherwise?

There were fewer media outlets then, and not all of them were highly effective at reaching the communities where most of our gas stations were located. While I didn't have clear data on how well the advertisements worked, I did what I could to be aware of our customers' buying patterns and what sorts of promotions and advertisements seemed to appeal to them.

For a few years, Martin Oil sponsored the Chicago Cubs on WGN, which had a huge listenership—and I came to know the Cubs announcers, Lou Boudreau and Vince Lloyd, and several players like Ernie Banks and Billy Williams. But did that help us sell gasoline? The truth is that there was no completely reliable way to judge how effective any particular TV, radio, or print ad was, which provided me with a challenge. How could I best use our marketing dollars? Promotion efforts often overlapped, and we didn't have data to work with as companies do today—the measurement tools were fairly crude, so we would have to decide whether the profits from extra sales during the promotion were enough to justify the cost.

In the late 1970s, when self-service became the popular model for gas stations and we were able to offer lower prices on gasoline, we reduced the number of premium and giveaway promotions and spent less on advertising. Even so, we kept our humorous, playful "Hey, we're the little guy, we have to try harder to get your attention!" reputation.

A Not-So-Benign Habit

Disruptions in the supply of gasoline and diesel fuel and unexpected spikes in costs were always a potential threat, so I was very focused on protecting the company financially. Adding convenience stores to our stations increased our profits. Food, candy, and household goods had a good markup. Cigarettes had a lesser one, but they were one of our best-selling items, drawing in customers.

Knowing what I know today about cigarettes, I wouldn't choose to carry them in our convenience stores, but it seemed almost everyone smoked in the 1960s and 1970s. Even into the 1980s, smoking around other people was very common. Martin Oil's offices were filled with smoke, and some executives and secretaries went through multiple packs of cigarettes a day. One of our VPs often had two cigarettes going at a time, leaving one perched in the ashtray in his office and lighting up again before he finished that first one. Cars came with cigarette lighters and ashtrays. Until the 1980s when smokers started to be pressured to restrict their smoking in businesses and in public, I took for granted that often, there would be a haze of smoke in places like offices, restaurants, and airplanes. In fact, I'm sad to say that lung cancer ended up taking the lives of several of our employees. We also lost some people to heart disease, possibly caused by smoking. Even as it became clear that cigarettes were carcinogenic, it was still some time before society recognized the toxic effect of secondhand smoke—and even thirdhand smoke (chemical residue cigarette smoke leaves on objects like walls and clothing). Like many Americans, I would come to change my perspective on cigarettes.

Even knowing about the dangers, some people still smoke—or vape. Why? Denial can be very strong. Or, they might vow to quit but don't. Why is it so hard for us to take the actions we say we want to take? In those days, it was just a question I might have pondered casually. Later, I would explore in depth—and write about—the topic of how to help people make positive changes that were somehow eluding them. For now, however, I was fully immersed in my work running a fairly large company. The self that was curious about the bigger questions was dormant.

Difficult Jobs

Knowing what I wanted to do in business and actually doing it with the help of my team kept me excited and motivated. One of the biggest challenges I faced at Martin over the years was dealing with our workforce. As president, I was balancing competing interests, seeing the control of labor costs and profit margins as important factors in keeping the business prosperous but also rewarding our employees so that they felt Martin was a good place to work. There were many moving pieces to manage and keep in balance if we were going to maximize our potential for profitability into the future.

We paid a fair wage, but many of the jobs we offered could be dangerous. For one thing, we were working with flammable materials. Over the years, we had a few explosions and fires involving our barges and storage tanks at our terminals. Some of our employees were injured or even killed. You could do a thorough check of every system to try to ensure people's safety, but all systems are imperfect, and human error can lead to disaster. We did our best to keep everyone safe, but it was always a terrible day when we lost an employee or learned that one had been injured.

The core of our business was filling stations, and turnover of the lower-level employees at these was always high because the jobs were difficult and even sometimes quite hazardous. Attendants could be promoted to manager, which offered more money and benefits. However, managers had to work long hours, and if something happened in the middle of the night, they had to drive to the station and deal with the problem.

As self-service became common and customers learned to pump their own gas, check their own oil and tires, and wash their own windows, we reduced our number of attendants. We now needed just one instead of as many as three or four on a shift. That saved us money, and customers quickly adjusted to the new model.

"Sorry, we're all out of gasoline"

In 1973, a huge change occurred in our business. OPEC suddenly announced that it would curtail sales and shipments to the US in response to America's involvement in the Israeli–Palestinian conflict. Most Americans probably didn't think about where their gasoline came from, and there were always domestic as well as foreign suppliers, but having all the supplies from the Middle East cut off suddenly was a huge disruption. I knew that my company had to shift quickly.

Around 1972, we had started to buy a large portion of our gasoline and diesel oil from overseas suppliers and now, we suddenly lost them. Our primary domestic supplier, Koch Industries, run by brothers David and Charles Koch, informed us that they were raising our cost of gasoline 9.8 cents a gallon, compared to an increase of two cents that other suppliers were charging our competitors. This was very worrisome. Although Martin Oil had begun investing in oil and gas exploration and other businesses by this point, our profits from these ventures were not enough to outweigh the skyrocketing increase in costs we were facing. Frankly, we were stuck. We lacked enough domestic suppliers for our stations and had to pay the Kochs' higher price. That meant we had to raise our prices to consumers. Our profits evaporated as our sales dropped by more than 60 percent.

At the same time, the Teamsters union was once again trying to unionize our stations. When I came to Martin Oil, all of our Chicago stations were unionized. Harold Martin had dealt with Teamsters Local 705 for many years and found it was better for him to be in the union than not. In fact, we were the biggest member of Local 705. As he became increasingly ill, Mr. Martin paid less and less attention to this union contract. Our wage scale became so much higher than our competitors' that our profits per gallon shrank drastically. No volume of gasoline sold could make up for that. Within a year or so of my coming to the company, I allowed each of our managers to lease their stations from us and become independent dealers. Most of them dropped out of the union and ceased paying union wages. It was too costly for the union to try to organize each of these stations individually instead of dealing with one bargaining unit: our company.

As the years went on, we took back many of our dealer stations, and we company-operated them to ensure better service and overall operating efficiency. These stations were not in the union, so when I learned that the Teamsters were once again trying to unionize us in the midst of the oil embargo, I felt it could not have come at a worse time.

I decided I would need to meet with Louie Peick, the head of the Teamsters Local 705. Teamster leaders were often seen as tough guys, and Louie was no exception. He had purportedly survived a kidnapping as well as a home break-in, an incident in which he was shot and beaten with a baseball bat but lived to tell the tale.

Louie's office desk was on a platform, allowing him to look down on visitors and adding to his already imposing physical presence. A big guy, somewhat overweight with thinning hair, he had a way of establishing his dominance immediately. Once, the president of a trucking company came to negotiate a union contract with him and was asked to come into Louie's office. As the story was told to me, Louie didn't acknowledge his visitor standing there; he just continued reading some papers he was holding. Finally, he looked up and said to the fellow, "What the f--- do you want, you [string of obscenities]?"

I called Louie to ask if I could stop by to see him on a Saturday to discuss his unionization efforts at our stations. I was in my early thirties and feeling the full weight of my responsibilities to the company—and my family. The oil embargo, the Koch Brothers' price increase, and the union's organizing efforts could have driven us out of business.

When Louie and I met, we reminisced together about Harold Martin, agreeing that he was a good man. I was discovering that I liked this union leader—he seemed amiable. I told him about our dire economic situation and respectfully asked him to stop trying to unionize our station attendants. He seemed to think about what I said but was noncommittal. Nevertheless, I heard nothing more about our employees being approached to join the union.

I offered Louie nothing in return for this favor, and he didn't ask for anything, but I felt very lucky that he seemed to have heard me and acted accordingly. After my meeting with him, Martin Oil Service eventually found other suppliers, and our costs and prices became competitive again. The crisis had been averted.

In my experience, when you don't think you will be able to change someone's mind but you want to try anyway, there's no substitute for a face-to-face meeting. I was glad I had gone to see Louie in person to plead my case.

During my time at Martin, besides getting to know Louie Peick, I met and negotiated with other union leaders. Most of them were trying to do the best job they could for the workers they represented, which I could respect. While we did not always agree, generally we were able to come together, find common ground, and end up with outcomes both sides considered fair.

"Sure, I lied, but I'm ticked off that he didn't believe me"

When I initially surveyed my team of executives and managers, I knew I wanted to bring in some self-starters who didn't need lots of direction. Some of the people I had inherited were afraid to take risks and use their creativity and experience to solve problems. They didn't want to make decisions and stand behind them.

One of my early hires was my brother, Kirk, who had worked at U.S. Steel after being discharged from the military, where he was a senior enlisted man. I knew he was a hard worker and smart and that I could count on him. Kirk eventually became a senior vice president in charge of our stations and wholesale operations. I also brought on a good friend, Bill Roberts, a fellow student from Columbia who became my financial vice president. Jack Elgin, another friend and one of the students I taught at Columbia, agreed to oversee our stations. In the years to come, I would hire a number of other exceptional managers—some of whom are still with me today.

In those early days at Martin Oil, I knew that what I wanted from managers or executives was follow-through without my having to micromanage them. Once, a few of us were trying to figure out what to do about a popular truck stop of ours where the trucks were getting backed up waiting to purchase diesel fuel. Truckers hated waiting in line and had a very high incentive to make stops for fuel go quickly. We decided to install high-speed pumps that would cut down the time needed to fill up a truck's tank. The new pumps were a terrific investment because the trucks could get in and out faster, allowing us to sell a higher volume of diesel as we attracted more truckers who knew they wouldn't have to linger in line. I was pleased that we solved the problem, but one day not long afterward, I drove by another Martin Oil truck stop and noticed a long line of trucks. It turns out the district manager had not thought to take our new, successful model and apply it to other busy stations. I had to tell my management team to look at every station to determine where high-speed pumps would be useful. It was a good reminder to me to double-check that my people would take a good idea to the next step and apply it in a general way—and come to me if they had any questions.

As a boss, under pressure to accomplish many things each day, I was probably moving too quickly at times. I made many good hires but also some that were not so good. In part, that's because I rushed the process and neglected to interview enough people for a particular job to get the right person. In those cases, I projected onto the people I was hiring skills they didn't possess and ignored the signs that these individuals might not work out.

My internal drive to get things done according to my schedule sometimes kept me from spending as much time with people as I should have—for example, engaging in collaborative thinking about how they could accomplish a goal. On the other hand, I was also aware that it was appropriate to have limits to each interaction if I was going to manage effectively. By trial and error, I was learning to give my people the amount of time and attention they needed to do their jobs well.

I wanted my executives to overcome obstacles and accomplish things on their own. If they couldn't, I wanted them to be honest and forthright with me. Once, I gave one of my executives the assignment to sell a hub of natural gas pipelines in Texas that we owned. We discussed potential buyers and any problems we might have getting the price we wanted. We agreed that I would periodically review progress with the executive but would leave it up to him to make it happen. More than once, when I checked in with him, he said something like, "I have some interest from that company I talked to you about, but they have to look into some more things." When pressed for details, he would give me vague promises about following through and needing to wait until a decision was made by someone else in the buyer's company—not his contact. After months of these conversations, I told my executive that I was going to call some of the people who were supposedly interested. I learned none actually were and realized that some people who worked for me would rather keep alive the hope of a deal rather than admit there was no deal to be had. That attitude kept us from moving on to explore other real possibilities.

I had to recognize that some people I had working for me simply weren't go-getters. Maybe that's because they were afraid of failure. Maybe they didn't know how to be assertive as salespeople. Were they consciously being dishonest? I don't think so—but these situations frustrated me. Fortunately, most of our people could make things happen when given clear directions to do so.

Once, I had to deal with an employee who did something worse than drag his feet on a deal. This particular executive—let's call him Sam—had been accused by a female department head of discovering how much she made and talking about it. Salary information was supposed to be confidential, so when this came to my attention, I brought each of them into my office separately to get to the bottom of what I considered a serious breach of confidentiality.

Sam denied knowing the department head's salary or telling her that he did. She insisted she was telling the truth. Not knowing whom to believe, I asked both if they were willing to take a lie detector test. Each was adamant that they would do so and prove they were not lying.

We sometimes used lie detector tests when an employee was suspected of stealing from the company, but it was a complicated endeavor to set up the test. Plus, the results weren't always reliable. I decided simply to tell the female department head that I would reiterate to Sam the importance of confidentiality and left it at that. She seemed satisfied with my response.

A month or so later, I was talking to Sam's direct boss, whom I'll call Pete, about another topic, and he said he had mentioned to Sam the dispute about the department head's salary. Pete asked Sam, "*Did you know how much she made?*" For whatever reason, Sam felt comfortable revealing the truth to his boss. Remarkably, he said to Pete, "Sure, I knew. And I was disappointed and angry that Carl Greer didn't believe me instead of her!"

I didn't want to compromise Pete's relationship with Sam, so I chose not to reveal to Sam what Pete had told me. And because the incident seemed to have long blown over and was not an offense I would fire someone for, I didn't speak to Sam and the department head again about what had happened. But I have to admit I had never expected someone would become indignant when I didn't believe their lie, as if *I* were the bad guy! It was a good lesson for me about the complexities of human nature.

Over time, I became more aware of people's different personalities and their peccadillos. I was learning to work with the people I had and didn't look to replace them. Becoming better at managing my team helped me keep our business prosperous and our workforce generally happy and contented. I was realizing that I had an excellent team and that without them, I would not have been as successful as I was.

In retrospect, I could be too driven and sometimes pressured my staff too much. I now know that "good enough" can be an acceptable standard and perfectionism can have very high emotional costs. While people who left Martin for other jobs never said so, I believe that in some cases, my impatient, demanding attitude could have been a factor in their leaving, which I regret.

I wanted the people who worked for me to be able to expand their horizons and opportunities if that was something they desired. I paid for college and graduate school for many of them. Some of our employees left after we sold the businesses they were involved in while others departed on their own. I'm pleased that many were quite successful after leaving Martin Oil, in some cases, becoming presidents and CEOs of very profitable companies. Whenever we sold a business, I made it a condition of the sale that the purchaser would hire any of our employees who wanted to keep their jobs.

I also have come to value even more the "glue people" who stuck around and helped keep my organization going. Some of the people who work with me have been by my side for as long as a half a century. Gladys Burow, my administrative assistant, worked with me for over fifty-two years; Don Waterlander, my senior vice president of operations and the executive director for the Greer Foundation, for over forty; and Tom Floyd, my senior vice president of finance, for more than thirty-five.

Even though I was in a tough business and it was sometimes difficult to orchestrate all the moving pieces, I loved my work and found it invigorating. I also enjoyed the competitiveness and the need to stay on top of changes that affected our business model and profits. In short, I felt very comfortable with the choice I had made to move to Chicago.

Many of my Columbia Business School peers were working in places like New York, Boston, and Washington, DC, earning more than I was. Would I have been happier in a more prestigious job? Over the years, I received job offers from other companies, none of which tempted me to leave Martin. One, however, was different enough that I briefly explored it. In the early years of the Nixon administration, I received a call from Martin "Marty" Anderson, a senior adviser to the President. I knew Marty because he had been a professor in the business school at Columbia. He had written a book called *The Federal Bulldozer*, about the pitfalls of urban renewal, and was a very smart fellow as well as a staunch free-market Republican. I got the impression that he sincerely believed some Democrats were evil! He invited me to the White House to see if I would be interested in working for the Nixon administration. We spent several hours together exploring the possibility, but I turned down the opportunity. In hindsight, that was probably a good decision—I certainly avoided getting swept up into the Watergate scandal and having that debacle color my career going forward.

In truth, I was satisfied with my compensation and with living in the Midwest with my family, so I really had no regrets. The intellectual challenge of my career, the interesting people I met and worked with, the measurability of our successes, and the creativity the job required gave me a strong sense of satisfaction for a long time. What's more, in the coming years, I would negotiate and strike some deals that helped solidify my financial security as well as that of my partners and my employees.

In the 1970s and 1980s, the part of me that yearned to feel a connection to nature and a sense of home that had too often eluded me was sufficiently nourished by vacations, getaways to go fishing, and time with my family. Business fed my soul to some degree because it was exciting and it allowed me to be creative as I solved problems and came up with new ideas about how to increase our profitability and stability. Being the boss, I could cultivate a culture that helped people at all levels to feel they were valued contributors to successful outcomes. During that period of my life, I was much too busy to feel a sense of anything missing—yet.

Change happens whether we like it or not. If we let go of our fear of change, it can be easier to see it up the road and plan for encountering it. At Martin Oil, we were not expecting our suppliers to make the huge changes in oil and gasoline prices that impacted us greatly. Having alternative revenue streams and fresh ideas turned out to be key to keeping us afloat during some very difficult years. As you think about changes that have been thrust upon you, and how you responded when facing them, you can start to see strengths you might be overlooking. You can also gain confidence in your ability to keep working with all the moving parts of your life as you face big transitions.

Questions for the Reader to Ponder

Relaxation. In my youth and early adult years in the Midwest, people commonly relaxed by drinking alcohol and smoking, sometimes to excess. As you think about how you relax, do you self-medicate with foods, beverages, or chemical substances? Do your forms of self-medication have downsides to them? Would you be open to replacing them with healthier ways of addressing your difficult emotions such as anxiety, anger, or grief? For example, would you be willing to exercise more to relieve stress? If you'd like to make changes, what, if anything, is stopping you?

Connecting and communicating with others. Do you prefer to work alone or with a team? What have you learned as a result of having to work with others? How have you changed because of this experience?

Vulnerability and crises. Have you ever felt vulnerable and exposed as you recognized that your life's circumstances had changed due to factors beyond your control? How did you handle this situation? Looking back, would you want to handle it differently? What, if any, lessons did you draw from that situation?

Mistakes. When you have made big mistakes, have you resisted looking at your role in them and blamed others instead? Why do you think that is? If you have been able to acknowledge your responsibility for your mistakes, did your honesty reduce any negative consequences? What do you think you need to change to be more consistently honest about mistakes you have made? Are you willing to commit to making those changes, if you truly feel they're necessary? Can you identify anything that will make it easier for you to learn from your mistakes without feeling so embarrassed or upset with yourself that you avoid reflecting on them?

Creativity. Before trying out a new idea or approach to a situation, do you do a lot of research and internal calculations? Does that typically work out well for you, or does your "overthinking" cause you to strike too late or not at all, missing the chance to make the best of opportunities? When has creativity helped you solve a problem? Would you like to be more creative and, if so, how can you make that happen?

CHAPTER NINE

Loose, Loose, Tight, Loose

My opponent and I bowed to each other, our sensei and a scattering of other judo students to the side watching to see who would be the first to throw the other to the mat and get them to submit. "Loose, stay loose," I thought to myself. My senses were alert and my muscles ready as I stood with bare feet on the mat, eyes looking straight at his. I was determined not to tighten up in anticipation of attacking or defending. The rhythm of judo—remain "loose, loose," then tighten up to move forcefully before becoming loose again—now felt as natural to me as the rhythm of my work life.

By the mid-1970s, I had achieved my goals of having a wife, children, a home we could call our own, and a firm foundation for a career that would support my family. What I didn't know is that I had also set myself up for financial stability that would allow me to step off the familiar path someday and write a very different story for myself.

At Martin, we made money from investment ideas that others brought to us, but the less control I had over a particular business, the more likely it was that our returns were not what I would have hoped. Those who brought opportunities to me probably believed they would turn out to be lucrative, but people often don't realize that making money is more difficult than it seems on the surface. I had some partners I initially thought very highly of who were excellent at selling me on an idea but, as it turned out, not as good at executing a business plan. They got in over their heads when it came to dealing with the complexities of management. I felt I was doing adequate due diligence when choosing to invest in some businesses, but in retrospect, maybe I should have looked more closely.

While I was a good operator, most of the money I made for Martin Oil came as a result of successfully negotiating some key business deals that I happened across. In business negotiations, I tried to employ principles I was taught when studying martial arts, which paid off well. For example, I learned this rhythm for expressing *kime* (KEY-may), meaning focus or power, at the right time: loose, loose, tight, loose. You remain relaxed until just the right moment and only then do you tighten up and focus as you strike, releasing an explosive burst of energy. With total concentration, you can deliver a single, decisive blow. Afterward, you immediately let yourself relax again so that you conserve your energy and are ready for your next move. When you are "loose, loose," you avoid telegraphing to your opponent what you are about to do. If you are too tight before you strike, you will lack speed and power and will waste energy. I find that making the most of business opportunities when they show up is easier when you practice kime.

Taking the right action if a challenge arises, responding the right way with the right timing, requires being attentive. Sometimes, the cues about how best to interact with people or a situation are subtle. Sometimes, opportunities dry up very quickly, and you can miss them if you don't act right away. Being aware of when a shift is happening and remaining flexible helps. I developed those skills by practicing martial arts—and also, to some degree, as a result of playing tennis and platform tennis.

I practiced judo for the first three years I was at Martin but stopped doing it for about eleven years as my schedule became more crowded. I occasionally played Ping-Pong or golf, but even just a round of nine holes could eat up half a weekend day. Back then, I'd get to the office by eight in the morning and often stay past six at night. It was common for me to work several hours on Saturdays, and occasionally, I worked on Sundays, too. Tennis was a competitive game I could fit into my schedule, and as the kids grew older, they would develop an interest in the sport. Jerri and I spent time playing with them. It was fun, good exercise and a way for me to unwind from the stresses of my job.

Tennis and martial arts were teaching me to be prepared to switch strategies quickly if necessary but not so quickly that you end up adopting a new one that's just as bad as the old one—or worse. It's easy for us to unconsciously fall back into old patterns, including patterns related to fear of failure. For example, a tennis tournament I was in reminded me that there's a big difference between playing to win and playing not to lose. The latter is rooted in a fear of losing that can trip you up in a competitive environment. I had been in the finals of a doubles tournament on the brink of winning the match. My partner and I were up 5 to 2 in the third set and serving at 40-love. We were one point away from winning but lost the match.

What happened? We stopped playing to win, abandoning the strategy that had taken us to the edge of victory, simply because we were flustered by losing a few points in a row. We could have recognized that something had changed and consciously decided to take a time-out to discuss whether we needed a new strategy or just a short break. However, we simply kept playing—and then lost another point . . . and then another. We were now focusing too much on defense. The outcome we feared came true. In a sense, our minds had been our most challenging opponents.

A very different experience happened once when I was being trounced in the finals of a men's singles tournament. The tennis courts were outdoors, and when it began raining, we postponed the match. I was saved by the rain, so to speak. When I came back three days later to resume play, the time away had allowed me to think up a new strategy. I knew my opponent had played competitive college tennis at a high level, and it was clear he was much better than I was. I could not outhit him, so I decided to become a backboard and keep the ball in play. I hustled to every ball, returned every shot I could, and showed no emotion when I missed one. I could see my strategy was starting to work when my opponent had to hit good shots consistently because I was no longer beating myself. He began showing signs of irritation and frustration and started missing shots. I wound up winning the match and the tournament.

Both experiences reminded me that even a brief time-out to reframe a situation, let go of any frustration or fear, and regroup can help turn around a losing situation. There is a martial arts saying—"winning without gladness, losing without sadness." That sort of equanimity can be very valuable in a stressful and challenging situation when you're in danger of allowing emotions to get in your way.

I have found it's important not to simply give up and quit situations out of frustration. Being patient and hanging in there is often a good strategy in a negotiation. I'm generally the tortoise, not the hare, steadily making my way and paying attention to what I'm doing. Like everyone, I can become annoyed when a problem is not resolved, but when I notice I'm starting to feel that way, I remind myself that it's important to take the time to get it right. There were some key deals in which people on the other side of the negotiation became impatient or tired out by the work involved in going over details again and again. Patience and mindfulness benefitted me in my deal-making, and so did my willingness to change strategies quickly and consciously—look at the situation differently, focus on a different aspect of it, and so on. Martial arts helped me to remember to stay loose rather than be constricted and on the defensive.

Once, at a karate tournament, I noticed a large, tattooed competitor pull up on a motorcycle with an attractive woman on the seat behind him. His dramatic entrance drew a lot of attention, and I wondered if I'd see him again. Sure enough, we ended up facing each other in the finals. He was a boxer and younger and faster than I was.

At first, neither of us scored with our kicks. Then I managed to get two quick points with punches. He was faster than I was and got the next two points, also with punches, by anticipating my moves. With the score tied 2 to 2, whoever got the next point would win the match. I thought he would go for the point with a punch. To throw him off, I faked a punch, quickly pulled it, blocked his attack, and countered with a punch. I won the point and the match. The experience reminded me that no matter how good we might think a particular approach is, it will not work in all situations. The real skill is being adaptable in the moment, remaining loose and open to the possibility that you will need to change your strategy.

"Watch out for the filing cabinet!"

My management style wasn't always conventional. I didn't want to be rigid and stubborn. Occasionally, I even engaged in what some might call zany behavior, and that worked for me. For the most part, the people I worked with seemed to enjoy my unconventionality and my particular sense of humor.

I remember an interaction in the office of Roger Flair, one of the lawyers who was working for Martin Oil, that took him completely by surprise—and he rolled with it, literally. We were standing and having a serious conversation about a negotiation we were involved in but were at an impasse in trying to figure out what would be our best strategy. Knowing Roger had been a college wrestler, I suddenly stepped forward and attempted a takedown, just to lighten the mood. As I suspected he would, Roger responded playfully. Within seconds, we were on the floor, trying to pin each other. Mel McCoy, a geologist who was in charge of our oil and gas explorations, stood watching us, incredulous. After we knocked over some furniture, Roger and I stopped and laughed. Realizing that our impromptu wrestling had been in good fun, Mel and the others who were there with us started laughing, too. It was clear that Martin Oil was not a stuffy place to work! After catching our breath, Roger and I continued with the conversation. Everyone seemed to have shifted into a more creative state of mind.

As president, I regularly talked to people on all rungs of the ladder in our exploration business—drillers, landmen (who secure land rights), supervisors of our pumpers and wells, geologists, and oil-field workers—as well as personnel at all levels in other companies with whom we were trying to do deals (major oil companies, large banks, and many other businesses both big and small). On the whole, I trusted my spontaneous impulses and my instincts when negotiating or having a conversation that could turn awkward or tense. I tried to pay attention to cues, however subtle, about what did and didn't make individual people feel comfortable.

My eye was always on the long game of the business, and I tried not to get caught up in dramas over losses and gains. My goal was to maintain equanimity when it came to money. I would try to maximize the payoffs in every deal I was involved in, but when I did walk away, unable to reach an agreement I was happy with, I had no regrets. I trusted that more opportunities would show up—and that I and my team could find them and even create them. I like win-win situations, and fortunately, that's often what I was able to bring about, even though at times, there was some wailing and gnashing of teeth by me and the person I was making a deal with. One way to look at negotiations is to consider whether the outcome will make a difference five years down the road. Usually, it won't—and remembering that can ease some of the anxiety and stress related to deal-making.

Martial arts training reinforced the lesson that you win some, you lose some, and it also made it easier to be clearheaded when presented with opportunities that could, at times, not be very obvious. In a judo tournament or karate match, you might see that someone is a little off balance, overly rigid, or inflexible about their strategy, like the guy with the motorcycle who had a plan he was determined to carry out, which made his moves predictable. Remaining present in the moment, focused on what is happening rather than what might happen, makes it easier to see openings for winning, opportunities that might otherwise be hidden. I found that applying these lessons to making money and negotiating deals was useful.

"Carl, this is to protect me from your men"

By the late 1970s, after the worst of the foreign supplier crisis was behind us, Martin Oil was doing well. Our oil and gas exploration business was generating strong profits while our bread-and-butter business of filling stations, now mostly self-serve and attached to convenience stores, had started to come back. During my time with the company, Martin Oil just about doubled the number of stations we owned, which helped us thrive. We had survived the worst challenges to our business we would ever face and stayed alive when many independents were bought up by bigger companies.

Our holdings were increasing as I looked for good ways to diversify by investing in other businesses. Some of these opportunities came through business partners, some through friends or friends of friends, and some through my serving on a board of a local bank.

It wasn't just the Martin Oil executives who were doing well, either. The minimum wage stretched further than it does now, and the gap between a CEO or president's compensation and the average worker's pay was not as large. The ratios seemed to change in the 1980s. Today, people are asking what I feel are good questions about salary and compensation. What is fair, given the work people do and the costs of living? What should the minimum pay and benefits be for workers at different levels of skill and responsibility? Should an individual be able to support a family on a full-time, minimum wage job? I think a higher minimum wage should be phased in by government mandate as well as through voluntary company action—with exemptions for companies that might be forced out of business by a too rapid change.

Should college be free—at least, community college or public universities—so that families headed up by minimum wage workers who might want to train for better, more lucrative jobs can more easily meet their goals? I believe that society would benefit if we were to provide education for those who can't afford it at present. Similarly, I believe that more people in the US should be able to receive good health care at reasonable costs than currently do.

I believe our economic system needs to be adjusted so that those at the bottom or middle of the pay ranges make more even if that means those at the top make less. This can be done through new tax policies and changes in how companies compensate their employees.

What should the role of unions be, and do we need them if the relationship between management and labor can be strengthened without them? I believe that in some situations, unions can play an important role in helping workers gain better working conditions and wages.

It will be interesting to see where this conversation heads: which companies lead the way in making changes and what new government policies might turn out to be effective at reducing income inequality and providing more opportunities to more workers.

When negotiating with unions as president of Martin Oil, I was not trying to turn us into winners and them into losers. I respected that they were trying to achieve the best results for their members, and they seemed to respect us, too. We strove to pay fair wages and still be able to survive and grow our business. And at Martin, we never had a problem with work rule issues where union workers refuse to perform tasks that aren't explicitly spelled out in their contract.

After that Saturday meeting in his office, I occasionally spoke with Louie Peick over the phone. But a couple of years later, I had to talk to him about a new, contentious issue. For most of its history, Martin Oil had maintained its own fleet of tractors and trailers for hauling gasoline and fuel oil. The fixed costs of running our freight operations had been increasing so much for so long that now we felt we needed to get out of the trucking business. It just wasn't profitable anymore, so we offered to sell the trucks to our drivers if they wanted them. Our plan was to start contracting with them, or with a common carrier, to haul our gasoline.

The Teamsters felt I should negotiate with them if I wanted to exit the business. I told Louie Peick I disagreed, but I was willing to meet with him to talk.

First, however, I wanted to speak with our drivers to explain what we were doing and why. When I got to our terminal around 5 a.m., there were already two big Cadillacs with hefty union business agents present. Seeing them, I went up to the business agent for our men and asked, "Why are your guys here? Are you trying to intimidate me?" He replied, "No, Carl, this is to protect *me* from *your* men. They're pissed at me."

I explained my decision to the drivers, trusting they would be able to appreciate what had led me to it. Among the reasons for the change was that we were no longer able to pick up and deliver several loads of fuel during a driver's route. Unfortunately, too often we had to deadhead, that is, run trucks empty to get them back to where they started. The drivers understood my position, and I could feel that as I made my case, they were beginning to accept the inevitable. They left our meeting resigned to the reality of the situation.

I then set up a meeting with Louie to resolve our differences with the Teamsters and part ways amicably. He was there with the union's business agent for our men, and I brought our attorney and his son, who was just starting his career in labor law. Also attending was Bob Bushek, who was in charge of our supply and trucking operations.

I tried to keep things calm, but the conversation became very heated. Suddenly, Bob Bushek and the business agent were going at each other, fists and curse words flying. I stepped in and separated them. Then, Louie and I cleared the room so we could finish our meeting together. As soon as the others left, Louie, who by now had some cardiac issues, shook his head at me and joked, "Greer, you give me heart trouble every time I'm involved with you!"

Despite that eruption, and maybe because of Louie's tension-relieving crack, we were able to continue talking calmly and reach an amicable agreement. I didn't feel I needed Louie to intervene in our relationship with the drivers. I would have taken care of them. But given how he had been so helpful to me before when I was in a tight spot, I wanted to let him take the credit for what our drivers received. We said our good-byes as friends, and that was the last time I saw him. Despite Louie Peick's reputation as being ruthless, he was honorable and fair in my dealings with him—another example of my learning the importance of forming my own opinions rather than being overly influenced by others or someone's reputation.

"Hmmm, maybe they only THINK they bought it . . . "

In the '70s and into the '80s at Martin, my time was split among running existing businesses, acquiring and starting new ones, and negotiating for the sale of some of our assets. I enjoyed all the many aspects of my job. If there was anything that aggravated me, though, it was executives working for other companies puffing themselves up and treating my company and me disrespectfully. Some of the deals I was involved with wouldn't have happened had the other side not adopted an arrogant stance toward us. We were a small company compared to many, but a contract's a contract, and I didn't take well to people treating us shabbily. I also remember some negotiations that almost fell through but didn't because I recognized that others needed to feel respected and heard during the process. And finally, some negotiations were fun because they were low pressure: I had the authority to act on behalf of my partners, whose attitude was that as long as I cut a deal that was better than the status quo, they would be happy.

Once, a company called Gas Production Operators, or GPO, invited me to a meeting with Colorado Energy Corporation, or CEC, which had partnered with us in some oil and gas wells in Colorado. My exploration manager Mel McCoy and I were invited to attend the meeting so we could explore ways in which GPO could help CEC and Martin Oil work together to sell our gas for the highest prices. Besides Mel and me, people from CEC, GPO, and Coors Brewery would be attending. (Coors was there as a potential gas purchaser.)

In the meeting, I noticed that the GPO spokesman kept bringing up what CEC would do in the future. After a while, I said, "You sound like you're speaking for Colorado Energy."

He responded, "We *are* Colorado energy."

I was puzzled. "Something must have happened that I'm not aware of . . . ?"

With a smug tone, he announced, "We bought Colorado Energy."

At that point, I told him that I hadn't known about the sale and that it didn't make sense for me and Mel to continue with the meeting. We excused ourselves, got up, and left.

As Mel and I walked to the elevator, I said, "Well, that was a surprise, wasn't it?" He agreed. Keeping big secrets from trusted business partners was not how we were used to doing things. We were shocked at the disrespectful attitude toward us. As our partner, Colorado Energy should have informed us about what was going on, and I didn't appreciate the GPO spokesman's supercilious attitude.

When we got down to the lobby of the building we were in, I located a pay phone and called our lawyers to tell them what had happened. "Listen," I said, "I'd like you to find a way to stop the transaction if it hasn't already been completed." I told them to explore our various agreements with Colorado Energy to see if we could assert a right of first refusal, meaning they couldn't sell the company to someone else without us being given a chance to make an offer first. I also told them I was going to call the president of Colorado Energy and say that whatever offer they had from Gas Production Operators, I would offer more.

Colorado Energy was a public company, and by law, they were required to seek the best offer for their shareholders. From a legal perspective, they could be in hot water with the SEC if they turned down a higher offer.

I flew back to Chicago that night, a Thursday, and the next morning, I was completely focused on stopping the CEC sale to GPO. I called the principals at Colorado Energy and offered them more than GPO had—a fraction of a cent more per share. "Why don't you come out here to Chicago so we can talk about it?" I suggested.

The CEC executives flew to Chicago that evening, and we negotiated all day Saturday and early Sunday. By noon on Sunday, Martin Oil owned CEC. Glad that I had achieved my objective, I went home that afternoon and spent the rest of the day relaxing with Jerri and the kids.

The deal would not have happened if GPO would have been forthright about their objective from the beginning of our meeting. It also would have been helpful if CEC would have told us what was going on. By keeping me in the dark and treating Martin Oil as they did, their executive team riled me up. What had served me well in this situation was remembering to practice kime (striking quickly with focus and power) and ma (which in this case meant maintaining enough emotional distance to have freedom of action).

There was another upside to the deal: After working with the Colorado lawyer who was representing CEC, Jim Henshall, I was so impressed that I hired him to come over to Martin Oil. He worked with me for some years and gave me valuable guidance.

Chugging Along

In the '70s into the early '80s, my story as a family man was fairly typical of the times. I was the father, husband, and breadwinner, and Jerri was the mother and wife. We could afford for her to be a full-time mother at home, and she was very involved in activities that had meaning for her. Jerri did volunteer work for groups such as the Infant Welfare Society and the P.E.O. Sisterhood, sang in the church choir, sometimes played the flute for the congregation, and played golf and tennis. She also pursued her educational interests and enrolled in courses at a local college.

Jerri made it a priority to take our kids to singing, piano, and dancing lessons that were part of their routine, and she and I were usually in the audience at their recitals, too. Caryn was a terrific dancer even when she was very little, and both she and Janet sang and played the piano. Jerri and I also attended the kids' sporting events as much as we could: All of my kids got into organized sports early in their childhood. Each played tennis, and by the time they were in high school, Janet and Mike were all-state tennis players. Janet and Mike also played soccer, and Caryn ran track.

I worked long hours but took time to go on family vacations with Jerri and the kids. We went to places like Green Lake, Wisconsin, where there was a pool and hiking trails, and Canada, where we fished in Eagle Lake, staying in a cabin for a week. At one point, we vacationed with the kids in Hawaii, too. We also traveled to see my dad in Pennsylvania and Arizona and Jerri's parents in Ohio and Arizona. All in all, it seemed we had a good, peaceful family life in a nice house in a pleasant neighborhood.

I wasn't a 9-to-5 business guy coming home and mowing the lawn, firing up the grill, and relaxing in the backyard. Even so, I tried to be more involved in my kids' lives than my dad and Mary Anne had been in mine. The kids played with their friends at each other's houses and in the neighborhood, but none of my children roamed quite as freely as I had after my mother's death. No one was disappearing into the woods far from home for an entire day or taking the bus back from another town when still in their single digits. Between Jerri and me, we almost always knew where our kids were. And while I wasn't in the audience at every one of my children's sports events or recitals, I attended whenever I could. Years later, when their own children played sports and music, Caryn, Michael, and Janet were much more involved. In a sense, I was a bridge between generations, more connected to my children than my dad and stepmother were to me but not as much as my kids are with their own children.

I was the solid provider I had always thought I should be and had no reason to question my choices. Life chugged along. The story unfolded before me without dramas that might make me wonder, "Is this really what I wanted?" or "Is this what makes me feel fulfilled?"

When I took time off from work, I was able to spend time outdoors, especially on vacations, but the demands of my job were never very far from my mind. I was always ready to go in when needed or get on a plane to handle a problem. However, there was one problem I faced that required the help of the police.

"Who are you and is that a gun?"

The business I was in, and being the president of an oil company, exposed me, my family, and my company to a certain amount of danger. As I said before, the service stations and terminal business had risks, including fires, explosions, and shootings over the years. Organized crime was active in Chicago when I lived on the South Side and still is to a certain extent, so that posed a hazard, too. Gasoline price wars put the economic viability of independent petroleum marketers in jeopardy, and sometimes, there were even threats and violence.

The suburbs I lived in, Olympia Fields and Flossmoor, were close to Chicago Heights, home of Al Capone, where in the 1970s and 1980s, there was Mob activity. At the karate dojo I went to regularly in the 1980s, members of law enforcement worked out next to men who were involved in organized crime—at least, this is what I came to learn. After a shooting on a golf course in Chicago Heights, one of the men from my dojo, who had witnessed it, disappeared into the Witness Protection Program.

Once, during a particularly contentious time when we were negotiating with the union, vague threats were made to blow up our office building and our terminal. But I didn't know how personal it could get until one day when the police contacted me at work to give me some disturbing news. They told me someone had warned them about a person in a bar talking about "kidnapping the Greer kids." The police had taken Caryn, Michael, and Janet out of school. I drove home right away, and as I pulled into our garage, I was confronted by an unfamiliar woman with a gun in her hand.

"Who are you?" she asked.

"I live here," I said. "Who are you?" She told me her name was Cory and that she was a police officer, sent for our protection.

I never knew anyone who had been kidnapped. How real was the threat? To be safe, we kept our kids out of school for a week while Cory and two policemen lived with us around the clock. Our family played board games with them, and they joined in on some of our conversations and shared meals with us. Nothing came of the kidnapping threat, so the police were taken off our case. Jerri and I became friends with Cory—in fact, we attended her wedding later that year.

The officers who stayed with us advised me to protect my family against any future trouble by getting a dog—they suggested a Doberman pinscher or a Rottweiler—and buying a sawed-off shotgun. Jerri and I knew we didn't want a gun in the house, but we were all set to buy a Doberman. Then, Caryn was scared by one who barked and lunged at her when she was at a friend's house. Her friend's parents had immediately asked Caryn, "What did you do to the dog?" which didn't help. Caryn was afraid of dogs after that, and we decided it was better not to get one.

When it came to pets, we stuck with animals that were small and cuddly—hamsters, rabbits, and the like, which the kids enjoyed. As it turns out, Caryn was allergic to dogs—and cats—so we made the right decision. There were no more threats issued, and the police never found out who had been talking about kidnapping our kids. However, we did have to explain to our children what happened to the baby rabbits and hamsters after a litter was born and a few disappeared—the parents ate them! It was an ugly reality, but nature is nature, I explained to the kids, who were understandably upset.

We lived in safe neighborhoods the entire time my kids were growing up, but I still felt that being able to defend yourself is a valuable skill to have. My son, Michael, ended up studying martial arts, and my daughters took some self-defense classes here and there as they were growing up. I remember once when Michael was about eight, he told me that a kid and his father, who lived in the neighborhood, had verbally bullied him. I told him we would talk to the boy and his dad together and make sure it didn't happen again. It was bad enough that another kid was picking on mine, but the fact that the father was doing it, too, really angered me. I wanted to show Michael that you don't back down from a confrontation, and we searched the neighborhood until we found the man and his son. I told the father never to threaten my son again or he would have to deal with me. That was the end of these two causing trouble for Michael.

"Carl, we're going to have to call you the Chicago Hammer!"

I was involved in a few outside boards of directors but not many. They were mostly bank or bank-related, but one industry board I was involved with was the Society of Independent Gasoline Marketers of America (SIGMA). I had good friends serving on the board and said yes when they asked me to negotiate something that was tricky for them. SIGMA had been defending itself against antitrust claims and was running out of money. The group had hundreds of thousands of dollars in unpaid legal bills and asked me to negotiate on its behalf. I agreed to fly to DC and talk with the lawyers on the condition that I could make whatever deal I thought would be best without having to go back and forth between SIGMA and the law firm.

I met with the law firm's principals at their offices. We talked for a long time and eventually, after caucusing among themselves, they came back and said, "Tell us what you'll pay, and we'll accept it." I had to decide now what would be fair for both sides and pick a number that SIGMA could afford and that would give the law firm something. The members of the SIGMA board were relieved and happy to hear the results. Some of them said, "Carl, we're going to have to start calling you the Chicago Hammer!" I laughed. The negotiation wasn't as dramatic as all that. But earning the nickname that felt a little more suited to Louie Peick reminded me that I was learning to manage probabilities and possibilities in ways that led to good deals for myself and for others.

The Value of a Rock-Solid Contract

A few years after the SIGMA negotiation, I was once again involved in a negotiation much like the GPO one. Had the company handled the situation with more respect for Martin Oil and me, we would not have entered into a conflict that involved lawyers.

Martin Oil had a deal with Panhandle Eastern Pipeline Company that obligated Panhandle to buy a certain amount of natural gas from us every year. Our agreement was that if they chose not to take the gas, they would have to pay us anyway and we would owe them the gas— to be delivered sometime in the future. At one point, Panhandle should have taken about half a million dollars' worth of natural gas but had not, so they owed us that money. They refused to pay up even though the terms of the contract were very clear.

The dispute could have been settled if they had given us what was essentially an interest-free loan for a short period of time. Instead, it ended up costing them tens of millions of dollars—because the Panhandle team turned out to be arrogant and unreasonable.

I started my conversation with their representative at their offices by letting him know that I was aware that Panhandle also hadn't fulfilled other aspects of our contract. I said, "You didn't keep to our agreement when it came to line pressures and other issues. I'm willing to let all that go. But you have to honor your take-or-pay clause and pay us." He said he would think about it.

When someone from Panhandle got back to me and said no, they weren't going to honor their legal obligation, I figured I would give them one more chance. I called their executive vice president but he, too, said Panhandle wasn't going to give us the money. I reminded him that the contract required them to do so. His response was blunt: "I don't care what the contract says."

I thanked him for his time and, after getting off the phone with him, called our lawyers and instructed them to prepare a lawsuit including all of our potential claims, which eventually totaled over $100 million.

As the case proceeded, Panhandle made offers to settle for much more than our initial take-or-pay claim. I rejected them. That made some of my executives and some on my legal team nervous. They thought it would have been best to settle. I explained, "I think we can do better, so let's just see what they come up with next. It's not 'eating money.' We're on the house's money now." I didn't feel that Panhandle was going to walk away from their offers: They knew their case was weak.

Finally, it was the day before the judge was to rule. That morning, I was on the phone with a number of lawyers, some on my side, some on Panhandle's. I told them I had an engagement later that day that I wasn't willing to break, so we had better settle this negotiation before 2 p.m. or we would have to wait and see what the judge ruled the next morning. I said Martin Oil would be willing to settle for $100 million; they counteroffered $30 million, a significant increase over the last offer they'd made. After many calls back and forth, they ended up settling with us for $62.5 million. Plus, as part of the deal, they would pay a higher price for the gas they were going to buy from us in the future. That meant millions of dollars more for us in addition to the $62.5 million.

And I made it to my appointment on time.

Remember, initially, they just had to pay us the $500,000 and they would get a half million dollars' worth of gas at some point. I would have overlooked their other contract violations had their team been conciliatory instead of acting as if they were above the law.

I believe there are two reasons Panhandle settled. One, they didn't want to risk losing and therefore setting a precedent that would make them liable in similar situations with other companies. Second, they had recently realized a one-time gain for more than $60 million, a situation I knew about and that allowed them to settle with us without a significant hit to their financial statement. (In the years following this settlement, we ended up receiving millions more as we eventually wrapped up all of our agreements with them.) Once again, remaining loose, talking to people over the phone and in person, and then striking decisively when it was clear I had to do so paid off.

Letting events unfold instead of getting impatient and trying to force them to happen when and how you want them to can be beneficial in a negotiation. And I believe it's best not to settle when your gut instincts and understanding of your opponent's weaknesses tell you not to.

Patience and Observation Pay Off

On another occasion, I negotiated my biggest and most lucrative deal by being mindful of signs that someone was overly eager to make the deal happen. The whole thing nearly unraveled, but ultimately, it came together.

In the late 1980s, I had been at Martin for more than twenty years, and things were going well. Out of the blue, I received a call from a banker at Goldman Sachs asking if we would be interested in selling some of our oil and gas wells and associated rights in Colorado to Gerrity Oil & Gas. I wasn't particularly interested, so I told the banker no. He persisted, calling me a few more times. I kept turning him down until one day, he mentioned that Bob Gerrity himself was flying into Chicago on a private plane with a team of executives and asked if I would at least meet with them. I agreed.

After a long discussion, Bob offered $250 million for our Colorado oil and gas operation, subject to their due diligence. In my mind, those assets were worth much less than that, so I said, "Let's proceed." I subsequently learned that Bob, who had been a successful real estate investor, was thirty-nine years old and wanted to make his mark in the oil and gas business before he turned forty. That gave me a sense of how eager he was to make this deal work for him.

The talks began in November, and the pressure to get a complicated deal done was tangible: The holidays were coming and on January 1, some tax laws would change, making it necessary for us to finalize the deal by December 31. Bob came back quickly with his engineering reports and said our assets weren't worth as much as he first thought. He felt the purchase price should be more like $80 million, not $250 million. I took his engineering report and went over it with our engineers. I found it quite thorough but dependent on a number of assumptions that I disagreed with.

In the midst of all this, I started experiencing terrific pains in my back. I was hospitalized on a Thursday, not too long after we had begun negotiating. Right away, I was diagnosed with kidney stones, but the doctors suspected I had kidney cancer, too. They scheduled exploratory surgery for Monday and told me I could go home and wait for the kidney stones to pass, which I did—on Saturday. Sunday, the stones passed, and the pain subsided. When I went in on Monday, presurgery tests revealed that I didn't have cancer, so I was sent home. This interlude set back our progress in the Gerrity deal for a few days, but we made up the time as soon as I was back on my feet. This experience reminded me of my mortality and planted seeds for changes in my life that I would come to make in time. The Mythopoetic Carl who liked to ponder the big questions about life and what it's all about was starting to stir, but having such a big deal underway caused that self to go dormant again quickly after I was discharged from the hospital. I was back to being all business.

Gerrity eventually agreed on a price of $125 million plus additional payments if we could validate that we had titles to land we held that they weren't sure we owned. I did everything necessary to close the deal by the year's end, a tight deadline. The transaction was very large for each of us, and we worked long hours to get it done in time. I started talking daily with Gerrity's executive vice president. But just a few weeks before our scheduled closing, he phoned one day to say they were calling off the deal.

I wondered what had happened. I didn't want to give up what I thought was a good deal that I'd put a lot of work into and that I believed was good for us. In the moment, I felt frustrated and disappointed, but I thought it was best to compartmentalize my emotions and act calmly. I told him I was sorry to hear that and wished him well. I said, "Some deals are meant to happen and some not. What will you do now?" We talked a bit longer, but before we hung up, I asked casually, "Just out of curiosity, why did you decide to cancel the deal?"

He said that his team felt that one of our executives had not given them accurate and reliable information. I asked, "Would you mind if I checked into this? I've not had that kind of experience with (this executive)." He said okay and told me the details he was concerned about, which had to do with a well and some leases that he didn't think we could prove we owned.

I called my executive, but I didn't tell him that his trustworthiness was being questioned by Gerrity. An emotional response of defensiveness was not what I needed from him, and I could understand why my executive might become upset by having his facts disputed. I just asked him about the wells and leases in question. His answers revealed it had all been a misunderstanding, and I called back the executive vice president at Gerrity. After I told him what I had learned, he checked further, and then the deal was back on.

I believe that had I initially tried to talk the Gerrity executive out of his decision, his resolve would have stiffened. By accepting his choice and not challenging him, talking collegially, and then offering to check further, I was able to keep the deal alive. It was a case of applying ma— not being too emotionally close to the situation, attached to the potential financial outcome, and not being too far away, that is, not giving up on reestablishing trust with my negotiating partner at Gerrity.

We were still racing against deadlines to close by year's end. On December 30, bankers from Nation's Bank and Goldman Sachs were meeting with us in Gerrity's office as we attempted to wrap up all that needed to be done. By early afternoon, the bankers said that they had to leave in a couple of hours. With that impetus, we got the paperwork signed before they left.

I had a hunch that I should stick around on New Year's Eve to see that the money actually got into our account that day. I discovered that Gerrity hadn't made adequate arrangements to transfer the money, and I had to intervene to make it happen. Otherwise, we would have had to pay many millions of dollars more in taxes. I was glad I stayed even though I missed some vacation time with my family.

This was the biggest of all of my deals at Martin, and Harold Martin's widow and daughters were very happy with the results. My relationship with them over the years was good for me and for them, which I think is somewhat unusual in family-owned businesses where an outsider is involved. Conflicts with the founder, spouses, children, and relatives who are either investors or work for the company can arise. I experienced moments of tension with the Martin family here and there, but overall, we had enough mutual trust and respect to develop an amiable, cordial, very successful partnership and maintain it for more than fifty years.

Whenever I checked with the Martin family about major acquisitions and sales, they paid close attention to what I was telling them and asked questions, but they always gave me permission to go ahead and do what I thought best, and the Gerrity deal was no exception.

That's My Story, But Am I Sticking to It?

From the beginning at Martin Oil, I didn't want to be too identified with short-term results, which could evaporate rapidly if something changed. Nor could I assume that things would take care of themselves—I had to check up on whether there was follow-through and whether deals were completely sewn up and difficult situations were effectively resolved. I was always looking into how various aspects of our businesses were doing and making sure nothing fell through the cracks. My job kept me on my toes. I tried to stay loose but ready to act quickly and to remain at a proper emotional distance from situations so I could maintain a clear perspective and prevent my decision-making process from going awry.

I was living according to a story that people in my social class found acceptable and admirable, a story called Successful Businessman Who Is Smart, Practical, and Unemotional. This story wasn't enough for me anymore. There was still a self deep within that had been latent for too long and was now yearning to express itself. This self had a capacity to dream and imagine. It was a self that cared about life's mysteries, including the mysteries of the psyche and of relationships—with myself and with others in my life. In the 1980s, just before the Panhandle deal, my life would change dramatically as I started on a new trajectory and adopted a new goal. I entered a time of change and uncertainty that would challenge me in ways I had not been challenged before.

Negotiating is a part of life, but many people aren't taught skills for doing it effectively. They may lack confidence when it comes to striking a good, beneficial deal for themselves. That lack of confidence can also cause people to hesitate and miss out on opportunities. They may also become scared and impatient, leading them to make mistakes.

Business school training and martial arts study helped me become decisive and make good judgment calls in negotiating. Growing up feeling I had to control my emotions and stay levelheaded affected my negotiations, too. My general approach was to strike a fair deal for the other party but also a good one for me and the people I represented. To do so, I kept in mind the idea of kime: remaining loose until the time of focus and then tightening up to act suddenly before becoming loose again. You have to be loose at the right time and tight at the right time.

I also kept in mind the concept of ma: maintaining the proper distance. I tried to make sure I was not too close to a situation, overidentifying with an outcome or too distant and detached. Practicing kime and ma helped me to remain open to opportunities and apply the right tactic at the right time.

As you reflect on negotiations you have entered into in your own life, you might discover insights into how to prepare yourself when you have to strike a deal with someone.

Questions for the Reader to Ponder

Playing not to lose. Have you ever been triumphing at something but then saw your opportunity to succeed slip away? Was it due to an outside variable you couldn't control or to something that happened inside you, such as suddenly becoming afraid you couldn't succeed? How did you handle the situation as you saw your opportunity to succeed waning—did you persevere, give up, or something else? If you had to do it all over again, would you use a different strategy once you became aware that you were losing? If so, what would it be? If not, what, if anything, did you learn from the "win that turned into a loss"?

Seizing an opportunity. What was the best opportunity you ever took advantage of? What prepared you for being in the right place at the right time? What prepared you to be able to seize the opportunity effectively so that it didn't slip away? For example, had you developed certain skills? How much of your success in making the most of that opportunity was due to luck and how much was due to your skills and talents? What was the best opportunity you didn't take advantage of? Why didn't you, and would you do something differently today? Are you able to remain cool-headed and not let emotions carry you away when faced with opportunities you'd like to take advantage of? What helps you to remain calm?

Right tactics/right timing. Have you ever had your ego trip you up when you were negotiating? How did your ego or insecurity get in your way? Were you too sure of yourself—or too unsure of yourself? Did overconfidence or a lack of confidence interfere with your ability to time your words or your actions? What did you learn from the experience? Have you been able to improve your negotiating skills? If you would like to be a better negotiator, what do you need to do?

Patience. When you are in a difficult situation, are you able to step back and consider your response and any conversations you need to have with others rather than rushing to get to a solution? What, if anything, can help you to improve your timing and patience so that you are more effective at communicating and negotiating?

Standing up for yourself and others. When it comes to standing up for yourself and others, what are your challenges? For example, are you comfortable dealing with legal situations, lawyers, and contracts but not comfortable standing up for yourself in other situations—or vice versa? Do emotions get in the way of your effectively advocating for yourself and others? If so, how might you better contain and control your emotions? Do you have trouble standing up for yourself but not for others? If so, how might you become better at standing up for yourself?

Deal-making. Have you ever been at an impasse in a negotiation? What, if anything, did you do to break the logjam? How did that work out? How could you be more creative in your negotiations so that you can salvage a deal in a way that works for you and the person you're negotiating with?

CHAPTER TEN

The Mythopoetic Challenge

By the time I turned forty-one, I had been at Martin Oil for fourteen years. On some level, I was sensing that being successful at running a business was not enough to fulfill me. I was still enjoying my job, the people I worked with, and the invigorating opportunities to make money and negotiate good deals. I was glad to be able to provide well for my family. And my personal life, including family time, socializing, and participating in various sports, was rewarding in many ways. Volunteering at the church Jerri and I had joined gave me a sense of community and belonging. But none of this was providing spiritual stimulation or sustenance. I couldn't articulate exactly what was missing, but I wanted something more.

I felt a call to return to the martial arts to assuage this longing, and to some degree, that strategy worked. This time, instead of judo, I decided to study and practice karate. I told myself that a stress-relieving workout at lunchtime or in the evening would be good for me, and when I found a conveniently located dojo that offered Okinawan karate, I started to attend classes three times a week.

I soon realized I would have to practice on my own, too, if I were going to keep up with my classmates, most of whom were ten to twenty years younger than I was. My competitiveness was pushing me to work toward mastery of this martial art that was new for me. Part of the appeal of Okinawan karate was that I was learning more about what's called "the way of the warrior"—having discipline, facing inner fears, and serving causes larger than your own self-interest. The rituals beginning and ending each class and each match against an opponent made me feel that I was a part of an honorable and proud tradition. And they served as a transition from my everyday business life into a centuries-old warrior lineage with spiritual, energetic, and physical aspects.

My instructor, Sensei John Nanay, was like a Hungarian James Bond—a real-life action figure. During his country's uprising in 1956, when he was just sixteen, he had been arrested by the Russians. They suspected that he had blown up Russian tanks with nitroglycerine—and he had. He was set to be executed but somehow had managed to smuggle a small amount of nitroglycerine into prison in his rectum. It was enough explosive power to allow him to blow the door of his cell open and escape. Eventually, he made his way to the United States and joined the military. He served in the Vietnam War and had life-and-death adventures as part of a US Special Forces group, including being captured by the Vietcong and escaping. Coming from someone else, these stories might have stirred great skepticism in me, but Sensei Nanay seemed to me to be a man of integrity whose ego was in harmony with his inner self.

He liked to set up challenges that tested his students mentally as well as physically. In one instance, he told us to hold one arm in an "upper block" position and maintain it until he said to stop. Most of the men in the class were not just younger but bigger, stronger, and faster than I was. I made up my mind not to yield to fatigue or pain. I wanted to see how far I could push myself. Twenty minutes went by, and one by one, my classmates gave up and dropped their arms. At the half-hour mark, I was the only one still holding my position. Finally, at the one-hour mark, Sensei Nanay told me to put my arm down. I think I had earned his respect. However, my shoulder was very sore the next day!

I would go on to practice with Sensei Nanay for more than twenty years and sometimes teach classes for him. We became good friends. I admired him for having won world championships in karate (and his students had won many national titles) and been an international referee. His last rank was that of a ninth-degree black belt, which took him decades to achieve. That's dedication.

Despite my sensei's impressive accomplishments, his dojo was traditional: He didn't teach large classes or have students sign onerous financial contracts for lessons. Success in business was not his priority, and he never made much money. I respected that he was very clear on who he wanted to be as a martial artist, teacher, and leader of his dojo.

To me, he embodied the best aspects of a warrior: He practiced daily. He was humble. He didn't berate or humiliate any of his students and was patient teaching them at whatever level they were at. He embodied the paradox of being a tough guy but also a gentle man. He showed respect for his teachers and for their teachings, which they shared with us in person or which we read about in books he recommended.

In the martial arts, when you delve deeply into warrior training, the goal is not just to defeat your opponents through superior skill and preparation. It's to operate out of your center so you will be in harmony with your higher self that is less ego-dominated and less concerned with achievement. The warrior's path enables you to overcome fear and anger and establish a new relationship with the world—one based on courage and risk-taking as well as compassion for the self and others. Walking the warrior's path lets you live more authentically, true to the self that longs for expression—something I wasn't doing at the time I started my karate practice.

As a kid, I had wanted to be like Robin Hood or the Three Musketeers. As an adult, I was applying kime and ma in my business dealings in order to be successful. Still, I wanted more outlets for expressing what was awakening inside me. Apparently, my mythopoetic self was still very much alive—and demanding to be fed.

A Call to Be a "Wounded Healer"

I had tried to burn out the more mythopoetic parts of myself through hard work and self-discipline as I prepared for and developed a career in business. Increasingly, I was recalling two of my dad's sayings that he had voiced often when I was growing up: "Happiness comes from within" and "You have only one life to live, so play it for big stakes." I was learning that my happiness was not based solely on external achievement. "Play for big stakes" seemed to mean worldly success or acclaim—or winning at a negotiation. Making great business deals gave me pleasure and a sense of accomplishment. But now, "play for big stakes" meant letting my responses arise from an inner source of knowing rather than from a script written by someone else, a script I hadn't been fully conscious of and hadn't questioned.

The unspoken message I had received growing up and later, as an adult surrounded by people who shared some basic values about success and happiness, was, "Do what you are supposed to do to be a successful man and a respected person in your community, with a good career and a healthy family, and happiness will naturally follow." If happiness was actually supposed to come from within, maybe I needed to introspect—and dare to make different choices.

As I became aware of my unconscious beliefs and began to question them, I wasn't sure what to replace them with. What was my own definition of success? What made me feel happy? I started to make changes around the margin, as I call them—small changes that would eventually lead to larger ones, such as expressing my emotions more often and being more authentic with myself and others.

There were many reasons I should feel consistently happy and contented, I told myself. I had much to be grateful for, yet I was restless. I longed for a larger purpose, a sense of contentment, and a connection to something larger than myself.

My dad was inspired by those two sayings I mentioned, but I don't believe he was ever able to internalize them and live from them as he would have liked. He didn't explore the unconscious parts of himself, and in his later years, he did not seem happy. He grew up in a time and place in which men like him rarely underwent therapy and analysis. Like him, I had internalized that people in therapy were different from me. Part of me also felt that men should take care of their own problems. Another part realized there could be value in men addressing their psychological issues that get in the way of achieving their goals, finding meaning, or dealing with their anxiety, anger, or depression.

I began thinking again about my earlier interest in psychology. An associate pastor at my church, Dave Owens, happened to know several psychologists and psychotherapists, some of whom were Jungian analysts. Together, he and I talked about Carl Jung, archetypes, and how Jungian psychology differs from other traditions. I had been reading academic psychology books about such subjects as theories of personality, object relations, psychoanalysis, and Jungian theory, but I had also been reading popular psychology books such as M. Scott Peck's *The Road Less Traveled*, Eric Berne's *Games People Play*, and Gail Sheehy's *Passages*. My readings and my conversations were steering me back toward the path I had abandoned back in college. Studying to become a psychotherapist or analyst would probably take me years if I attended school part time, but I felt pulled toward it.

I was confident that I could fulfill my obligations to Martin Oil and my family as well as complete psychological training without stretching myself too thin. However, I didn't know which branch of psychology to pursue. The books I'd read had introduced me to several, including gestalt, cognitive-behavioral, Freudian, and Adlerian. I had always liked the more mystical realms of stories and fairy tales, which I associated with Jungian psychology, but wanted to see what the other possibilities were and what programs were available nearby, as I would continue to work my job full time. I knew I could get a master's degree in social work in less time than it would take to get a doctoral degree in clinical psychology, but I felt the latter would give me more options.

I visited the offices of the Psychoanalytic Institute of Chicago, the Adlerian Institute, and the Jung Institute and talked to people at all of these to get a feel for their training programs and whether they would be a good fit for me. The people in the Psychoanalytic Institute and Adlerian Institute seemed severe, withdrawn, and even, perhaps, unhappy compared to those at the Jung Institute, who seemed more inviting, warmer, and more positive and optimistic overall. My impressions might have been projections of my shadow nature—in other words, what I was seeing in others were either qualities I didn't want to see and acknowledge in myself or qualities I had but wanted to express more fully and consciously. But at the time, I simply paid attention to what I felt was the right focus for me—and decided to study Jungian psychology.

One day in the mid-1980s, I called the Jung Institute and inquired about applying for their training program. The head of the institute then asked me a series of questions:

"How much analysis have you had?"

"None."

"Do you have any educational background in psychology?"

"I took one course my freshman year in college."

"What clinical experience do you have?"

"None."

He did not hang up the phone.

"To apply here," he told me, "you need a terminal degree in the field, you have to be in analysis, and you must have clinical experience."

These were formidable obstacles, and he may well have thought he wouldn't hear from me again after that, but I made up my mind to someday apply to the Jung Institute. As for undergoing analysis myself, it made sense: It would better equip me for helping others later when I had completed my training. I could also see the benefits of dealing with my conscious and unconscious issues and experiencing how an analyst works with a patient. Today, I'm amused to remember how very logical I was about starting analysis—and how little awareness I had of my need to reflect on my shadow qualities, my unexplored and dormant emotions, and my hidden beliefs. Most likely, I had some unconscious desire to undergo analysis so I could experience healing and transformation. I didn't realize it, but I needed to break out of some old patterns.

As I thought about my future, I felt that helping people change their lives for the better would be as rewarding as making money or negotiating lucrative deals—and maybe even more so. With hindsight, I can see that while I wasn't fully conscious of it, I also wanted to be looked up to as an effective healer—to be special in some way.

I'm not sure I realized at the time how much hard work over many years would be involved in becoming an analyst or how challenging and humbling my experience of undergoing analysis could be. Maybe it's good that I didn't know how exhausting the journey would become at times. I wanted to pursue this path and was determined to make it happen—as determined as I was not to let my arm drop that day at the dojo.

Carl Jung identified the wounded healer archetype, represented by the god Chiron in Greek mythology, and although I did not see it at the time, I had unhealed wounds. Exploring them and working to heal them would help me become a better analyst—or so I would learn. Improving my listening skills would help me, too. However, these insights about my need to work on myself would not come to me until after I had done some therapeutic work with others and begun to do more self-reflection. My mentors would help me see my weaknesses and address them. For example, they would help me reconcile the part of myself that wanted to receive accolades for my accomplishments and the part that wanted to be seen as humble. For now, undergoing analysis was, to me, just part of the training that would lead me to my goal. I had yet to understand how my pursuit of psychology would help me access my mystical side and unacknowledged emotions.

Much as patients might like to intellectualize their experiences, a good analyst will lead a patient to emotional honesty—but at this point in my life, emotional honesty wasn't my strongest suit. After my mother's death, my father taught me that grief and pain should be swiftly swept out of the way so that life can carry on.

Reattachment, Reintegration

Around this time, I had a vivid dream that I suspected was giving me an important message about my life. In the dream, there was a judo competition and the competitors' bodies were arriving at the event frozen and decapitated. They were to meet their opponents with a head not their own and, after competing, have their own head reattached. My task was to sew one of the heads back on to the body of a participant who had completed his competition, but I didn't know how to do it. I became wounded in many ways, including being shot, before I could get the body and head to a hospital, where a surgeon could help me. The competitor's head was correctly reattached to his body, and my own wounds became healed, but both of us were told we would have scars from this experience. The competitor and I looked at each other, man to man, and realized we were the same person. We embraced and knew we would never be separated again.

Who was this self I had detached from, the body that was cut off from the head? It was the self I had stored away somewhere while I competed in the world of work. Now felt like the right time to reintegrate it into my life. My interpretation of the dream was that parts of me were frozen and disconnected—in particular, my emotions and some of my thoughts. In the dream, I had been wounded in many ways and sought healing and reintegration or wholeness. I wanted to acknowledge and incorporate the essential part of myself that had been missing for too long.

It was painful to reunite with myself and mend the split between the two competitors. Later, as I thought about what the dream meant, I realized that my unconscious might have been warning me that the work of healing would not always be comfortable. Having on someone else's head when I was competing might be effective for my work life with all its competitiveness and deal-making. But I was cut off from my head—its feelings, beliefs, and desires—and needed to have it reattached.

Increasingly, I wanted to reflect on my life and the decisions I had made in the past so that I could be more conscious in making choices in the future. I knew that studying psychology would help me better understand myself even as I got training to be able to help others.

Several schools in the Chicago area offered doctoral programs in clinical psychology. The one that seemed to give the most practical training, which would help me get clinical experience, was the Illinois School of Professional Psychology. If I earned a doctoral degree, I would have to do coursework and then practicums, which would involve administering diagnostic testing and providing psychotherapy to patients. Then, I would have to serve an internship with an institution, hospital, or state agency, fulfilling a requirement of working a certain number of hours. Since I would still be working full time at Martin, I calculated the program would take me longer to finish than the usual five years. It ended up taking me eight.

As difficult as this schedule might seem, it was easier than my engineering schedule at Lehigh had been. The Illinois School of Professional Psychology operated on a three-semester system, allowing me to attend school year-round. Otherwise, my training would have taken even longer.

When I showed up for my first class, it was a bit of a jolt to realize I was older than most of the students—just like with my karate class. Also, the majority of my fellow students were working in the field of psychology. Here I was, the CEO of an oil company with almost no background in psychology, even though by then I had read a fair amount in the field. Listening to my younger classmates talk about what they had learned broadened my perspective on what psychology was and how it could be used to help people.

Together, we delved into theories of psychopathology, the effects of trauma on mental health, different types of therapies, and the physiology of the brain. All this provided a welcome balance to the mechanistic world of engineering and the pragmatic world of business. I felt my soul was getting long-needed nourishment. I realized how hungry I had been for this reconnection to the part of myself that was interested in the mysteries of the human experience.

Compartmentalization was key to running a company, studying psychology, working with clients during my practicum and, later, my internship, while still training in martial arts and having a personal life. While I was at work, my focus was on the business and my responsibilities. I put it all away in a corner of my mind when I transitioned from being in the office to stepping into my home or the classroom. When I was at school, I kept the rest of my life sealed off from my coursework and client work. When I was at home, I was pretty good at being present with Jerri and my children, setting aside work and school concerns. Earlier, I wrote that I had an important engagement I was not willing to change on that last day before a judge would determine the outcome of the Panhandle lawsuit: The engagement was a class at the Illinois School of Professional Psychology, where I was scheduled to take a test. I was skilled enough at compartmentalization that I could go down to the wire in the negotiation with Panhandle yet also know that once I walked into the classroom, my mind would be completely focused on taking the exam.

However, there was a shadow side to my ability to compartmentalize. Typically, I would put my inconvenient emotions away and then forget about them. My habit protected me from the discomfort of what I thought were unnecessary conflicts, but it made me less authentic and emotionally expressive in my relationships with others, which I didn't realize was problematic. With people I was working with, I often resorted to joking to deflect from an uncomfortable emotion, such as anger, sadness, or embarrassment. I had learned this from my dad and his side of the family. In the moment, joking could help me feel better, but I was shifting the discomfort to others. I would have to learn to handle my emotions differently to be more direct and authentic as well as to express and nourish a side of myself that had become closed off long ago.

In midlife, I was beginning to learn that you can't split off parts of yourself and put them into a deep freeze, so to speak, without consequences. Those heads and bodies I reattached in my dreams would always bear scars, just as I would, because my lack of emotional integration significantly affected my marriage.

Changes at Home

In 1980 or so, Jerri, the kids, and I moved from Olympia Fields, where we had been living for about ten years, back to Flossmoor into a house that we had first seen one night when Jerri and I were there to attend a charity benefit. A beautiful Georgian with huge oak trees in front of it, the house was adjacent to a country club and a forest preserve. The property included four acres, a pool and pool house, and a creek with a little footbridge. Being lit up to create a festive mood for the party made the house and grounds seem even more attractive. I felt it was the most magical home that I had ever seen. It came on the market not long after I first saw it, so I bought it. The kids liked swimming in the backyard, and switching school districts didn't seem to upset them. After all, many of their friends were still connected to them through sports and other activities.

I ate dinner at home each night if I could, although sometimes it was late. I wanted to spend time talking to Jerri and to my son and daughters about their day. I had often read or told stories to the kids before they went to bed, but at this point, they were reading on their own. Sundays continued to be family time, however. We would spend it attending church, eating at a local deli, and playing tennis or going on a bike ride together.

All my kids were good students, and I might help them with their homework if they asked me, but they didn't need much guidance from me. I don't remember any stress about school obligations. Jerri and I didn't emphasize grades or make a big deal about how the kids did on any particular test. I wanted them to get into the best schools they could, feeling that would give them the greatest number of options, but we didn't obsess about what colleges would accept them. I figured Caryn, Michael, and Janet would all end up at the right schools for them.

But while there was much that was right in our home, and Jerri and I had spent many good years together, I felt disconnected from her for a variety of reasons. I was very busy and would not normally reflect on how happy or unhappy I was, but analysis was making me ask questions and take a look at why I felt so strongly that something important was missing from my life. The exploration was uncomfortable but necessary for me. I didn't know where this transformative process would take me, but I was increasingly sensing that my marriage might not survive it.

While in some ways I was good at compartmentalizing my various roles, I didn't always do so successfully at home. Although it was hard to admit it, in my relationship with Jerri, I have since realized, I had not been accepting enough of who she was. To some degree, I brought home my "boss" energy, and that caused me to be critical and impatient with her at times. I'm certain it was hard for her when I was like that, and in hindsight, I wish I would have handled some things differently.

I had grown up in a culture where men were expected to handle their feelings privately, letting them out here and there before quickly returning to a logical, analytical mind-set. Talking about painful or difficult experiences or feelings was regarded as a weakness, but of course, the work of therapy is to bring to the surface that which makes you uneasy. My focus on embodying the skilled warrior archetype at work, being competitive and not getting too close or attached to my opponents, had its upside. But it also had led me to stifle my emotions, which meant I wasn't fully present in some of my relationships. I knew intuitively that it took more courage to talk about something than it did to endure it in silence, deny it, or minimize it. Even so, I didn't always have the conversations I should have had.

I had seen what happened when men felt they had to repress their grief or pain. My father had been married three times at this point and was starting to pay the price for years of smoking and drinking, habits that had helped him relax and dampened some of his anger, frustration, and sadness. Many of my relatives and people I knew had the same habits. I took the edge off by doing martial arts, yet I still had a sense of emotional constriction that I wanted to be freed from.

Constriction of a Lifetime

A few years ago, I did a shamanic journey—a practice for engaging what is hidden in the unconscious. In this journey to a place called the lower world—a transpersonal realm you can set your intention to travel to so you can learn more about your past—I sought insights into how my past was affecting my health in the present. In my trancelike state, I became aware that I had been exposed to toxins from alcohol and tobacco when I was in my mother's womb. Memories of my parents smoking and drinking rose up, and I felt a sense of constriction in my body and my personal energy field that surrounded me. As a child, I was surrounded by cigarette smoke, and of course, over time smoking hardens the arteries and makes it more difficult for lungs to draw in air. Even just breathing in someone else's cigarette smoke can cause strokes, heart disease, and lung cancer. By the time in my life that I was doing the journey, I had some arterial plaque and vascular disease. I have to wonder whether the emotional experience of constriction combined with actual exposure to pollutants affected my circulatory system years down the road. Using shamanic and Jungian-influenced practices, I have worked on myself energetically to release any stagnant energies, and I believe it has helped alleviate some of my constrictions, including those of the heart. Growing up, I saw the men around me contain their emotions and do what was expected of them, not what their hearts urged them to do. In my childhood, I had seen that letting go of restriction and letting emotions arise could lead to violence. Maybe years of allowing my mythopoetic self to be expressed in small increments, like a valve opened to relieve a little pressure, supported me. For a long time, I had feared that if I didn't contain my emotions and compartmentalize them, disaster would strike. I was beginning now to let go of that fear.

Constriction as a theme was playing a role in my life even after I had spent many hours reflecting on myself and my experiences. I asked my analyst, Lee Roloff, PhD, whom I worked with in the '80s and '90s, if he thought we ever free ourselves from unconscious themes carried over from the past that affect us in the present. He said he didn't think so but believed they could eventually affect us less intensely, less frequently, and for shorter periods. He also believed that the more people free themselves from past themes, the easier it is for them to experience equanimity and peace with the old issues, whatever they were. This has been my experience as a Jungian analyst.

While working with Lee, I confronted other emotions I had suppressed or tried to eliminate so I could bring them into harmony with my conscious life. Jungian psychology deals with conflict—within oneself, between the analysand (person undergoing analysis) and the analyst, and between the analysand and others in their life. Martial arts principles also relate to conflicts, and I've found them valuable for gaining insights into how to be a better analyst.

My martial arts training and studies have helped me to acknowledge and confront conflicts not just in my outer world but in my inner life. Shosan, a Zen master who influenced the philosophy of the martial arts, stressed the importance of knowing oneself: "No matter how much you have learned and how much you know, if you don't know yourself you don't know anything. Indeed, if you don't know yourself you cannot know anything else."[1]

The Buddhist monk Bodhidharma, who had brought martial arts to China in the fifth or sixth century AD, preached that the goal of the martial arts is to promote spiritual development and health rather than fighting for its own sake. He talked about martial virtue, which includes discipline, restraint, humility, and respect for human life, a virtue the practitioner was expected to apply at home, in business, in relationships, and in all walks of life. Westerners often place more emphasis on martial arts showmanship and winning tournaments while Easterners emphasize the spiritual dimensions of the art. The Eastern practitioner is not as concerned with winning and flashy techniques.

There are two major styles of this ancient tradition of martial arts: external (hard) and internal (soft). While each has aspects of the other, generally, external styles such as judo and karate involve the practitioner becoming physically hard and strong. These qualities were more like those embodied by the warriors I had seen in movies and in the dojos I had attended. In the external style, the warrior delivers force through punches, strikes, kicks, and blocks that the opponent attempts to counter with greater force. However, practitioners of external styles often lack good flow of internal energy, or qi, and die at relatively young ages because of the ravages of physical stress.

Starting in my twenties, I was very dedicated to the external martial arts and experienced some broken toes and fingers, cracked ribs, dislocated joints, pulled muscles, and so on in those years of doing judo and karate. However, I would not come to appreciate the internal martial arts until many years later when I would study their foundation: qigong (CHEE-gong), a practice of working with energy. Performing its gentle, flowing movements offers physical benefits of balance, flexibility, and stamina—and I would find it easier on my body than the external martial arts had been. My shift from being highly competitive and driven to being more engaged by inner explorations would not happen right away, but much would change in my life, especially in my early forties.

Important Questions

In the mid-1980s, Kirk's wife, Rita, and I were teachers in the confirmation class at our church. I noticed that the teenagers I was working with weren't interested in the bigger spiritual questions: Why are we here? What happens after we die, and do we exist somewhere before we are born into this life and these bodies? They were more interested in what they were going to do on Saturday night and whether their friend was going to be angry at them for sitting with someone else in the school cafeteria.

Rita and I showed the students how Christian theology and the teachings of other great religions, such as Buddhism, Judaism, Islam, and Hinduism, could help them wrestle with their day-to-day issues. We went to other houses of worship to experience what their services were like and talked afterward. Having grown up exposed only to Christianity, I was learning a lot, too.

More so than the kids, I was the one quietly pondering the big questions. I was exploring them on my own even as I was unpacking my choices past and present in my analyst's office. I started to realize that there are many spiritual paths, and some seem less rote and routinized and some more so—or perhaps how people experience their religion varies a great deal within those traditions. I wondered whether the doctrines and strictness of some of the paths distracted people so much from the experience of God that the religion often seems to have become more about itself than a quest for a relationship with Spirit.

I was also thinking about the challenges I was facing in my family life. It was a painful time for all of us. My children each had their own response to the news that I was moving to an apartment in Chicago and Jerri and I were separating (later, we would divorce). There was sadness, confusion, and denial. Some were angrier and less understanding than others were. I felt that as a father, I had to allow my children to express those difficult feelings toward me even though it was hard for me to be on the receiving end. Being in analysis and studying psychology made it easier for me to listen to others express things I was uncomfortable hearing—their disappointment and judgment of me, for example.

I had done the best I could as a father but now realize I could have made different choices about how to spend my time and how to parent my kids. Much of my self-worth was tied up in winning at business and athletics and the need to prove that I was strong, smart, and capable of besting formidable opponents. That often got in the way of my humanness in relationships. I had done what the culture I was raised in had expected of me. But in midlife, I was beginning a long journey toward evolving into someone who is more emotionally connected to people and less focused on competition and achieving success as it has been defined traditionally. I've had to learn to be honest with myself about my shortcomings and my choices. Altering old patterns and beliefs takes a lot of soul searching and a lot of feedback from people who make you uneasy because they call you out for what you say and do.

One young lady in the confirmation class I was teaching seemed to view me as a role model and phoned to ask me a question I felt compelled to answer, difficult though it was to have the conversation.

"Mr. Greer," she asked, "how can you be teaching us about becoming good people and leading Christian lives when you're getting a divorce?"

I respected her curiosity and desire to understand the seeming contradiction of me being a spiritual mentor of sorts and yet being poised to dissolve my marriage. I asked her if she would like to talk over lunch and took her to a restaurant where I answered all her questions. She was surprised and appreciative that I'd taken time to talk to her, but I got something out of the conversation, too. Having to explain myself wasn't the easiest thing to do, but it made me think—and this was a time in my life when I needed to do a lot of thinking.

"People throw that term around a lot"

My father had married a third time after Mary Anne died, to a woman named Elizabeth. She was not severe and withholding as Mary Anne had been. Elizabeth and my dad's marriage broadened my father's life and coincided with him retiring from U.S. Steel.

Elizabeth had two sons and a daughter, whom my family and I came to know, and we all got along well. Char, Elizabeth's daughter, saw my dad as a positive father figure. He spent time listening to her and giving her patient guidance and advice about her future plans. Char was an artist, and after an early life of trekking around the world seeking adventure, she founded a graphic design company called Softimage. She later sold it to Microsoft for tens of millions of dollars. Recently, she reminded me that I turned down a chance to invest in her company and the few thousand dollars she asked me to put in could have turned into a bonanza! Sometimes, your best opportunities are right in front of you, but you don't recognize them. Elizabeth's oldest son, Tim, built custom log houses, and her youngest son, Michael, was a fitness trainer who ran his own gym. Sadly, he died in a car accident in his twenties not too long after our family first met him.

After his retirement, Dad's illnesses started taking a toll on his body and his mood, amplifying his critical, judgmental nature. I could see this shift toward greater irritability was straining his relationship with Elizabeth as he too often seemed to be finding fault with her. I can remember being on vacation with him and Elizabeth and my own family, and she was telling a story about what they had done recently. He felt the need to correct every detail, however small, that he felt she had gotten wrong, interrupting the flow of the story. I thought, "What does it matter if you played golf on Tuesday and not Thursday?" But then I had to acknowledge he had been this way as far back as I could recall. Maybe he felt a sense of power or control being able to right the "wrong" of how Elizabeth was telling the story. That inflexibility seemed to prevent him from relaxing naturally. This was true even in his retirement despite his being financially comfortable and not having the pressures of work hanging over him. Dad always seemed to have trouble being at ease.

I found myself reflecting on how I was like my father—too irritable and impatient, too brusque with others who wanted me to relax and spend time with them, to listen to them sympathetically and enjoy the experience of being together with them. I started to see that in some ways, my father lived in me; I had adopted some of his less stellar qualities.

To change, we first have to be honest about our present situation. Though it was difficult to admit my flaws, I knew I had to stop denying the parts of me that I didn't like. I wanted to see myself as someone who was open-minded and adaptable. In the years to come, I would become increasingly aware of my habitual ways of responding to people and situations. I also came to see that the gulf between wanting to change and actually changing could be very wide. Bridging it could take much time and dedication.

Dad had been on a trip to Vancouver with Elizabeth when he ended up in the ER. Kirk and I flew in to be with him. The doctors diagnosed congestive heart failure, but Dad had also suffered from arteriosclerosis for years, along with type 2 diabetes, glaucoma, and fibromyalgia rheumatica. His lifestyle choices were contributors to his diseases but for whatever reason, he didn't follow through with surgical options or begin to radically change his drinking, eating, and exercise habits.

When he was in the hospital and lying in his bed, the reality that we might lose him weighed on me, and while I knew it might make him feel a bit embarrassed, I said to him, "I love you, Dad."

He let that sink in for a moment and replied, "People throw that term around a lot, Carl."

I understood. We were men of a certain time and place where you just didn't say those words explicitly.

"That may be true," I admitted. "But still. I love you."

"I love you, too," he said awkwardly.

In his remaining years, I noticed my dad was better able to listen to someone say "I love you" and say it himself.

My father's orneriness and need to have things exactly as he wanted them had led to a big argument between us years before when my kids were still little. It was at Kirk and Rita's wedding in Pittsburgh, late at night, after the reception. My family was staying at my dad's house, and Caryn, Michael, Janet, and Jerri were already in bed while Dad and I were up talking. Mary Anne had recently died, and my dad hadn't remarried yet, and I suppose the wedding might have triggered some grief in him about his own losses. He had been drinking and was in a foul mood—irritable and morose.

He was particularly upset because after the wedding, people had toasted Rita's father, but nobody had toasted him. He kept turning this slight over and over in his mind and was becoming increasingly belligerent and accusatory. I had put up with his bad mood all day but finally, I'd had enough. Although there was a snowstorm outside, I left him in the kitchen, went to the bedrooms, woke Jerri and the kids, and told them to get dressed because we would be leaving now.

On our way out, I saw my dad sobbing in front of the sink, looking out the window at the snow. Through tears, he muttered, "I don't think I can take anymore."

Suddenly, I felt really bad—and sorry for him. I walked over, hugged him, and held him for some time.

Jerri, the kids, and I ended up staying the night. And the next day, after the snow had stopped, we all went out for brunch with my dad before parting ways.

I was one of the few people who confronted my dad, and in our remaining years together, we had no more incidents as raw as this one. I think at some level, he was proud of me for being on my own from an early age, escaping what he must have realized was a toxic home environment. Some years later, after he married Elizabeth, I remember him telling this to her while the three of us were at dinner when I was visiting them in Pittsburgh.

My dad was a good man but a hard man, sentimental yet cruel, critical, and judgmental—but somehow lovable. In analysis, I came to see how my experience with a rigid and sometimes volatile father affected me. My dad simply didn't know what to do with intense feelings like hurt and anger, but he did his best to temper them—and felt guilty when he failed.

I also explored with Lee Roloff how losing my mother at such a young age, and in such a dramatic, abrupt way, only to have my father marry a woman who lacked warmth, affected my relationships with women in all areas of my life. Lee asked me tough questions that sometimes made me a little defensive or irritated. But I was committed to the work, to the learning, and to being more authentic—not just with others but with myself.

I was reading books on psychology, including textbooks for my courses, but also ones on shamanism, often pulling them from the shelves of the library at the Jung Institute. Carlos Castaneda's books and Lynn Andrews's *Medicine Woman* made their way into my hands. I also read other books on consciousness and mystical experiences by authors such as Hyemeyohsts Storm and Sun Bear. The topic of shamanic healing especially piqued my interest. Over the years, many have questioned whether Castaneda's adventures were confabulated, but as stories, they worked well. They also helped me better understand nature-based spiritual traditions.

As I studied Jungian psychology and Carl Jung's writings and continued with my own analysis, I became increasingly intrigued by how healing could happen when in altered states of consciousness. I could see overlaps between the work of this European psychologist from the twentieth century and ancient traditions of indigenous people in the Americas. I also read some books by Aleister Crowley on the magic tradition in England, but I didn't feel drawn to exploring those ideas in the way that I was to Jungianism and shamanism.

Around this time, my high school sweetheart, Pat, and I reconnected and ended up getting married. We both had a shared interest in psychology: She had become a marriage and family therapist and later would become a Jungian analyst. Pat and I began spending time with our respective children and with all of them together. It took a while, and a lot of understanding on everybody's part, for everyone to start feeling comfortable, but today, our extended family group seems natural.

Unfortunately, my father died before he could spend much time with Pat, me, and her family. I remember his final visit to Chicago. At one point, I was with him in my car when I had to take a business conference call. After I hung up the car phone, he said, "You handled that well. I couldn't have done that." He told me that my style of dealing with a team was clearly effective and better than the way he had managed others.

The compliment was quite unexpected, and I wondered briefly, "What brought that on?" The conversation with my team was nothing particularly special, and I didn't feel I had done anything out of the ordinary. Even so, I was glad to hear my father was proud of me.

Maybe the reason he made this effort to connect with me and praise me for moving beyond his example and discovering my own way of operating was that on some level, he sensed he didn't have a lot of time left. Within days, he ended up in the ER with chest pains and had quadruple bypass surgery. I talked to him just before he went under and was there afterward, but he passed away a day later, never regaining consciousness.

Driving home from the hospital, I felt tears coming up and suddenly, the old Protestant hymn, "Blessed Assurance," came to mind. I cried as I sang:

Blessed assurance, Jesus is mine;
Oh, what a foretaste of glory divine!
Heir of salvation, purchase of God,
Born of His Spirit, washed in His blood.
This is my story, this is my song,
Praising my Savior all the day long.
This is my story, this is my song,
Praising my Savior all the day long.
Perfect submission, perfect delight,
Visions of rapture now burst on my sight;
Angels descending, bring from above
Echoes of mercy, whispers of love.
Perfect submission, all is at rest,
I in my Savior am happy and blest;
Watching and waiting, looking above,
Filled with His goodness, lost in His Love.

The lyrics brought me some comfort as I processed the reality that my father really was gone.

We buried my dad in his family's plot in the cemetery at Paris, Kentucky, rather than near my mother's grave in Indiana or Mary Anne's in Ohio. I don't know why he made that choice, but we honored it.

160

"Living in the shadow of death makes life sweeter, more compelling, more intense"

Later that year, I experienced another shock. Pat was diagnosed with breast cancer, which had spread to her lymph nodes. She had a lumpectomy, chemotherapy, and radiation. Pat would explore her experience of the illness in a book published by Chiron Publications called *Breast Cancer: A Soul Journey.* In it, she wrote about her journey to access inner wisdom and to live more fully and more authentically.

She underwent treatment, and the following spring, we were vacationing in Oak Creek Canyon, Arizona, near Sedona, when an incision the surgeons had made became infected and started to ooze pus and blood. Inspired by what I had read about shamanic journeys in Michael Harner's *The Way of the Shaman,* I talked to Pat about using visualizations to see if we could affect the wound. Having worked in imaginal realms, Pat was open to the experience.

While packing for the trip, I had placed in my luggage a quartz crystal I had recently bought. I did not yet know that shamans use crystals to amplify or extract energies from a person's energy field for the sake of healing. I only knew I was drawn to it when I saw it for sale and, for whatever reason, decided to bring it with me. Had my intuition told me to bring it along because we would be in a place where, it was said, there were energy vortexes with healing powers that could be accessed and directed? In retrospect, I wonder.

Pat and I decided to work together for healing, intending to let our unconscious minds guide us. I sat with the crystal in my hands and my eyes closed. Soon, images began to appear in my mind's eye. I saw myself sitting under a tree, a crystal in my hand. I also saw a woman sitting in a pool at the base of a waterfall. Like me, she was holding a crystal. I could see our two crystals were exchanging energy and pure white light with each other and with the crystal I was holding as I sat in the room with Pat. In this vision, to heal Pat's wounds, I was using the quartz crystal I was actually holding, imagining it was sending her healing energy. While I was having this experience, Pat was visualizing that her inner healer was mobilizing her immune system to attack the infection. We ended our visualizations and shared with each other what we had seen. Within less than an hour, Pat's wound was healed—no more pus and blood. It could have been a coincidence, but it didn't feel that way to us. It was my first experience of shamanic healing, and it felt mysterious to me. At the same time, I felt reassured that working with transpersonal realms to change our everyday reality could be quite powerful.

We completed our trip and came home. Pat finished her chemotherapy and radiation. Then, a few months later, we learned from a scheduled biopsy of Pat's breast that more cancer had been detected. The surgeon recommended a mastectomy.

Before she was due to have the operation, Pat and I did more healing work together in the hope of destroying the cancer cells. The same vision of the crystals and the woman in the pool by the waterfall came to me. Meanwhile, Pat was seeing the cancer inside her being destroyed and coming out of her body through her belly, and she felt this energetically. Then she experienced a vision of those spaces in her body filling up with a healing blue-green light. She and I did this work together several times over the next few weeks, hoping it would be beneficial.

As the date of her scheduled mastectomy neared, she made a request of the surgeon. She wanted him to stop and do several frozen C-sections (biopsies that show any cancerous growths) while she was under anesthesia before removing her breast. Her hope was that the cancer might have disappeared. Her surgeon went along with her request, and each time he saw the results, he came out to the waiting room to tell me that there was no trace of cancer. When Pat woke up from anesthesia, she realized indeed, the surgeon had not removed her breast—and I told her what had happened.

We were both thankful for the gift of healing and savored life more deeply. As she wrote in her book *Breast Cancer: A Soul Journey,* "One of the paradoxical gifts of breast cancer is that living in the shadow of death makes life sweeter, more compelling, more intense."

I was now answering my long-repressed calling to be a psychologist and would experience many changes, starting with my discovery of the connection between my healing and that of others I helped on their healing journeys.

Many people put aside their dreams and set new priorities that are out of sync with their authentic selves in order to be practical and gain approval from others. In midlife or during crises such as experiencing health problems or losses (jobs, loved ones, marriages, and so on), we often will awaken to how much we have constricted ourselves and compromised our values. Exploring themes of authenticity and transformation can make us feel frightened as we face truths about ourselves that we have tried to ignore. Yet, these themes can also lead us to breakthroughs and positive changes. I was able to reclaim my mythopoetic self and gain greater satisfaction due to the inner work I did: I looked at how I had repressed my desire to explore the realm of psychology and how the mind works. As a result, I became a psychologist and changed the direction of my life.

If you are thinking about making changes in your life, you might want to reflect on the compromises you have made and what your current story is. If it's dissatisfying, it might be time to examine it and begin the process of writing a new one.

Questions for the Reader to Ponder

Compartmentalization. Are you easily able to compartmentalize your emotions and your personal life so they don't get in the way of work and career? Do you have difficulty accessing and expressing your emotions and sustaining healthy, rewarding relationships with others because of your work and career? If so, what would you like to do differently so your ability to compartmentalize serves you better?

Authenticity. Have you taken steps to reclaim your true self? If so, what are they? If not, what steps would you like to take? What is stopping you? What if you could begin to break through those obstacles beginning today—what might your life look like in the future?

Making the unconscious conscious. Do you value a relationship with the unconscious and invisible realms and, if so, do you take time to connect with them? How do you do that? Or, have you been so "grounded" that you have not been connected to the invisible realms of nature or of your unconscious? If you want a relationship with them, what is stopping you from having one? Are you afraid of facing uncomfortable emotions and thoughts that you may have relegated to your unconscious? If so, what do you think might happen if you did confront them? What might happen if you did it with the help of a therapist or analyst who could support you? On the other hand, have you been too involved with the invisible, spiritual realms of life and not grounded enough in the everyday world? How has that kept you from living the life you would like to lead? What can you do to establish and maintain a balanced relationship between the conscious, everyday world and the invisible, spiritual realms?

Transformation. If there are changes you'd like to make in your life, what is stopping you? How could you begin the transformation process today?

CHAPTER ELEVEN

Discovering What Had Been Hidden

It was a recurring dream: I could feel that the fish on the end of my line was a big one, but I couldn't see it below the surface of the water. Parts of the lake were becoming shallower, and I could see clear through to the bottom in spots, but as I sat in the boat trying to land the fish, it continued to be hidden from me.

In dreams, water often represents the unconscious. My dream was telling me that the psychological work I was doing was revealing parts of myself that had been hidden from my awareness for years. "Don't give up," my unconscious seemed to be saying. "You're onto something big."

Extracting the information that was hidden in my unconscious and examining it was helping me let go of old beliefs and feel emotions that had long been buried. Through studying psychology and undergoing analysis as well as through my relationship with Pat, I was feeling a greater sense of fulfillment and purpose even as I continued to get in touch with parts of myself I had long repressed because they made me feel uncomfortable.

I'm sure I seemed resistant to the analytical process at times, but Lee, my analyst, was patient and excellent at guiding me to do the work I needed to do. Any defensiveness I displayed probably helped me later on to empathize with my clients when they pushed back against my questions and observations. My job as a psychologist required me to challenge them at times. That could bring up difficult emotions they didn't want to feel but needed to if they were going to experience transformation.

Working with Lee and, some years later, with analyst Mary Dougherty, helped me become less ruled by my unconscious and better understand its influence on me—including its influence on how I interacted with others.

A big discovery was that I needed to work on my relationship to the archetypal feminine energy: my internal, unconscious relationship to women. On the one hand, I had learned to be somewhat independent of the feminine because I had lost my mother so young and under such mysterious circumstances—and because I had not bonded with my stepmother. Meanwhile, at an unconscious level, I longed for feminine approval and acceptance I feared I wouldn't receive. That makes sense when you look at the relationships I had with my mother figures when I was a child. I needed to make conscious my unconscious struggle with the feminine to be able to break out of old patterns and heal my wounds from the past.

I continued to keep my own counsel rather than confide in others, just as I had as a child. The work of analysis pushed me to share more about my internal life—my thoughts and feelings—than I ever had. Part of me still felt that real men didn't go to therapy, but I decided to trust in the process even though initially, it did not feel natural to talk about my problems in a one-to-one setting. What I learned as a result, however, was eye-opening.

Analysis helped me see that while I perceived myself as strong and confident, the truth was that I felt very vulnerable in my relationships with women. I was afraid of upsetting them by voicing my needs or wants. In one session, I recalled being in a store by myself as a boy of nine or ten in Gary and talking with a saleswoman who wanted me to buy something. I was able to remember the feeling of not wanting to disappoint her by saying no. That reluctance to disappoint others, but especially women, has been a theme I've had to work on throughout my life.

In my analysis with Lee, I was discovering that some of my conflicted feelings about women stemmed from my father's attitudes. My dad had a need to win and dominate that might have originated in a sense of inadequacy. He was outwardly gallant to women but seemed to have an unconscious desire to control them, which I could see in how he interacted with my mother, Mary Anne, and Elizabeth. Part of my psychological growth has been to recognize and deal with my own such tendencies.

I had learned that central to Jungian analysis was the challenge of looking at uncomfortable aspects of my character that were hidden in my shadow—the part of my unconscious where repressed emotions, thoughts, and urges lay—and integrating them into my consciousness. The idea is to acknowledge what you don't want to face, no matter how embarrassing it might be to admit what you see in yourself. After that, you can start to relate to it differently and will likely find it easier to make changes in your relationships with others.

Carl Jung pointed out that all shadow qualities have both positive and negative aspects: They can serve us well, but they can also hurt us. I was seeing this in my own life. For example, compartmentalizing was helping me to stay on top of all my goals, yet it had also made me less emotionally available in my marriage to Jerri. Being competitive was an asset in business and led me to engage in sports that kept me physically fit, but a need to triumph and dominate has to be tempered when dealing with family and friends. The goal wasn't to stop compartmentalizing altogether and repress my competitive tendencies but to change my relationships with these qualities. Then, I would have more freedom of choice instead of going along with the old programming that had me reacting to life in predictable ways rather than engaging it with curiosity and creativity.

Once, toward the end of a difficult business negotiation, I casually suggested to my counterpart on the other end of the deal, "When this is over, perhaps we can get together for coffee or lunch." He replied, "What makes you think I would want to get together with you?" I had a few other similar experiences that woke me up to the truth that how others have viewed me didn't necessarily fit with my image of myself. Why would someone perceive me to be stubborn and difficult instead of as a friendly competitor? I wanted to be more mindful of how I was expressing my personality traits—for example, not letting my competitiveness cause people to not want to do business with me again.

In my thirties and forties, I highly valued winning athletic competitions and accumulating money. Over the years, those goals became less interesting and the triumphs less satisfying. Today, I am not attempting to beat thirty-year-olds in a martial arts contest. I am also not drawn to negotiating deals and making money as I was in the past.

My work around these themes of compartmentalization and competitiveness has made it easier for me to know when to act versus when to let things be, allowing for differences and disagreements. I am more conscious of when something is sticking in my craw and better able to handle conflict without letting my competitive nature get the better of me. I used to push myself to quietly tolerate situations rather than express my feelings. I told myself I wasn't all that upset, but meanwhile, I would be building up a head of steam—something I was in denial of. Eventually, I would erupt, maybe saying something I would later regret. I now can better listen to the other side and respond earlier, making my point before I get too irritable. The other person and I can then agree to disagree or to see each other's side well enough to go forward in a new way that works for each of us. That's a very different way of relating to people than being a domineering boss. This new way of communicating and interacting with others felt awkward at first but feels comfortable now—and it nurtures my relationships. I suspect that none of these changes would have happened without confronting what was hidden from my conscious mind.

Another example of how analysis was affecting me was that I was starting to become less driven. Always rushing to get on to the next task had made me very productive but posed problems in relationships. It served as a defense mechanism for avoiding emotional experiences. If a conversation veered into emotional territory, I wanted to resolve it quickly and move on to a safer subject—or end the dialogue and go on to some task or action that served as a distraction from my discomfort. Wisecracking was a fallback that worked for me. Focusing on work became an avoidance behavior.

Emotionally, I was closed off for a long time, checking items off a list instead of recognizing how important it was to give more time to other people and be sensitive to their emotions and reactions. Being the boss, I could, ultimately, let people go if they didn't follow my guidance or figure out their own solutions and implement them. However, for me to have better relationships with other people called for more subtle, complex emotional responses to their telling me about their problems and expressing their disappointments. I hadn't put much thought to how hard change is for anyone, but now I was coming to see that it could take a lot of effort over a long time. It wasn't a great solution for me to just say, "Well, if that's not working for you, do something else." Transformation isn't that easy—and often, people don't want advice as much as understanding and listening.

As I came to view my life differently and better understand my unconscious drives, I slowly gained more freedom to choose other ways to interact not only with women but also with other people in a variety of situations.

I also discovered that repressing uncomfortable feelings and beliefs takes enormous energy. When we bring those emotions and stories about ourselves and our lives to the surface, we free up energy that can be used for other purposes. The work I was doing brought up anger, regret, curiosity, sadness, and many other emotions I had no idea I was holding on to. Releasing them felt good.

During my early analysis, when I was out of touch with my emotions, I had dreams of living in houses that were gray and barren. At one level they reflected my need to develop and relate to an inner life that was more vibrant and colorful, with greater vitality. At another level, they indicated a need to change what I was doing in the outer world so I could live more soulfully and in line with my deepest desires. Until then, my inner light was dim—I was putting great effort into maintaining the status quo of interacting with others as I always had. I was repeating patterns set back in my childhood—common patterns that I would come to see as nothing to be ashamed of. After all, they had served me effectively when I was trying to protect myself from being hurt as a child. As I began to discard them, I no longer felt so weighed down: I felt a greater sense of vitality and more color or vibrancy.

I was no longer willing to remain at the surface of my life, avoiding the risk of being hurt or feeling abandoned. I was finding the courage to imagine what my life would be, and who I would be, if I stopped dimming the lights, repressing my feelings, and holding back my thoughts. I was taking on the responsibility of writing a story that illustrated what I wanted to experience instead of remaining stuck in my old narrative. You might say my old life story was "I'll keep on truckin'": I was moving along the same path without questioning what I was doing and why. Now, I was writing a new story: "I want to get out of the truck and occasionally take a walk in the woods."

Competitiveness Begins to Fade

My relationships with men were less driven by unconscious factors than my relationships with women. With men, I have been aware of the theme of competitiveness being present in my academic, business, and sports life, and even in the areas of shamanism and psychology. Many men like to compete and be the "alpha dog" while others may choose to not engage in the competition. They may not realize why they are more—or less—competitive than they would like to be. Not being conscious of the reason for the imbalance can create problems for them. I am more comfortable than ever with not wanting to always win, but I am aware of the echoes of the strivings.

The idea of a story that we can become trapped in was still nascent in my mind at the early stages of my studying psychology and undergoing analysis. I wasn't sure what I wanted my new story to be, but I knew I no longer wanted to pay so much attention to reaching certain goals that would make me feel successful and accomplished. The task now was to choose what to focus on and what to devote less energy to. Later, I would think of this work as owning my power to be the storyteller in my life instead of having it ruled by hidden, unconscious influences.

I began to more highly value being true to myself and honoring my feelings and desires—for example, by spending time in nature, where I felt more in touch with my spiritual side. Instead of just reading about shamanism in books, I was taking shamanic journeys while listening to recordings of drumming or didgeridoo-playing. These hypnotic recordings were said to help quiet the conscious mind's activity and awaken a portal to the unconscious, including the collective unconscious: the field we all share where we can access hidden insights and energies for healing ourselves mentally, emotionally, and even physically. Taking actions that fit with the desires of my true self moved closer to the top of my agenda.

My psychoanalytic work involved, in part, breaking with the culture I had grown up in. As I described earlier, I didn't have a lot of exposure to people with different values. Consequently, there was much about my cultural conditioning that I had never thought about. The work now was to discover who I was and become a man on my terms rather than automatically assuming the role of stoic or warrior that had been modeled to me in myriad ways.

The process of evolving into my own person—individuation, in Jungian terms— meant examining my life and uncovering insights. Individuation involves consciously integrating what we discover in the unconscious and beginning to heal our sense of separation between our conscious and unconscious parts. This alchemy, so to speak, transforms us, helping us break out of old patterns. For me, sewing heads onto the bodies of judo tournament participants in my dream was a call from my unconscious to work on my individuation. Carl Jung believed that although no one ever completes the journey to total integration, "the true value of individuation lies in what happens along the way."[2]

In the coming years, I would learn more about myself and make a serious effort to be more easygoing and less controlling and stifled in my relationships with others, but I would never rid myself of these tendencies completely.

At last, I was consciously making different choices and beginning to establish new habits that were making me feel happier, freer, and more authentic.

When Dad Screws Up

By the time my kids were teenagers, I had discovered the pleasure of fishing on remote lakes in Canada. Twice, I had traveled to them by seaplane to fish, accompanied by some people I worked with. On those trips, we ate many of the fish we caught and cooked our meals using supplies we'd flown in with us. Being so far into the wilderness reconnected me with my mythopoetic self, and now that my son, Michael, was eighteen, I wanted to go on a fishing trip with him—just the two of us.

We portaged into a remote lake in Ontario, where we stayed in a century-old trapper's log cabin that we hadn't realized was quite so dilapidated. So many mosquitoes flew in at night through the chinks that, according to Michael, they were diving in and out of my open mouth while I was sleeping. It didn't wake me up, however, and I wasn't particularly bothered.

We swam, caught lots of fish, explored the lake, and drank beer and smoked cigars as we talked or sometimes, just listened to the sounds of nature all around us. At the end of the week, we started the trek back to our base camp so the seaplane could pick us up. We had to cross several lakes: Once we reached a shore, we would leave our boat and then, using a map and compass, find a land route to the next boat on the next lake we had to cross. At one point, after a long time walking through thick brush in the hot, humid weather, attacked by mosquitoes every inch of the way, we reached what I thought was the lake we were searching for, but there was no boat. Mike and I retraced our steps, tried what we thought was another way, and ended up in the same place, with no boat.

We decided that Mike would start walking along the shoreline to find the boat, and I would wait where I was. We called back and forth until I could no longer hear his voice. Hours went by and still, I heard nothing.

Overhead, I could see helicopters and planes. There had been forest fires in the area all week, and we had seen planes dropping chemicals and water on the fires to put them out. Now I waved at them in the hopes of getting a pilot's attention, but I must have been too far away for them to see me. I didn't know exactly where we were, only that we were many miles from other people.

By this time, the sun was starting to set, and I was conflicted about what to do. Should I stay put, where Mike knew I was, or should I try to find him? I wasn't particularly concerned about myself. I had water to drink from the lake, but I was concerned about Mike. It occurred to me that a forest fire might come toward him or me. A fire could easily cross over to the bay where I was, and while I could jump in the water to avoid the flames, the superheated air would kill me if I tried to breathe it. This wasn't too likely to happen, but I was aware that it could—for me or Mike. What had I gotten us into?

As I waited in the fading light, I was surprised to find myself relaxing into the situation. I was willing to be patient and trust that Mike and I would be okay. Knowing I might be there for a while and not knowing what I was going to do or what was going to happen, I focused on my natural surroundings. When I did this, I became calm and accepting of my situation.

Eventually, I heard the *putt-putt* of a motor and soon saw Mike in a boat coming around the shoreline, heading straight for me. When I got in, he told me his story: He had walked along the shoreline until he came to some impassable stretches, which forced him into the water for part of the journey. He came across a boat but discovered it didn't have the rubber tube that connected the gas can to the engine. He finally found the tube, but it took him a while to figure out how to start the motor, which was partly why he had been gone so long.

We drove around the lake to where he had found the boat. Mike realized—and now I saw it—that the boat he had picked up was the same one we had dropped off on this lake! When I had been leading us through the brush, thinking we were getting to another lake, we had merely walked across a peninsula and ended up on another section of the same lake where we had started.

Now it was dark. We docked our boat; I took our bearings with the compass and started leading us back into the brush again. We hadn't gone too far when Mike said, "Dad, I think we need to be going this way, not that way." I had started to take us right back to where we had gotten lost before! At this point, despite me being the father and him being the son, I didn't let my ego get in the way and start insisting I had to be right. I had been humbled by my mistakes of the day and yielded to Mike's advice. Finally, around midnight, we got home to the base camp and were able to eat some dinner at last.

The next day, as we were flying back to Red Lake, our guide, who was piloting the plane, pointed down and said, "Lost point." He knew from our description exactly what had happened and where we had gotten sidetracked. I realized that my cheap compass had been thrown off by the iron in the rocks and hadn't given us true directions.

The trip had been a coming-of-age experience for Mike: He had challenged my authority as his father. I let him know I was glad he had the confidence to speak up to me and trust his sense of direction. For me, the trip was a lesson in letting myself be still and allowing nature to inform me when I am in the presence of the unknown instead of bulling my way through the situation. I had taken the right action by yielding to the moment and staying where I was. On the other hand, I obviously needed to become more observant, since I had tried to lead us on the same path that had gotten us lost before. In our own ways, Mike and I had both learned something about ourselves. It was an experience of growth I will never forget sharing with him.

I didn't have the same kind of perilous adventures with my daughters that I had that time with Mike, but we shared many good times together, and there were occasions when my daughters got me to laugh at myself and my ineptitude. I remember once when Caryn and Janet were adults, I joined them in Northern California for a short vacation, and the three of us drove around singing along to the Indigo Girls' *Nomads Indians Saints* album. Even after we'd nearly worn out the CD playing it in the car as we made our way through Napa Valley, I couldn't seem to remember the words to the chorus of the album's hit song "Hammer and a Nail." The girls teased me, but I didn't mind. After all, hadn't my high school vocal group adopted the name the Inepts? Singing was not my forte. I was just grateful to be spending time with my daughters in such a relaxed way.

Many of my fondest memories of spending time with Caryn and Janet included being outdoors boating, fishing, hiking, and biking, but we also loved going to movies and even some Broadway shows together when we were able to meet up in New York City.

When they were young, I would take my daughters on business trips when I could instead of leaving them at home as my father had done with Kirk and me. On one trip, Janet and I drove through rural Indiana as I visited service stations. In the car, we would play simple word games to pass the time and then stop to eat at a drive-in like the A&W or a small-town diner like the ones I remembered from my childhood. I took Caryn to Denver when I had to travel there on business, and in my free time there, the two of us played tennis, went sightseeing, and ate at good restaurants. Having one-on-one time with each of my kids helped me feel more connected to them.

I'm fortunate to have good relationships with my children. All of them were physically active, so it was easy to find things I could do with them that we could enjoy as a family—a game of tennis or a day canoeing on a lake, for example. As a consequence, I have many good memories of our being together and becoming closer to each other.

Spending time with my kids was often a good reminder not to bring my "take charge" energy into my everyday life, where it could be intrusive. I knew that they needed space to make their own decisions and mistakes without me getting in their way, and I hope the way I fathered them was supportive without being overbearing.

"Why are you going easy on them?"

Another lesson around my vulnerability and being adequately supportive of someone dependent on me happened during my analytic training, when my case review committee required me to present reports on two clients I was working with. While I didn't realize it, this requirement would give me deeper insights into myself, too. It seems my choice of clients was driven by my unconscious more than I realized.

I chose to write about Ernie and Tim. Both were more comfortable being dependent on others rather than taking on greater responsibility for their lives. I could see they were sabotaging themselves in some ways, being too strongly influenced by those around them instead of having the confidence to make their own choices. Both set goals for becoming more successful in their careers and their relationships. I thought I was doing a good job working with them in achieving those aims, and they seemed to be getting something out of analysis.

After reading my reports, the committee members asked me two important questions. First, why did I pick these two men to write about? And second, why did I feel guilty when doing something that might cause either of them emotional pain, therefore inhibiting a potentially useful part of the analysis?

I hadn't thought much about why I had chosen them. My initial answer was that they seemed to be good analytic cases according to the parameters I had been given: Both individuals were willing to explore unconscious factors that were influencing them. Also, I thought that the two men would help me better understand people I was close to who had similar issues. I didn't see myself in Ernie and Tim, but with prodding from the committee, I started to realize I had been drawn to writing about these two particular men because, in part, they represented my own hidden desire to not have to grow up and be responsible, which I had needed to be at an early age.

The second question—why was I going easy on Ernie and Tim, not making interpretations that might make them feel angry or hurt?—compelled me to think deeply. With other clients, I had little difficulty pushing them into uncomfortable conversations in the interest of the work, so what was the difference here?

My well-meaning approach was keeping Ernie and Tim from growing up and taking on adult responsibilities. Unconsciously, I was giving them something I had lacked as a child: support in remaining dependent and, in some ways, childlike and free. In some sense, I wanted to be a kid again. That hidden desire was affecting my choices when working with these two men.

Unlike Ernie and Tim, I had prepared myself rigorously for success in the world. I had been responsible and done what was expected of me—but at a cost to my inner life. Prodded by the committee, I was beginning to get a glimpse of still-raw wounds inside myself that needed healing. I started to realize I strongly identified with Ernie and Tim and by not confronting them, it was as if I were protecting myself from being hurt. I still bore emotional scars from my father's volatility and physical punishments and from feeling emotionally neglected as a vulnerable child, and I felt great empathy for my patients.

As Ernie's and Tim's analyst, I needed to get beyond this overidentification and help them look closely at their wounds, begin healing them, and take on greater responsibility for their lives. Both had to start acknowledging that they had choices and could make different ones. It seemed likely that I had unconsciously chosen these two men not just to help them but to heal myself as well. Treating them had the potential to make me see at last what I had been avoiding for a long time: my desire to be nurtured and supported.

Difficult though it was to talk about this, I shared these insights with my case review committee. I felt very vulnerable. Then, something unexpected happened. I developed a growing sense that the members cared about me and genuinely wanted me not just to become a better analyst but also to feel supported by them rather than judged. They indicated that while I clearly had room for improvement, they respected my work.

The experience brought home how much I both needed kindness, which they were expressing to me, and how much I believed I wouldn't get it. I had been so convinced that I could never have it that I unconsciously told myself I could live without it.

Now I could see why the warrior's life had appealed to me so much: It allowed me to feel in control and powerful and to disconnect from the emotions that made me feel exposed. I had learned to be the soldier protected by armor. I could see out, but others couldn't see in— and that kept me safe. It also kept me from fully feeling and expressing my emotions.

I was ready to shed the armor.

A true warrior must overcome the fear not only of injury (or even death) but also of being touched by kindness, love, or sympathy and having his emotional vulnerability revealed to the world. Going forward, I wanted to work with the warrior archetype differently so I could have a greater sense of purpose, fulfillment, and connectedness to others. The classic Jungian book *King, Warrior, Magician, Lover: Rediscovering the Archetypes of the Mature Masculine* by Robert Moore and Douglass Gillette helped shape my thinking about my relationship to this archetype.[3]

Once during my training to become an analyst, I was asked by a committee member, "What did you feel in that situation?" I replied, "I don't know. Sometimes, I don't know in the moment, and it takes me a while to sort it out." The committee member was irritated that I couldn't answer on the spot, but I know I'm not alone—for many, it can take practice to reconnect with what they are feeling. I still need to take some time to process my emotions about situations, but I'm better at accessing them and recognizing what they are than I was back then.

You could say that at this period in my life, I was not only working with the warrior archetype but also with the magician, engaging in an alchemical process as I tried to become creative and generative outside of the world of work and making money. Reshaping the way I interacted with others and the way I saw myself required using new eyes to look at myself and the situations I was in.

The process of personal analysis was life changing for me. It was an arduous and sometimes tortuous process, as I had to confront who I thought I was versus who I really was. The in-control, confident image of myself I had constructed hid a much less secure person. I had come full circle from the high school senior who had wanted to burn out the mystic in me to the warrior who now needed—and wanted—to acknowledge and embrace my mystical tendencies.

My experience of undergoing analysis did make me better at helping others achieve their therapy goals. As I gained experience, I learned to better support and guide my clients in their self-exploration by slowing down and listening more, leaving pauses in a conversation. That helped my clients to find the answers themselves rather than looking to me to solve problems for them. And I was finding new ways to express kindness toward Ernie and Tim so that I could feel comfortable challenging them, too. I wanted them to be open to change—and I was experiencing that feeling awkward and vulnerable was part of the process of their, and my own, transformation.

"John Barleycorn and the still. What do you think about that?"

In time, I had to leave the classroom and begin to do the two practicums required for my clinical psychology training—one involved testing and diagnosing people, and the other, being a therapist at the Lorene Replogle Counseling Center, now called the Replogle Center for Counseling and Well-Being. At the time, I had no idea I would end up on staff at the center a few years later.

During my practicums, I saw clients at different locations to gain real-world experience in the field. Later, I would do an internship treating patients in a clinical setting. These training experiences deepened my understanding of how to apply what I was learning. Theory met up with the realities of what it is like to deal with people who do not always behave according to the examples in textbooks.

My diagnostic practicum took me to a variety of locations that included the State of Illinois Department of Rehabilitation Services (DORS), where I did psychological and neuropsychological diagnostic testing on patients. The tests could bring to light a client's perceptions and thought processes, personality traits (such as introversion versus extroversion), and IQ. They could also help detect whether the person might have suffered brain damage and, if so, where in the brain it might be located. I wrote up reports on the results and went over them with my supervisors to decide on how best to treat any given client.

Every time I assessed a patient, I learned a little more. For example, a person's anxiety can skew test results, and experiencing that to be true, I realized I had to find ways to put people at ease before and during testing them. I also came to see that life circumstances, such as where people were born and how they were parented, have a strong effect on personality and perception. And while I felt I was doing important, beneficial work, I couldn't help but notice the mental health system is strained by a seemingly endless number of people in need.

Occasionally, I would come across patients who were more challenging than others. One of the men I was testing had been diagnosed with paranoid schizophrenia. In his everyday life, with medication, he was functioning well despite his mental illness. I spent a morning and afternoon giving him a battery of psychological tests. By the late afternoon, possibly because of the stress of the testing process, he was starting to decompensate, losing his ability to rely on his usual ways of preventing a psychotic episode involving an eroding sense of reality. In decompensation, the boundary between the unconscious and conscious mind becomes porous, letting unconscious thoughts seep through—thoughts that make no sense to someone who is in an ordinary state of consciousness. My client was saying things like, "John Barleycorn and the still—what do you think about that?"

I didn't want him to leave the testing site in this condition, so I tried to get him back to a more coherent state from which he could maintain a stronger hold on reality. I listened for a long time as he talked. Occasionally, I asked questions in between trying to answer bizarre queries from him. I hoped to get at possible metaphorical meanings of what he was saying and understand his associations to "John Barleycorn." Taking him seriously and showing that I genuinely wanted to listen to him seemed important if I was going to help him come out of his decompensated state. I sensed that if I gave him enough time and support, he could do this.

After working with this patient for a while, I was relieved to see him talking rationally again. I had been prepared to hospitalize him but now felt confident about letting him leave. I was reminded that being in a test situation can be very stressful, sometimes even enough to cause people to lose their normal grip on reality. I learned it's essential not to panic when this happens and to do what you can to restore a patient's ability to function. If you can't make that happen, you have to hospitalize such patients so they can get the support they need to return to their usual state.

Another case taught me about some of the difficulties people from impoverished socioeconomic backgrounds have in accessing adequate mental health care. I was administering psychological and neuropsychological tests to an African American Vietnam veteran in my office at the Illinois School of Professional Psychology. I had treated other men who had served in Vietnam and who were struggling to put their lives together, and this client had many issues that by now were familiar to me: He was an alcoholic, had suffered repeated head trauma, and had been in and out of prison. Even though he was unkempt and lacked personal hygiene, I was fond of him and enjoyed our work together.

On one occasion, we had to take the elevator to my office at the school. When the doors opened, a few professors were already inside. They took one look at us and backed away as far as they could. My patient and I stepped in and continued to talk. I thought it was ironic that with all their training, the professors were not seeing this man as a person but only as a disturbing "other."

Things got steadily worse for my patient as the day went on. He began muttering to himself, and I realized he was decompensating. My efforts weren't restoring his grip on reality, and I decided he needed to be hospitalized to get evaluated and treated. I then called the police to arrange for them to take him to the hospital.

As I waited for them to arrive, I felt some misgivings. I'd heard stories that the police would pick up men like my client and then drop them off in some alley instead of going through the hassle of taking them to the hospital and writing up the necessary paperwork on transporting someone. I wasn't sure the tales were true, but I didn't want to run any risk of this happening to my client. When the officers showed up, I impressed upon them the need to deliver my client to the emergency room and asked them to call me when they had done so. I was relieved when they reported he was safely in the hospital.

After seeing how he had been treated as inferior by professors at the school, I thought about the fact that what I was seeing in him was hidden to people who were only looking at him from the outside. Clearly, some individuals have difficulty seeing the humanity of a person who is disheveled and has body odor. I have noticed this on the streets of Chicago near my downtown office: Many homeless men and women find spots on the sidewalk to sit or stand and ask passersby for spare change. They often become invisible to people who walk by without making eye contact. Having experienced working with clients like the troubled Vietnam vet, I know I perceive homeless people differently than I would have if I had simply remained a businessman.

"Was it something I said?"

I was fortunate that my supervisor for my diagnostic practicum, Eli Schwartz, was a well-known expert in diagnostic testing as well as in neuroscience because he taught me a great deal. From him, I learned more about how to interpret tests for each individual client. He also taught me how the different parts of the brain interact with each other when it comes to feeling and thinking, and how they interact with different parts of the body, including the gastrointestinal system, which reacts to emotional distress. I was getting a scientific perspective on mind-body psychological connections and found it especially helpful when dealing with clients who had many issues going on.

My problem-solving skills learned working in business—and sometimes, through practicing martial arts—helped me develop as a therapist. I had a diagnostic case very early on that required me to give a mental status exam to a man in a wheelchair. Before I could begin the process, he suddenly took off down the hospital hall. I didn't know what to do. Chase after him? Wait for him to come back? Find someone who could assist me in coaxing him to return so I could begin the testing? Why had he sped away after I introduced myself and began explaining what I would be doing? In this case, I intercepted my client in another hallway and loped beside him until we could finish the exam. My textbooks hadn't exactly prepared me for this situation, in which I literally had to learn on the run.

Jim Wyly was my supervisor for my therapy practicum at the Lorene Replogle Counseling Center. He was well trained in both Jungian analysis and clinical psychology. From him, I gained a deeper understanding of how Jungian and psychoanalytic concepts were applied in a therapeutic setting. The two of us discussed how I could help my clients recognize when they were repeating old patterns of behavior that were no longer useful. We looked at various ways to do that, including methods for accessing the unconscious and archetypal energies.

Jim also schooled me in exploring my clients' everyday lives and the transference and countertransference that occurred in each session. In other words, he helped me recognize my unconscious reactions to my clients and theirs to me. In a session, we can act out old stories from our pasts without realizing it. For example, a client might not realize that he was beginning to relate to me as if I were his authoritarian father, causing him to rebel against my simple request for more information. I might see this type of transference in a client who kept getting fired because he was unable to stop rebelling against his boss—and rebelling against any interpretations I might make—as he reenacted childhood patterns of challenging his father's authority. My job was to notice patterns, offer my insights, and ask questions that could help a client recognize what he was doing and why.

I was discovering that the timing of what I did was important, that words matter, and that often, fewer words from me were better than more. Our ability to truly listen often needs improvement. We want to be listened to, but listening to others attentively, staying present in the moment, can be challenging. Sacred listening means listening patiently, tuning in to what is said and not said, rather than hearing what we want to or expect to hear. Too often, we listen impatiently as we try to get just enough information to be able to quickly offer a solution. Sacred listening is a gift that helps us to experience our connection to others and to Spirit.

Part of good listening is patience and observation. When we are talking, it's hard to truly take in what we are observing. Even when we are silent, we can find ourselves half-listening and being oblivious to what the other person is communicating, perhaps in subtle ways.

The skill of sacred listening is especially important for analysts to develop. As therapists, we only listen and talk. When we're just listening, we need to be aware of the quality of our listening. When we're talking, we need to be mindful of what we're doing: Clarifying? Affirming? Repeating their words? Interpreting what they said? Helping them see possible connections between their past and present? Offering information at the right time can help clients see how their unconscious is affecting their behavior. Once they become aware of this influence, they can make a conscious choice to change if they want to.

I had to do a lot of thinking about balancing the roles of listener and talker as a therapist but naturally started thinking about this balance in my personal life and my business life, too. I liked being able to just listen and not be a focal point expected to impart wisdom and manage people. Plus, I was starting to see that good listening helped me support people in finding their own solutions to problems. I was realizing I didn't have to be the authority figure with all the answers telling them what I thought they should do.

"How exactly would you like to hurt me?"

One of the clients I treated during my therapy practicum, a young man I'll call Dan, had suicidal and homicidal tendencies. He had been referred to me by a psychiatrist who was afraid to continue to work with him. Soon, Dan was telling me how much he wanted to hurt me and why.

While the threat of violence in my own office surprised me, I quickly began thinking about what I would do in response to any attack he might make. I asked him to describe all the ways he would like to hurt me, and we discussed this for a while. My reactions in the face of Dan's aggression impressed him and allowed us to explore the ways he fantasized hurting me and why and how this related to other people and experiences in his life. As we talked over a period of months, Dan's aggressive energy dissipated and was replaced by an undercurrent of anxiety, hurt, and sadness that we were able to address.

During my years of training to be a psychologist, I also was reminded that while we may receive verbal threats, on rare occasions, clients can become violent, and we therapists have to find ways to contain physical aggression and protect ourselves. Once, I was seeing a family who had been referred to me by a state agency, and they started to fight among themselves and knocked over a lamp and a table. Another time, a couple physically attacked each other. In both cases, I had to separate those who were fighting and calm everyone down. Then, at a time that I felt was right, we talked about what happened so the people involved would gain insights and understanding that would make them less likely to resort to violence in the future. In both cases, there was no further fighting in my office.

I worked with some therapists who were concerned about handling violence if it were to flare up in a session. They asked my advice. I suggested that if an angry, volatile patient came at them, they might want to scream loudly so as to startle and perhaps frighten the attacker—and simultaneously alert anyone within earshot. (In martial arts, this loud scream is known as *kiai* and is said to put fighters in touch with their power.) I also suggested that they could try to hit the attacker in the nose. I explained that a punch to the nose typically draws a lot of blood—and seeing it often can snap a person out of an aggressive state, just as hearing someone suddenly scream can be disorienting. I also showed my colleagues how to use their knees and elbows to protect themselves. Fortunately, the outbursts the other therapists and I witnessed were rarely serious enough for anyone to get hurt or be frightened off from doing what could sometimes be very challenging and even perhaps dangerous work.

A Dream, a Tree, and a Breakthrough

As I continued to hone my skills in treating clients, often, it seemed my work mostly served to lay the foundation for a potential breakthrough, mediated by the patient's own unconscious.

Sandi had worked with me for more than a year when she had a breakthrough. She had previously been given a diagnosis of paranoid schizophrenia, which I disagreed with. Sandi was shut off from her feelings because she thought she'd be overwhelmed if she let them arise.

She came across as very constricted and robotic. At each session, she would describe her week in some detail but without emotion. I noticed she held her body in a guarded and restrictive posture: hunched over with her arms folded tightly and her legs crossed.

Together, Sandi and I did some dreamwork and made some connections between what occurred in her dreams and what was happening in her life. But as the months went on, I wasn't seeing any changes in her. She had very little affect, and some sessions felt tedious to me—and maybe to her as well. But we persisted, and I continued to listen to her.

Then, one night, Sandi dreamed about a magnificent tree that was growing and unfolding before her. The tree sent its roots deep into the earth and spread its branches toward the sky. Shortly after this session, Sandi said her boyfriend had recently told her he was not going to ask her to marry him. He thought that by waiting and keeping himself available, he might meet someone better.

After Sandi told this seemingly devastating story, she seemed to transform. I have never seen anything quite like it before or since. Her whole posture changed as she became more open, relaxed, and receptive. She said something within her had been freed by hearing what her boyfriend had told her. Like the tree in her dream, she seemed more rooted and expanded. I was glad we had worked together long enough for me to observe this remarkable transformation. It was a privilege to witness, and I was very touched emotionally. Why it happened, I never really knew. The dream and her boyfriend's declaration seemed to have played a significant role. Sandi was more animated for the rest of our sessions together—and in the end, her boyfriend asked her to marry him.

"Please don't put her in a cage"

After my practicums, I served an internship at the Chicago Stress Center on the southwest side of the city. I was in charge of the center for two years and provided some supervision for the practicum students working there. During the time I was working at this clinic, the Chicago Greater Lawn Mental Health Center closed, and we received a sudden influx of severely mentally ill people. I had to up my game to serve these clients, who could be quite challenging to treat, particularly if they weren't taking their medications consistently, which was too often the case. Some of our patients had been ordered by the courts to get help with anger management, so the psychology students and I were often dealing with emotionally volatile individuals. We also had a number of people come for our services from the neighborhood around the center. They had various psychological problems, some severe, some less so.

My supervisor, Bonnie Rudolph, PhD, gave me excellent guidance in working with people with a wide range of psychiatric disorders, which was especially fortunate given our new, challenging caseload. Bonnie was a nationally recognized expert in brief psychotherapy (meaning the number of sessions was limited). Eventually, as an analyst, I would be treating people long term, sometimes over several years. Bonnie's perspective helped me better care for clients I might only see for eight sessions—if that. She taught me to set some goals with them, work on those goals during sessions, and toward the end of the treatment, prepare clients for when the therapy would wind up by summarizing what we did together and what they could do in the future as follow-through. This model seemed very helpful for many patients.

The cases we dealt with at the Chicago Stress Center were often quite heart-wrenching, especially when the client was a child. Sara was ten years old when I first saw her. Her home life had been abusive and chaotic when she was a toddler: Sara had been sexually abused by her father before she was two. As a three-year-old, she would take raw hot dogs out of the refrigerator to feed herself and her mother, who was an addict at the time. When I began seeing her, she was in a healthier home situation but experiencing academic, behavioral, and emotional problems in school.

At our first session, Sara came into my office and slammed the door on her four-year-old sister, bloodying her nose. Then, without taking her coat off, Sara crawled under my coffee table, where she cowered, whimpered, and refused to talk. For the next hour, I sat at my desk, hoping she might come out, and occasionally spoke to her. She didn't respond. I didn't want her to feel ignored, but I respected her need to be underneath the table, where she felt safe. As the hour ended, I told her our time together was up and I would see her next week. Without objection, she crawled out from under the table and left with her mother and sister. It was not an auspicious beginning to our work together given that she hadn't said a word, but I hoped she would begin to open up.

In the next few sessions, she didn't crawl under the table. At least that was progress! To encourage her to communicate with me, I would get down on the floor with her, and we would play with toys I had on hand. I noticed it was very important to Sara to be in complete control when we played. She dictated what we did and how we did it and was resistant to any of my observations or suggestions—particularly in the beginning.

Finally, after getting to know her a little more, I would occasionally start a story: "Once upon a time there was a little girl . . . " Then, she would continue the narrative, and then I would take a turn. Working back and forth like this, I gained insights into her inner world, listening to how the characters in the stories interacted with each other and what they experienced. I understood that these stories were reflecting her own inner processes, so when it was my turn to co-tell the story, I chose scenarios I thought she might want to explore.

We also played "circus," a make-believe game we made up together. Sara assumed the roles of most of the performers. I didn't try to overinterpret each of the roles she played from trapeze artists to animals, but her play seemed to be helping her address some of her psychological issues in an emotionally safe way. She would jump around the room and adopt roles, telling me who she was—or I would guess. Occasionally, I would make comments such as, "That clown seems sad," or "That trapeze artist was really brave," or "That lion was scary," and let her respond if she wanted to. If she did, the conversation would go where it needed to go.

I felt our playtime was diagnostic as well as therapeutic: It helped me understand her better and guide her to be able to manage her inner world. Sara started to make progress in being able to relate to me, becoming more emotionally expressive and less volatile during our work together. She was doing better in school, too.

A couple of months after she first came for treatment, I could see the excitement in her face and hear it in her voice as she told me she had been cast in a class play. But then, on the day of the performance, she came in deeply distressed and began crying. I asked what was wrong, and she tearfully told me that her teacher had put her in a cage in the classroom—an actual cage.

I was shocked. Sara said the teacher had told her she couldn't be in the play because she had misbehaved. This made me angry, and with Sara and her mom's permission, I called the school and arranged to meet with Sara's teacher.

The school was in a rough neighborhood on the South Side of Chicago.

I was prepared to confront someone who was abusing her power but instead found a teacher who was at her wits' end when it came to dealing with Sara.

"What else can I do?" she asked. "I have all the other children to teach, and I don't have time to deal with her when she's unruly."

Clearly, the teacher felt overburdened, so I said, "The next time Sara acts up, call me before you put her in the cage. Will you do that? I'll talk to her on the phone or come over to see you both."

The teacher agreed and seemed relieved to have an ally. Although Sara hadn't been allowed to perform in the play, her mother let me know that Sara's grades and behavior at school were continuing to improve. I don't know if her teacher was given more options for helping her students who had behavioral issues, but at least I know that Sara wasn't subjected to being placed in a cage again.

From Ducking into Alleyways to Walking amid Skyscrapers

While I had many memorable clients during my time at the Chicago Stress Center—families, couples, and individuals—one, whom I'll call Jane, stood out because of her courage in trying to transform her life.

Jane was a widow whose husband had been abusive and whose son had stepped into his father's shoes in some ways, being very controlling of his mother. Agoraphobic and unable to be comfortable outside, Jane suffered so greatly from her phobia that it was keeping her from living her life fully. Her son had to drive her to and from sessions. Despite how stressful it was for her to come in to work with me, she was determined to change and reclaim her freedom.

I did some cognitive behavioral therapy with her, helping her to see how her thoughts were often distorted and negative and feeding her fears. I also taught her how to use systematic desensitization, a technique based on the idea that it's hard to feel anxious when you're relaxed. Jane first learned to calm herself as I guided her to tighten her forehead muscles for several seconds and then relax them, and do the same with her other facial muscles, her neck and shoulder muscles, and so on, all the way down her body. Once Jane had learned and practiced the relaxation technique, I asked her to visualize an anxiety-provoking situation and rate her anxiety level from one to ten, with ten being the maximum. After that, I asked her to use the relaxation technique again and then visualize the fearful situation a second time. As I expected, she rated her anxiety level as lower. This sequence taught her that using the technique would be helpful when she was starting to feel anxious. A memory or scene evoking a ranking of ten might be only a three or four once we had used the relaxation technique.

After practicing in my office for a few sessions, Jane and I then did in vivo desensitization by walking outside. As we walked together, we stopped periodically when she became anxious, and she used the relaxation technique. Soon, she was able to walk around her neighborhood by herself, using systematic desensitization as needed. She told me she ducked into alleyways here and there to calm herself, and she brought an umbrella with her to open up and hold over herself for additional comfort.

Little by little, Jane regained her ability to be outdoors. Although we solved her immediate problem, I knew she had other psychological obstacles that were unconscious in nature.

Jane's big breakthrough came when she had a dream about a man who was holding her down and another man, who was a neighbor, rescuing her. She believed the rescuer represented a masculine aspect of herself that was unafraid to act and take risks. Previously, she had been unable to access this masculine energy within her. She said the man holding her down was her deceased husband. Somehow, this dream served to liberate her from the prison of her agoraphobia.

Afterward, she began making big leaps forward in her progress. By the end of my time working with her, Jane had a job in downtown Chicago amid the skyscrapers. I believe the work I did with her to help her alter her thought processes and better manage her fears was useful.

Perhaps it prepared the way for that which followed. However, just as with my other client, Sandi, it seemed to be something out of my control—a message from her unconscious—that finally liberated Jane.

My internship and my practicums gave me a far more varied perspective on life and helped me "re-member" myself in ways I could never have done in the world of business alone. At the Chicago Stress Center, in particular, I gained experience dealing with people who had a wide variety of psychological issues. I also learned to advocate for people unable to take care of themselves. I became better able to be fully present and in service to another. I honed my listening skills, recognizing how important it was to tune into what clients needed. Often, it was just a listening ear.

Dialoguing with What's Found in the Unconscious

My encounters with clients also stimulated my own unconscious, which in some cases expressed itself in my dreams. In one, I was taking care of a young boy, about three to four years old. He was not mine to take care of and seemed to have been captured by others. My heart went out to him, and I tried to reassure him even as I took responsibility for him in the absence of anyone else to do the job. As I took him away from what seemed like a guarded compound and spent time with him, he had fun and said it was the best day of his life.

From time to time, I imagined I was with this young boy again and creating positive memories for him that he could draw on if he felt hurt or abandoned. This visioning exercise was helping me to slowly reclaim the parts I had split off from myself out of fear or anger.

Many times over the years, I conversed with this inner figure of the boy. In other words, I used dialoguing, a technique for an imaginary conversation, to learn what my unconscious mind could tell me about myself and what I was experiencing. In dialoguing, there are three aspects of consciousness, or three selves, participating in a conversation that is informed by the unconscious: There is the self asking the questions, the self you're talking with that embodies the unconscious part of you with which you're dialoguing, and some part of you that is observing the conversation.

I had learned about dialoguing early in my training and used it to ask questions of inner figures, symbols, and even emotions I was experiencing—such as my frustration about a situation. The answers I received provided me with insights. I used dialoguing to help my clients as well. Over the years, I customized the way I do it, integrating not only ideas from gestalt therapy (in which you talk to an empty chair as if someone or something you wanted to address was sitting there) but also from Jungian active imagination and shamanism.

I explain to my clients that any answers they receive from the energy they are dialoguing with will be coming from their unconscious. Some believe the answers are coming from outside of them—perhaps from an entity such as an angel or power animal. Some believe that a part of them is simply making things up. Whatever the source of the information received, in all my experience of working with the dialoguing technique, what comes forth into the conscious mind is always helpful, even if it can be somewhat painful to encounter. For example, a dialogue with your inner child might reveal that you have lost your sense of playfulness, a revelation that might make you feel hurt or embarrassed because you like to think of yourself as a fun, creative person.

The technique of dialoguing is useful for revealing truths—including hidden obstacles to personal transformation. For example, dialoguing with the boy from my dream helps me to be honest with myself about whether I am paying enough attention to the part of me that wants to play, be nurtured, and be free of responsibilities. This aspect of myself can reveal inner wisdom my conscious mind isn't aware of.

Dialoguing is just one way to tap into insights that are hidden when we are in everyday consciousness. I would come to learn other techniques in the future as I furthered my study of psychology, Jungian analysis, and later, shamanism.

Hanging in There

In 1993, at last, I received my doctoral degree in clinical psychology. Shortly afterward, I began my postdoctoral training necessary to become licensed, and I started to work again at the Replogle Center for Counseling and Well-Being. The director of the center, Tom Schemper, was my supervisor, and he has become a good friend. He offered me many useful suggestions about the practice of psychotherapy. One that stood out was to frame the idea of change as an experiment: He would ask clients to "conduct an experiment" when encouraging them to try out a new behavior or response to a situation. If they didn't like the results, they could choose to go back to the old behavior.

As for the center, initially, it was located in a building next to the First Presbyterian Church of Chicago, but now it's integrated into the original church building, a space that is homey and comfortable. I was glad to be part of a group that does good training for aspiring clinicians, offers services to clients from all walks of life and religions, charges on a sliding-scale fee basis, and has a supportive staff. Everyone there is dedicated to the healing work we do—and I continue to be on staff at the center.

Still, I wanted to get trained to do Jungian analysis, so right after I received my doctorate, I called the Jung Institute, hoping they would accept me now. They told me I needed more experience in the field before they would consider my application, so over the next two years, I continued to see clients to acquire the experience I needed.

I was increasingly able to handle clients' more hostile or frightening emotions without judging or overreacting to them. Once, when I asked my own analyst, Lee Roloff, what he did that was most helpful to his clients, he gave me an answer that surprised me: "I guess I'm pretty good at hanging in there." I was hanging in there and recognizing, too, that incorporating into therapy techniques for accessing the unconscious was sometimes leading to breakthroughs like the ones experienced by Sandi and Jane. Experiences like these increased my interest in working with the unconscious using various techniques.

In 1995, the Jung Institute accepted me for training to become an analyst. The work would take another five years to complete, but it fed my soul. I was especially intrigued by Carl Jung's writings about his relationship with nature because they reminded me of certain childhood experiences I'd had, especially seeing the light around the apple tree. In *Memories, Dreams, Reflections*, he described his earliest memory:

> I am lying in a pram {baby carriage}, in the shadow of a tree. It
> is a fine, warm summer day, the sky blue, and golden sunlight

darting through the green leaves. The hood of the pram has been left up. I have just awakened to the glorious beauty of the day and have a sense of indescribable well-being. I see the sun glittering through the leaves and blossoms of the bushes. Everything is wholly wonderful, colorful, and splendid.[4]

Jung went on to paint a picture of other times he felt a closeness to and sense of wonder in nature—seeing the sunset sky glow a shimmering green after the explosion of Krakatoa and sitting by a lake and being mesmerized by the light on the water and the ripples in the sand made by the waves. At one point, when sitting on a favorite stone, he found himself wondering, "Am I the one sitting on the stone, or am I the one on which *he* is sitting?" The answer seemed unclear, but Jung felt certain that this stone had some secret relationship to him.[5] This experience of his influenced my own belief that even as we observe nature, it is observing us, and that it has a consciousness that is connected to our own and to all consciousness.

Jung is a somewhat controversial figure, but I found I could separate his writings, ideas, and experiences from him as an individual, setting aside his flaws so that I could better understand his teachings. They seemed to me to have value on their own. Later, when I studied shamanism and began working with shamans, I could see they were able to do much good for those they worked with—people who sought healing and received help from shamanic practitioners. At the same time, some of the shamans I encountered had significant personal failings. It seems they had not done their own psychological healing work, yet they still could be powerful healers. The contrast was intriguing. However, this much I knew: From the beginning of my foray into studying to be an analyst, I aspired to help people, and I'd also become a healer willing to put effort into healing himself.

It's been a lifelong process.

As a therapist, I have tried to be aware of my views as to why a particular patient was having certain issues, what I might do to help, and whether I was doing any good. I didn't always know how to answer the questions a patient might raise in a session. At such times, I just listened, listened, listened. Usually, by doing so, I gained some clarity about what to do.

Since my training, I've spent thousands of hours working with clients as a clinical psychologist, Jungian analyst, and shamanic practitioner. I hope I have been of service to my clients in their healing, evolutionary processes. Along the way, I've learned much about myself and human nature. Each individual's story that I have listened to is unique but also contains universal themes. There's no one right way to resolve life issues, and I hope I've helped my clients discover ways to relate to their innate inner wisdom and craft lives that are more pleasing to them and Spirit. A psychologist friend of mine who is now deceased, John Boyle, PhD, described his work as a therapist as being on a journey for a while with each of his clients. Eventually, the two of them would part ways, having recognized that it was time for the client to continue onward alone. John hoped that his client would be better off for having shared the journey with him. I like that image.

Each of us who becomes a therapist brings our own life story, education, and experiences to our work with clients. It's important to think through what strengths we bring to the therapeutic encounter, to hone our favored approaches, and to be true to ourselves. At the same time, we should be aware of our weaknesses and try to enlarge our repertoire. In martial arts, you might have a favorite move or technique and become very skilled at using it, but you need to develop other ones, too. Similarly, a therapist might be terrific at dream analysis but not at dealing with what's going on between therapist and client in the session. Or, the therapist might be adept at offering advice at the right time but not so good at listening and letting clients find their own inner wisdom.

A good therapist is always self-reflecting. A new approach may help clients tap into their inner resources and identify what they can do differently to be more successful at reaching their goals. As a therapist, I tried to remain open to new ideas about how to help my clients.

Cultivating the Life Force

As the end of the millennium approached, I was nearing the age of sixty. By now, psychoanalysis was accepted by millions of people. For decades, martial arts had been part of mainstream American culture and

194

respected for their ability to train the body and mind. Exploring the unconscious was no longer considered "mystical" but a pragmatic way of resolving trauma and psychological problems. I was moderately aware of the counterculture of the 1960s and its influence on the human potential movement and on attitudes toward consciousness, meditation, and consciousness-altering substances. However, my own explorations were more personal. I dabbled in meditation but didn't practice with any seriousness. I had ended my own analysis but was continuing to treat patients. I had not yet used consciousness-altering substances. Now, however, a new chapter of my life was about to begin.

I was more comfortable than ever exploring Jungian ideas, the martial arts traditions, and the very edges of Western thought. After everything I had done to achieve business success, become a Jungian analyst, gain my license as a clinical psychologist, and attain a fairly high level of martial arts skill, it seemed my soul was leading me into the realm of the unknown once again.

Around the time I turned sixty-two, I stopped my active training in karate. I had noticed my reflexes were slower and my body took more time to heal after injuries. Even more concerning, I developed high blood pressure and an aneurysm in the root of my aortic artery. I stopped attending the dojo where I had taught and let Sensei Nanay know what was going on. I turned to practicing qigong instead.

Friends had told me about a woman named Mrs. Chen, who had been a professor in her home country of China and who had worked as Mao Tse-tung's translator. She was teaching qigong in the US now, and I participated in several of her workshops. I even had a chance to go with her to China for a few weeks, where I studied with other qigong practitioners.

Qigong—from the word "qi," meaning the life force, and "gong," meaning cultivation—is said to be a way of moving energy that comes from the earth and the heavens to develop balance and harmony within the body and with nature herself. It also involves working intentionally to do an energy exchange with a part of your body—for example, releasing an energy that may be related to pain and replacing it with a more beneficial one. Qigong can also serve as a spiritual practice that connects you to the creative forces of the universe. All of this reminded me of Jungian psychology as well as shamanism—which I continued to read about.

The internal, or soft, martial arts are based on knowledge of the human energy system, which also underlies such healing arts as acupuncture—and shamanism, as I had learned. Both Zen and Taoist meditations help the practitioner achieve a balance between the energies of body and soul. Through the interplay of the physical and spiritual, masters of the internal arts gain abilities that seem to transcend normal physical limitations.

I began to suspect that my study and practice of qigong was making me more aware of the movement of energy and preparing me for something new in my life's journey. All the healing and re-membering I had done seemed to have brought me to a turning point. At the time, I had no idea just how far beyond Western "reality" I was about to go.

In becoming a therapist, I had to build up my listening skills. That helped me in other areas of my life. I also had to learn how to discover what was hidden in my unconscious so I could have a relationship with it that allowed me to gain information and motivation for change. As you consider your own listening skills—how well you listen to others and how well you listen to yourself, facing your true thoughts and feelings—you might want to answer the following questions.

Questions for the Reader to Ponder

Hanging in there. Sometimes, others don't want us to offer solutions to their problems or rescue them from their dilemmas so much as they want us to hang in there and listen to them—and even support them in finding their own answers. Have you offered anyone the gift of listening and hanging in there? If so, what were the payoffs to doing this? Has someone ever "hung in there" and listened to you when you needed them to do so? What benefit did you achieve?

Re-membering. Do you feel parts of yourself became split off as you grew into adulthood and took on new responsibilities? What parts of yourself did you lose? When, and why? What would it look like to reclaim these lost parts of yourself and reintegrate them into your life?

The wounded healer. If you work as a healer or have ever tried to help another person on a healing journey, did your own unhealed wounds get in the way? If so, how? Did having wounds that were healed or healed to some degree help you in your attempt to assist someone else on their healing journey and, if so, how?

Breakthroughs from your unconscious mind. Have you ever had a dream or an experience within a shamanic journey or visualization exercise that led to a breakthrough in the ways you think, perceive, and act? Why do you think that experience was so powerful for you? If you gained insights from the experience, do you think they came solely from your personal unconscious and inner wisdom? Or do you think something else might have influenced that breakthrough, such as larger, archetypal energies outside of you? Why do you think you were able to achieve this big shift in how you think and perceive? Looking back, did you lay a foundation for it? If you want to experience a breakthrough with the help of your unconscious, have you laid a foundation for that to happen or consciously set your intention to experience it?

CHAPTER TWELVE

The Jaguar's Call

Sitting in my study, I turned yet another page in Alberto Villoldo's best-selling book, *Shaman, Healer, Sage*. Pat had bought it for me as a present, and the mystical stories of being mentored by indigenous shamans in Peru, learning their wisdom and practices, engaged me late into the night. My leather chair was comfortable, yet as I read another tale of spiritual exploration along the Amazon or another dialogue between the author and a wise shaman, I knew I wanted more. I longed to be challenged as the author was—to examine my beliefs and start using shamanic practices guided by someone with great knowledge of shamanic ways. The part of me that had been drawn to exploring the unknown as a child and young man and that had dabbled in shamanic practice here and there was yearning to be expressed more fully. Reading about someone else's adventures wasn't enough for me. How could I have experiences like the author was describing?

When I saw that Alberto Villoldo had a school that trained people in shamanic practices, I contacted it and signed up for a two-year training set to start in August in Joshua Tree, California. I had no idea at the time that I would come to not only study with Alberto but also eventually teach at his school and do shamanic journeys and rituals and ceremonies in the US and Peru with him and other shamans. What's more, I would also develop a friendship with this like-minded spiritual seeker. I would then go on to spend time with and work with shamans on several continents, in countries such as Australia, Ethiopia, Mongolia, Peru, Canada, and the United States. Those journeys I took at home while following the instructions in shamanism books had nourished my mythopoetic self to some degree, but now I wanted more.

Reading *Shaman, Healer, Sage,* I felt the same kind of affinity to Alberto as I had to other shamanic authors: Lynn Andrews, Hyemeyohsts Storm, Michael Harner, and Carlos Castaneda. For one thing, I could relate to their desire to find answers and a sense of connection to something larger than themselves by spending time in untamed nature. The woods near my home when I was very young awoke that yearning in me. The jungles along the Amazon River and the mountains of Peru seemed to call to Alberto. There, he met and worked with shamans who mentored him and helped him become a shaman himself.

By embarking on this new adventure of becoming a shamanic practitioner, I hoped to gain a deeper sense of purpose and fulfillment. I wasn't altogether sure how this new pursuit would change me but felt a strong sense of possibility and a desire for further transformation. And I was willing to become a student once again.

What exactly is a shaman? Shamans are men or women who work with energy and nature for healing. During a shamanic journey, shamans enter an altered state of consciousness that allows them to perceive what is otherwise invisible. Their consciousness travels to supernatural, transpersonal realms that people who aren't shamans can learn to access as well. In their journeys to the past and the future, shamans gain energies and information that can help them and others live better lives in the present and set a new course for the future. They do this for the sake of achieving healing for themselves or someone else—even, perhaps, their community.

Shamans believe the places they visit on shamanic journeys are real. I believe that, too, based on the experiences I have had working with shamans around the world. I say to people who have chosen to walk the shamanic path, "Check in with yourself about what you are experiencing. It's up to you to decide what to make of it." Shamanism is based on learning to value your own perceptions, recognizing that there's more than one way to interpret an experience. Ultimately, we are all left with the task of weaving into our everyday lives the energies and information we may have gained as a result of doing shamanic work.

Perhaps the transpersonal realms shamans interact with are places that exist in other dimensions: places we can be transported to when we leave behind ordinary awareness and our identification with our bodies. Whatever the nature of these realms, shamans mediate between them and the world of their communities, all the while maintaining personal consciousness and will.

In the indigenous traditions of the Q'ero people in Peru, shamans journey to transpersonal realms called the lower world and upper world on behalf of others or themselves. The lower world corresponds with the unconscious and the past while the upper world corresponds with the future, celestial beings, and the possibilities we do not see when in ordinary states of awareness. Shamans can also work in the middle world, which is the realm of our everyday lives, consciously incorporating their findings from the lower and upper worlds. We can do the same.

Shamans work with the past to change the way people's previous experiences affect them today and with the future to connect them to a better outcome than the one they were headed toward. Like hunters, shamans track for a better future that can be brought back into the present energetically. Shamans also help people to dream into being a new future and new possibilities so that they do not have to continue to live as they have or stay on the same trajectory. All of this work is done to affect minute-to-minute decisions in the present so that ultimately, people can live in ways that are more pleasing to themselves and Spirit.

As an analyst, I saw similarities between what I was doing with my clients in my practice and what shamans do. I had been helping my clients identify past influences on their mind-sets and behaviors and guiding them to set goals for what they wanted to experience in the future as a result of undergoing treatment. It's often easier to focus on current problems and fixing them rather than try to come up with long-term solutions and imagine what can be experienced in the future beyond just relief from the pain being suffered in the present. For many, exploring new ways of being or living often takes a backseat to more immediate concerns.

I find it's common for people to lack clarity about what they want to experience in the future—at least during some periods of their lives. I was the type who would walk to the highway, stick out my thumb, and be open to where my adventure took me—until I got stuck in a story that felt confining, one that was not entirely of my own making. As an analyst, I recognized that for many of my clients, not knowing where they were going was stressful and even paralyzing. In talking about what the future holds, they often revealed to me fears about bad experiences they might have while they didn't have a sense of what kinds of experiences they would find enjoyable or helpful. Shamanic work, I find, can stimulate people's ability to begin envisioning new ways of being and operating in the world.

Some might say that having studied, taught, and practiced shamanism, I can now be called a shaman myself. I prefer to think of myself as a shamanic practitioner. I have found that while some shamans identify as such, many simply do the healing work that shamans do and don't try to label themselves or their work. They leave that to others to do.

It has also been my experience that the best shamans are always open to learning and further developing their skills for healing. They don't let their egos get in their way, perhaps because the work is so humbling and moving.

At the beginning of my training in shamanism, I wasn't sure where it would take me, but I was ready to start the process. Also, the shamanic work I'd done with Pat when she had breast cancer, which may have helped enhance her healing, increased my eagerness to learn more about shamanic techniques for physical healing. The Western medical community is aware of the mind-body connection—the ability of our thoughts and feelings to affect our physical experiences and our health. Carl Jung believed that all physical ailments have a psychosomatic component, meaning that our minds affect our bodies. To me, shamanism was another way of acknowledging and working with the mind-body connection for healing that can be both physical and psychological.

However, my main desire in entering a shamanic training program was to satisfy my longing for a richer experience of my life and a closer relationship to God, or Spirit. I wanted to not just believe that we are all interconnected, or accept that idea intellectually, but actually experience it. I wanted to feel that I was a part of a web of energy that encompassed all life and all of creation. Reading about other shamans' experiences and being an armchair shaman was not enough for me anymore.

I've come to believe that I always had a shamanic destiny, one that revealed itself to me when I saw that glowing light around a tree those many years ago as a child in a farmer's field. I believe this light was the light energy field that *Shaman, Healer, Sage* was describing as surrounding people and animals, too—and it is what mystics call an aura.

Shamans can perceive people's energy fields and work with them— which I wanted to be able to do. I had read that every individual's field is woven into the energy grid shared by all creation, not only on earth but also in the cosmos. Shamans believe that the separation between us and Mother Earth, her trees, her creatures—and the sun, moon, and stars— is an illusion created by the conscious mind. Had I been experiencing this illusion ever since that day as a child when I was aware of the unity of all things? I had craved that feeling of connectedness ever since that day, but only now, many years later, was I reconnecting with that desire and actively pursuing a path that might get me back to that blissful state of consciousness.

Nature's Messages

Soon after reading *Shaman, Healer, Sage*, I vacationed with Pat on the island of Anguilla. During our time there, I felt more connected to the elements in nature than ever before. It could be that reading the book triggered something hidden in my unconscious. Maybe my martial arts training and practice and my qigong work, along with my exploration of Jungian ideas and techniques, had primed me for something exceptional to happen. Maybe a combination of these experiences or something else entirely—fate, destiny, or perhaps a soul contract I had signed before being born into this life—was responsible for what transpired while I walked the beaches of Anguilla. I didn't quite have that mystical vision I'd had as a child before the tree in the farmer's field, but my senses were heightened, and a powerful sense of vitality coursed through me. The warmth of the sun was comforting me in a new way. Every step I took seemed to be in harmony with the sands I was walking on and the wind that was brushing against my face. The sparkling blue waters were teeming with energy and life. I felt a sense of unity with the ocean and its abundance.

I had been to tropical islands in the past but had never experienced anything like this. It was as if I were having a lucid dream, real and intense yet infused with a mysterious quality that seemed to awaken something within me. I felt filled, even overflowing, with the desire to express the richness and beauty that Source was sharing with me and to reciprocate in some way.

My spirit was calling to me to move in a new direction, and I thought about where I was in my life. I was nearing the age when most men retire. My health challenges had awoken me to the passage of the years and the finite nature of my life. It became crystal clear to me in Anguilla that now was my time for spiritual exploration that I hoped would lead me to have a more direct connection to the force known as God or Spirit. My relationship with this force had been neglected for too long even though I had been religious in a conventional way, being involved in a church community and attending services.

Back home, I had already begun winding down Martin Oil because I and my Martin family partners felt it was time to liquidate our operating businesses and make safer and more diversified investments. I had started selling off the gas stations, terminals, oil and gas wells, and the rest of the companies and assets we owned together. The Martin family knew I was grateful for the opportunity they had given me more than three decades before. And I was proud of what I had been able to build for the good of everyone involved. But now, I was letting it go, starting the process of shedding the past through strategic divestment—a process that would be enhanced by my engaging in shamanic work.

Learning about Sacred Technologies

In August of 2001, I attended the first of four eight-day workshops in Joshua Tree in Southern California. I'd signed up for them as part of a shamanic training program that, as I mentioned, was spread out over two years. I assumed I would be joining an intimate group of eight to ten other students. When I arrived, I realized there were many more participants than I expected—about 120 people. Apparently, I was not the only one who wanted to take the experience of reading *Shaman, Healer, Sage* to the next level.

Frankly, I was a little disappointed. I'd pictured myself being one of the rare and special students allowed to study with a master shaman and receive personalized attention, not being a part of a big crowd in a room. I had no choice but to leave behind my fantasy of what this experience would be, so I found a place toward the front where I could sit and hear Alberto, my good ear turned toward him.

The air outside in the desert was oppressively hot, and at times, the room was stuffy, but Alberto's teaching was engaging. First, he let us know the origin of the knowledge and wisdom he was offering us. When the Spanish Conquistadors came to the Andes, the land of the Q'ero people, to conquer and convert them to Catholicism, many of the Q'ero shamans fled high into the mountains to safeguard their cultural traditions. For nearly 500 years, they remained isolated until recently, when their elders said it was time to come down from the mountains, fulfilling an ancient prophecy about returning when the world had become dangerously out of balance. These keepers of the old wisdom wanted to offer their shamanic training to others to help bring the world back into harmony again. They begin sharing their knowledge with the people of North America, in an exchange that Alberto called "a meeting of the condor and the eagle."[6]

However, Alberto and the other instructors he works with also weave into their school's trainings knowledge and practices from other shamanic traditions, various North American medicine teachings, and Asian and European mysticism. For example, during the two-year training, students are taught about how chakras, the energy vortexes that Eastern traditions recognize, are a part of the light energy field (LEF) or light body surrounding a person's physical body: They can be found along the acupuncture meridians identified by traditional Chinese medicine. Clearing chakras energetically so they spin easily and in the correct direction is just one technique for affecting the LEF. In *Shaman, Healer, Sage*, Alberto described one of his mentors, Don Antonio, working with chakras.[7]

Alberto explained that shamans use spiritual or sacred technologies to help them change their perceptions and to work with various types of energy. These technologies not only include specialized knowledge but also rituals, chanting, and such tools as rattles, drums, musical instruments, objects from nature, special clothing, sacred plants (ayahuasca, San Pedro, peyote, and so on), and mesas. A mesa ("table," in Spanish) is a sacred bundle of objects that are wrapped in a special cloth and holds healing energies. A mesa serves as a traveling altar used by shamans in ceremonial and healing rituals. During the training, we students would begin to assemble our own mesas. We had been told to bring to the workshop three stones to work with. These would represent the teachings of the medicine wheel direction we would be learning about and interacting with energetically (the South). We were to wrap them in a cloth to protect them from taking on random energies that they might encounter.

In all honesty, I didn't put much thought into the cloth or stones I chose, but over the course of my training, my choices for what to place in my mesa became more intentional as I came to better understand the importance of these traveling altars in shamanic work. I would also eventually experience for myself that stones can contain a specific energy, I would even teach others how to work with rocks energetically. Years later, I would guide students in a workshop to dialogue with stones, as described earlier. When I asked one of the students to share what the stone had told him, he reported, "It said, 'Why are you asking me all these questions? I'm only a fucking stone!'" I said, "Well, that's an honest reaction!" Later, I helped my students to see that a rock could be more than just a rock and actually be an embodiment of something, but this man's experience was a good reminder that these ideas are foreign to many people and they may resist them. I've found that if you give yourself plenty of time to connect with your inner wisdom and don't entertain the thought, "This isn't going to work," insights almost always show up.

Some of the ideas presented during that first eight-day training at Joshua Tree were familiar to me from my reading over the years and compatible with many aspects of Jungian psychology. I recognized that the course was drawn from a blend of traditions and spotted several different influences, including ones from Alberto's own life journey and his interests in psychology and medical anthropology. A cross-cultural approach is controversial in some circles because some feel it involves cultural appropriation or stealing. Others recognize that spiritual traditions evolve over time and influence each other. I believe it can be helpful to learn about the teachings and techniques from healers around the world. Most of the indigenous shamans I have worked with have encouraged me to share their teachings; none have discouraged me.

In my shamanic work with clients, I have used a variety of approaches and applied the theories of several different pioneers in psychology. What is effective for one person might not be as effective for another, so I appreciate Alberto's creative combination of various techniques, ideas, and sacred technologies. In my psychoanalytic work, I have primarily used traditional Jungian techniques, but my understanding of the unconscious and working with it has been deepened by my shamanic training.

Most of the attendees in that initial workshop were Westerners. Over the years, I've come to learn that in many places, shamanic traditions are dying off as young people who might otherwise study with medicine men and women move to the cities to look for jobs. Many Western shamans I have met feel an obligation to preserve ancient teachings and help support indigenous healers they have met and trained with by honoring their request to bring the healers' spiritual wisdom to the world in larger ways.

The teachings were informative, but now, we were told, we would be doing some actual shamanic work. Already? I wondered. We were less than two days into our training and hardly seemed prepared. Nevertheless, as instructed, I paired off and had my partner lie on his back with his head cradled in my hands. We would begin doing what was called an illumination, a technique for clearing blocked or stagnant energy in an individual's energy field or what Alberto called the "light" or "luminous" energy body. As directed, I alternated between touching and releasing acupuncture points on my partner's skull. I felt him begin to relax as I focused on the work of tuning into his energy field.

Suddenly, I was distracted by moaning and guttural sounds from others who, like him, were lying on the floor, supported by strangers. The cacophony grew. I felt uncomfortable with the lack of restraint. Was this a case of people wanting change so much they were loosening their inhibitions for no good reason? I worried that all of this unleashing of old energies might be dangerous in some way. My analytical, engineering-trained mind wanted to know how this work was healing for people. What were the energetic mechanisms involved?

Despite my unease, I decided to trust in the process and Alberto. I continued the clearing and then exchanged places with my partner. I did feel a release of stress and later, wondered if this was indeed a case of removing some sort of blockage that was making my energy field unbalanced and incoherent—something that could affect my emotions, my thoughts, and even my health, according to the teachings. I sensed there was real potential for transformation when using the techniques we were learning. And by the end of the week, it appeared that no harm had been done and good had come out of it for many of the participants.

In doing the work over the eight-day training, we learned about journeying, clearing our own energy field as well as someone else's (the illumination technique was just one tool for doing that), and working with sacred space, which I knew was the demarcation of ritual space that serves as a container for the energies being worked with. I learned Alberto's ideas about what the forces were that we call in to help us in our work. His ideas were somewhat familiar to me, but to actually perform the rituals with others and try out the practices whetted my appetite for more.

This initial training session was focused on the first direction in the medicine wheel, the South, which Alberto explained is associated with the serpent. The South challenges us to shed our past the way a snake sheds its skin so that our past experiences live differently within us. The next work is that of the West, associated with the jaguar and moving beyond the fear of death, discarding the energetic influences of the past, including our genetic and karmic legacy. We would be facing our fears, engaging the Death Principle (also called the energy of endings), and learning to work with death as an ally instead of an adversary.

Some might consider the work of the West to be the hardest work of the medicine wheel: releasing the ego's need to pretend that death will never come to us. It's our fear of death that keeps us stuck in old patterns, deluding ourselves that if we keep on doing what we always have, everything can stay the same and we can avoid the discomfort of facing change. In fact, *everything* changes—it's the nature of life. Until we let go of our need for control, we can't work effectively with the natural cycles of life. We tend to deny them or fight them, wasting energy and getting stuck in our fear. However, through using rituals of self-protection and calling on spirit allies to assist us, we can transcend the fear and complete the work of the West.

I was starting to realize that one of the reasons I was interested in shamanism was that I wanted to learn how to die a good death: with equanimity, satisfaction with how I had lived, and as much consciousness as I could bring to the moment. I couldn't help thinking about my own mortality as I saw people I knew get sick and die. My stint in the hospital during that difficult Gerrity negotiation had shattered the illusion that I would be young and healthy forever. I stopped running from the thought of my life ending and began contemplating it more. Dying in a way that was peaceful and not dominated by fear or regret appealed to me—even though, of course, I hoped that my own death would be far off in the future.

The work of the West, in turn, takes us to the North and the work of the hummingbird—replacing our old stories with new ones that are heroic rather than confining. Our new stories relativize the challenges of our lives as we recognize our connection to those who came before us and those who will come after us—our spiritual sisters and brothers. To acknowledge our infinite nature as an aspect of a greater consciousness that is eternal is the work of the North. The medicine wheel ends in the East, the realm of new beginnings, where we do the work of opening up to new possibilities and achieve the clarity of the condor, whose vision encompasses the small details as well as the big picture. In the East, we integrate the old and the new, the past and the present as well as the future, and our mystical experiences with our everyday lives. Thus, the work of the medicine wheel is similar to the Jungian concept of individuation.

How it all would fit together—my training, my work as an analyst and my work selling off the Martin Oil holdings, my relationships with my family and with myself and Spirit—would begin to reveal itself as I worked the medicine wheel with Alberto and the other teachers of the Healing the Light Body School.

I imagine that the attendees experienced and took away different things from those eight days at Joshua Tree—a vacation, a social experience, a thirst for more clarity about their life's purpose, guidance on how to walk the shamanic path, pleasant memories of feeling part of a group of people searching for a better connection to Spirit and themselves, or perhaps some combination of all of these things. For my part, I learned a great deal. It also felt good to get a break from my routine and spend some time in nature (even if it was the hottest time of the year in Joshua Tree!). Those eight days confirmed that I was on the right path for me. I wondered what next awaited me as I moved forward in my quest to become a shaman.

Being Pulled Up the Mountain

In June 2002, while I was still in the Four Winds Society training program, Alberto Villoldo invited me and some other students to travel to Peru to study with both mountain and jungle shamans and visit ancient, sacred sites. I was very eager to take advantage of this rare opportunity but first, I had to confront my fears both real and imagined. I had very recently been diagnosed with high blood pressure, and tests had revealed an aneurysm in the aortic root of my heart, which, as I said, had caused me to give up karate and instead take up qigong. Cusco itself was over 11,000 feet above sea level. The peak of the mountain we would be ascending, Pachatusan, was at 15,886 feet. I had never been so far above sea level and knew such heights could bring on altitude sickness. Further complicating matters, I had plantar fasciitis, making walking painful. The plan was to go from Lima to Cusco and slowly acclimate to the altitude: Our group would climb a smaller mountain first before ascending Pachatusan, one of the twelve sacred mountains of the Inca. I might be in some pain walking, but maybe it wouldn't be too bad. After pondering the risks, I decided to make the trip anyway and hope for the best.

My plane landed in Lima late at night, and I was somewhat disoriented by being in a strange country where I didn't speak the language. Then I realized my luggage hadn't made the flight with me—not an auspicious beginning. I found my way to the other students who were in my group, and we stayed overnight in a hotel, planning to return to the airport very early the next morning. The next day, I was relieved to learn that my bags had shown up.

After arriving in Cusco, our group was told that drinking coca tea and chewing on coca leaves as the locals did would help us acclimate to the altitude. To the people of Peru, I learned, these stimulants were considered quite safe—on par with drinking coffee or eating a candy bar for an energy boost.

We also learned more details about the practice hike we would do in nearby Pisac, where we would ascend a mountain in preparation for the more challenging Pachatusan climb. Upon reaching the summit, we would explore the Temple of the Sun there and perform an *ayni despacho* (EYE-nee des-PAH-choh), a traditional ceremony of gratitude to Pachamama, or Mother Earth, that would bring us into balance and harmony with her. In Quechua, *ayni* means mutuality or reciprocity, that is, being in right relationship with the universe and the natural world as well as with all aspects of our being.

Don Manuel and Don Francisco, two Q'ero shamans, were introduced to us. Along with Alberto, they would lead us in making the despacho by selecting and placing symbolic items within a piece of paper that would be folded up at the ceremony's conclusion and buried or burned so that the prayers that accompanied the placing of objects could be released to Spirit. Despachos often involve objects such as paper money, grain, sugar, shells—and red and white wine are used during the ceremony to represent respectively the feminine energy of Mother Earth and the masculine energy of Father Sky. The traditional stack of three coca leaves that we would blow our prayers into would be used, too, just as in ancient times.

Thanks in part to the mild coca stimulants I took, I was able to complete the climb and participate in the ayni despacho ceremony. As I stood under the blue skies, hearing the prayers spoken aloud as we spontaneously stepped forward to offer them, I felt connected to the land, its people, and the tradition of shamanism here, as well as to the others in my group. But at the end of the day, having descended to the base of the hill, I was winded and tired. Walking had been difficult, and my feet ached, making me acutely aware of my frailties and vulnerabilities.

That night in my bed, I tossed and turned for several sleepless hours, wondering if I should attempt the climb up Pachatusan the next day. Would I be endangering my life? Would going through with my plan be brave—or foolish? My rumination finally gave way to a determination to do the climb. Peace settled over me after that, and I drifted off to sleep.

The actual journey to the mountain the next day turned out to be a learning experience in itself. To reach the spot where we were going to start the climb, we had to backtrack from roads damaged by landslides. Then we encountered police roadblocks set up to keep us out of areas where a group of Shining Path guerrilla fighters was active. It was clear that this was nothing out of the ordinary for our guides. Alberto seemed unruffled by the unexpected turn of events and the hours seemingly wasted.

This was the beginning of my experience with shaman time. Unlike in the United States, where the clock rules our lives, things in Peru had their own rhythm and happened when they happened. I was having to acclimate to that as well as to the altitude.

With all the delays, we didn't start our ascent until later than we had hoped. I mentally prepared myself for what promised to be a long, painful, arduous climb for me.

But first, at the base of Pachatusan, Alberto asked us to find a stone into which we were to place our possible genetic or preprogrammed deaths. I understood by now what he meant about placing something into a seemingly inanimate object: We would use our intention to blow the energies of these deaths into our individual rocks. Then we would rid ourselves of this energy when we reached a lagoon the next day where we would cast the stone into the water.

I found a stone and, despite my foot pain distracting me, did my best to focus on transferring to the stone death from cardiac disease. This was the death my father suffered and that might have been passed down to me through our family's genetic legacy.

With the stone placed in my pocket, I began making my way up the mountain with the others, led by Alberto, the Q'ero shamans, and another shaman, Don Martin. Don Martin was the son-in-law of a man known as a famous "sorcerer": Don Benito, who was called the "Falcon of Cusco." Don Martin, who had a different lineage from the Q'ero shamans I was meeting, was said to be the "keeper of the mountain" (Pachatusan) and have a close affinity with its condors. I witnessed him calling them—and their circling in the sky above him in response. I knew animals communicate in ways we humans can observe but have difficulty understanding—such as when a flock of birds all turn in the same direction simultaneously. However, this was my first experience with a person who could communicate so directly with nature, tapping into that hidden field of energy that the animals share with the land, the water, and the sky. It was extraordinary to watch.

We reached our camp by nightfall, and I felt that somehow, the energy of the mountain had been pulling me up the trail, too. A shaman named Don Pasqual offered to do individual healing work for those who were interested. I and a few others in our group took him up on the offer.

Together in my tent, he and I opened sacred space and began our ceremony. In the midst of it, Don Pasqual accidentally knocked over the bottle of red wine he was using, spilling it all over the tent floor. Instead of getting excited or upset, or seeing this as a foreboding omen, he just laughed and said, "It is food for the Pachamama." We cleaned up the spilled wine and continued with the ceremony, finishing it by closing sacred space. For all the mystical qualities Westerners project onto shamans, almost all the ones I've met—Don Pasqual included— are very grounded and not at all impressed with themselves. They are able to laugh at their mistakes and themselves. Even so, they take their work seriously.

The next day I arose at sunrise and did qigong, bridging heaven and earth, relaxing and harmonizing with their energies, and being a conduit for them. It was my birthday, and I thought, "What a good way to start my sixty-second year."

"Release it to Pachamama"

Later that morning, our group ascended higher and higher up Pachatusan until after about three hours, we arrived at the sacred lagoon. In a ceremony, we threw our stones into the water and, with them, the toxic genetic legacies we wanted to discard. As I threw in my stone, I felt a sense of relief. Maybe further constriction of my blood's flow through my veins and arteries, wearing down my heart until it no longer could support my body, did not have to be my destiny. I stood looking at the sparkling aqua lagoon. My fear of dying, which had plagued me before my trip and had intensified that stressful night before our climb, seemed to dissipate. I felt strong, alive, and woven into the energy of all that surrounded me—part of the land, the sky, and the lagoon that had received our stones and the energy they held. We remained in silence for a time, reflecting on what we had given to the earth, to Pachamama, so that we might experience healing.

After the ceremony, we began the steep descent down the mountain, a trek as hard on my knees and feet as the uphill climb had been. The strenuousness of the descent made it hard to keep our footing, but together, we all made it down with no mishaps. Afterward, we did a fire ceremony to close out the day, gathering together around a fire we started in a fire pit. We committed to the flames sticks into which we had blown energies we wanted to discard and other sticks into which we had blown energies we wished to gain. As I listened to the crackling of kindling and logs transforming to ash and smoke, I thought about how many humans over millennia have shared such an experience, gathering around a fire together. I felt a sense of communion with Pachamama and others who had performed similar ceremonies in the past, and I reflected on what I had just experienced.

I had conquered my fears about my physical ailments, pushing myself to take the risk of the climb yet feeling supported as I connected to Spirit through the spirit that was Pachatusan. I had felt the mountain communicating to me that I could always draw on its power if I needed help, if I felt weak or fearful. I had experienced being part of something much larger than myself, larger than my personal thoughts and emotions—a force that was loving and supportive. Of course, fears return to me sometimes, but ever since that day when I first climbed Pachatusan, the mountain has been a powerful protector and source of energy for me. Even now, thinking about it, seeing it in my mind's eye, I can feel its strength within me. Pachatusan is wherever I am.

"Is that a pig peeing on my foot?"

The day after our experience on Pachatusan, our group visited a more famous site: the ancient ruins of the sacred city of Machu Picchu on the steep slopes of a mountain northwest of Cusco. I engaged in personal and group rituals and explored the terraces built hundreds of years ago by the Inca who lived there. Photographs do not do justice to the experience of actually being in the spot where sacred ceremonies were held for many centuries. With bright green grass interspersed with stone ruins and terraces along the slopes of a steep mountain, Machu Picchu has a quiet beauty that creates a sense of the numinous.

Even so, some humorous experiences awaited me—experiences that would remind me not to take myself too seriously.

After visiting Machu Picchu, we flew to Puerto Maldonado, where we used motorized canoes to travel up a tributary of the Amazon, the Mother of God River, to a lodge where we would spend the next few nights. There, we would work with jungle shamans whose traditions differed from those of the mountain shamans. Yet, I found they taught the same lesson the mountain shamans had: that we all have the ability to communicate with nature and work with her to achieve healing.

The jungle shamans said that ayahuasca, which they considered a sacred plant, taught them about healing and nonordinary states of reality. The plant's potential for inducing higher states of consciousness had not been discovered by relying on trial and error, they explained, but through respectfully communicating with the plants themselves.

Was I actually in danger using a substance illegal in the States? I had never used a mind-altering substance other than caffeine, nicotine, alcohol, or the mild stimulant of chewing coca leaves. Yet, there on the Mother of God River, I set aside any reservations so that I could have this experience said to help a person become initiated into spiritual awareness. I decided I would use ayahuasca to facilitate my ability to communicate with transpersonal realms, with nature, and with all that lay hidden from my conscious mind.

My readings had taught me that shamans around the world work with sacred plants to open a portal to the unseen, connect with Spirit, and actually experience their oneness with what we Westerners call God. Their traditions are thousands of years old, passed down from generation to generation. I felt the risk to my safety was small.

Scientists know that ingesting these plants, called entheogens (from Greek roots meaning "the divine within"), in carefully prepared forms stimulates the brain (specifically, the pineal gland). The result is unusual experiences of consciousness. LSD, derived from a fungus found on grains such as rye, was studied in the 1950s to determine its benefits for treating mental illness but in time became very controversial and was outlawed. Research stopped, but recently, it has begun again. Psychedelics (from Greek words meaning "mind expansion") derived from plants and even, in the case of LSD, fungus, are being looked at as potential treatments for anxiety, depression, and tobacco and alcohol dependence.[8] However, people who take certain psychiatric medications could experience adverse effects when using ayahuasca.[9]

Entheogens seem to cue the brain to let go of the ego's fear and need to be in control while sometimes creating a euphoric sense of oneness with creation, which can relativize someone's problems and result in their everyday perspective transforming dramatically. Even though every experience is different, and not always pleasant, I had heard that using ayahuasca could be life-changing—and that would turn out to be true for me.

A molecule found in the ayahuasca plant's vine, DMT (short for dimethyltryptamine), can be extracted and rendered bioavailable, meaning it enters the bloodstream and the brain of an individual drinking the ayahuasca brew. This allows the user to experience what we in the West would call hallucinations but what shamans say is a sacred journey to transpersonal realms that they will guide to ensure the safety of the one who is journeying. DMT has been called the "spirit molecule" by author Rick Strassman because it is related to mystical and near-death experiences.[10]

Our "ayahuascaro," that is, the shaman trained to prepare the brew and guide our journey, was Don Ignacio. We were told he would perform his task with great reverence for the sacred plant.

The Q'ero say that some ayahuascaros are silk while others are steel, meaning they concoct a brew that can be so strong it induces retching in almost all the ceremony participants. I hoped Don Ignacio was "silk" but was prepared for "steel," having heard that as uncomfortable as the retching can be, it energetically releases energies that no longer serve you.

It was after nightfall when we arrived at the destination for our ceremony. The jungle canopy blocked all ambient light, forcing us to rely on flashlights to see our way up the trail to a large hut constructed of plant materials with bare earth as its floor. Several candles provided illumination as we followed the instructions to lie down on the floor and prepare for our journey. Quietly, we began to meditate, knowing that soon the ayahuasca would be passed.

Suddenly, someone alongside me jumped up screaming. I was snapped out of my reverie. As someone else yelped, I felt sharp, burning sensations all over my body. I scrambled to my feet along with the others, and we ferociously brushed away the fire ants whose mound nest we had lain on.

This was not exactly the deep spiritual experience I had been expecting.

We moved to another hut, checked the condition of the floor this time, and started over. As I sat in a meditative posture, I closed my eyes to relax once again. Don Ignacio began singing his *icaros*, or songs that communicate with the sacred ayahuasca plant and spirits of the natural world. The Quechua words, we'd been told, offered thanks and asked for protection for all who were making the journey that night.

The time came for us to drink, and Don Ignacio passed to each of us a cup of the brew. I found the ayahuasca warm and bitter. At first, nothing happened. Don Ignacio started to rattle along with singing his icaros. Then, the sounds and smells of retching filled the hut. I realized that despite his reputation as a "silk" ayahuascaro, I might end up vomiting like others were—but so far, I felt little nausea.

With my eyes still shut, I began to see intricate patterns of color shifting and realized suddenly that this was the first sign that the plant was taking effect. Then, in an instant, fearsome, otherworldly creatures and apparitions appeared—some animal-like and some demon-like. I remembered having read once that when encountering such manifestations, it's better to face them than to cower or flee. So, with some trepidation, I moved toward them. Their fearsome aspects changed, and very soon, the apparitions disappeared.

At that point, I suddenly had the sense of being worked on by extraterrestrials in a spaceship. I knew my body and nervous system were being adjusted in some way, although I couldn't tell exactly what was being done. I wasn't afraid—just curious. I was starting to realize that on this journey, dramatic changes could happen instantly, so I might as well get used to it.

I continued to see geometric shapes shifting in front of me in a kaleidoscopic set of images when suddenly I heard a tremendous noise, like an explosion. I had the sense I had broken through a membrane in the universe. Then, I found myself in an infinite blackness punctuated by globes of light all connected to one another. I knew I was in the presence of the living, aware matrix that contains and connects all things that ever were, are, or will be. I had read and been taught that this awareness resides not only in humans but also in rocks, plants, animals, molecules, stars—in the entire cosmos—but now I no longer merely believed that this was true. I felt and knew it to be real.

As the journey continued, I met a different version of myself, another Carl, who seemed to have a much broader perspective than I possessed and a very cosmic, wry sense of humor. I wondered what secrets of the universe he might share with me. I asked this Wise Inner Carl why we have to go through all the storms and stresses of our lives. He just gave me a small smile in response, suggesting it was something I needed to figure out for myself.

Areas of extreme darkness and extreme light appeared before my eyes, and I somehow knew I had been called to be among those who defended the light. But I also knew that I needed to journey into the dark places with my awareness and return safely with new insights gained. Later, as I thought about it, I would be reminded that in analysis, I had gone to these "dark places" when I recalled painful memories that I'd pushed out of my consciousness so I would not have to bear looking at them again. But those explorations in an analyst's office had been nothing like this.

The ceremony continued for hours, and to my surprise, my altered state of consciousness didn't completely shut me off from ordinary reality. I could move in or out of the journey state or change it simply by altering my position—standing up or sitting back down again or opening or closing my eyes. I sensed that within me was an observer watching everything unfold before me.

At one point during the night, I went outside of the hut to the edge of the rainforest to urinate. As I stood emptying my bladder, I felt a presence, looked down to my side, and saw that a wild pig was waddling up beside me. It took a spot right next to me, so close I could have pet it. It seemed that the ayahuasca had removed the ordinary barriers between me and other beings, including this creature that would normally be afraid of me but instead joined me. Then the pig urinated on my shoe before trotting away. One of the most profound spiritual experiences of my life interrupted by having a pig relieve itself on me! The mystical world had integrated with the world of pigs and pee.

My ayahuasca journey did not end at that moment but shortly later as I felt myself return to ordinary time and space. The plant had provided me with a powerful experience of awareness—of myself, the universe, and my interconnection with all creatures. It was just what I had been seeking, and I felt deeply grateful to Pachamama who had helped me feel my connection through her sacred plant.

The next day, I spent time alone in the jungle by the Amazon, listening to the buzzing of insects and the calling of the rainforest creatures. I pondered my experiences from the night before. The wise Carl had left it to me to piece it all together, to make sense of it in a way that was meaningful to me. Was the spaceship real—did that experience happen in another dimension? Was the near-deafening sound of the membrane breaking caused by barriers between hidden realities having been breached? Is that what had allowed me to have these strange experiences that felt as real as my experiences in the world of my senses? Were they real or an illusion? And did I have more demons to encounter in the dark spaces?

That night, I dreamed I was visiting a nearby travel agency and was angry that the people working there knew nothing about profits and sales. Even worse, they kept their records disorganized, in a cardboard box. I became particularly infuriated with a German man who was much taller than I and seemed to be in charge. He let me know that sales and profits weren't important. I left and walked back to go to work in my own business, but to get there, I had to squeeze through a narrow walkway.

When I woke up, I thought about this dream and how angry I had been that no one in it had been doing things the "right" way. Then I realized the inner figure of a German man had given me a message: For some types of travel, you can't measure outcomes through ordinary costs and benefits. It's the intangible rewards that matter. My logical, analytical self had to step back if I was going to travel the shamanic path.

Where Realities Intersect

Before leaving Peru, I would do another ayahuasca ceremony. This one caused me to vomit, but I had no complaints because it was just as profound and powerful a journey as the previous one.

We bundled up against the cold night air and traveled by motorized canoe to an island where for the first time, I saw jaguar tracks. Then we lay on the ground and settled in to start the journey. Don Bandura, the ayahuascaro, began to walk among us, singing his songs and interrupting himself here and there to blow dark, acrid tobacco smoke over each of our energy fields. One by one, we drank the ayahuasca brew and waited to feel the effects.

On this journey, once again, I found myself in a spaceship—and I knew somehow that it was a mother ship. As a passenger, I felt a sense of kinship with the other beings on the spaceship with me. The German man from my dream was nowhere in sight . . . My businesslike self did not intrude.

Later during the journey, I felt called by some force greater than myself to do certain things that I understood were initiatory in some way. I performed some physical movements, and, at one point, I fixed the broken jaw of a fox that was starving and gave it food and drink. Grateful for my help, it became my energetic ally. The fox's message for me was to recognize the importance of being crafty and even cunning at times rather than casting myself in the role of the naïve "dumbling," which is how I have sometimes thought of myself.

After our shamanic experience, we took another kind of journey—one to return to the lodge, which proved more difficult than our trip to the island. The river had receded, and some of our party were still retching as we hiked a considerable distance through the dark jungle to find a spot where the motorized canoe could reach us. We slid down the muddy bank to the water and climbed into the canoe that was waiting for us.

On the way back to the lodge, I gazed tiredly into the moonlit waters where caimans could be seen floating and looking for prey. Despite the nearby danger, I felt a sense of calm.

As it turns out, the lodge was no longer illuminated, so we accidentally traveled past it. Once we discovered our mistake, we headed back in the other direction and finally got to our beds.

I thought about what had happened to me under the influence of the sacred plant. What was I to make of all this? How were my experiences in the transpersonal realms going to integrate with my everyday life? The fox has helped me to see that I need to be more savvy about my shamanic path and the challenges and even, perhaps, dangers that I might face in my quest for nourishment and healing. I was reminded of the power of my dreams to offer valuable information and now realized that shamanic journeys mediated by sacred plants could also lead me to discover profound insights. I recognized that it might take time to fully process what I had experienced during the shamanic journeys I had just undertaken, but already I could feel something significant had happened to me.

The shamanic work of the West, associated with the jaguar in Peruvian shamanism, is the work of letting go of the fear of death. It's important work if we want to achieve transformation because when we let go of our biggest fears, we can surrender to the unfamiliar and the unknown. Resisting change can have payoffs, but facing our fears can lead to changes that allow us to live more authentically. I believe that doing the work of the jaguar can even lead us to our destiny.

As you think about your own fears of uncertainty and change, you might want to open yourself to the possibility that you will be able to transition to living more authentically, more in sync with your values and desires, without risking anything vital—your health, your well-being, your relationships, and so on.

Questions for the Reader to Ponder

Transpersonal realms. Have you ever visited transpersonal realms through a shamanic journey or a dream and wondered if that place and your experience were real? Have you had your view of reality expanded through visiting a transpersonal realm? If so, did your everyday life change afterward? How did it change—and if it didn't, why do you think that is?

Synchronicities. Have you ever experienced a synchronicity: a meaningful coincidence? Did your feelings, thoughts, beliefs, or actions change as a result of it? Were they reinforced by a synchronicity? Do you think being open to synchronicities can help you with personal transformation? If not, would you be open to the possibility of paying attention to coincidences and pondering any possible meaning they have for you?

Transitions. How do you know when it's right to move forward into unknown territory and when you need to back away? What can keep you on course when your fear tells you to quit? And as you look back at your life, how would you describe its chapters? What has characterized your transitions from one chapter to another? Which transitions have been voluntary? Which have been involuntary? Is there a new chapter that you would like to experience now? What would you call it? What first steps can you take to transition into this new chapter?

CHAPTER THIRTEEN

Letting Go

On my return to the States, I found it challenging to reconcile the sharp contrast between my mystical experiences and my everyday activities of running a business, treating clients, and interacting with family and friends. I couldn't exactly describe why I felt different, but the changes in me felt profound. It seemed that Pachatusan and the ayahuasca had actually given me beneficial energies. Something powerful and very real had happened. I was not the same person who had stepped on the plane to Lima two weeks before. I was transforming, but who was I becoming?

I knew I wanted to walk a shamanic path—to have more experiences in transpersonal realms, to meet other shamans, and to develop my skills as a shamanic practitioner. I was being challenged to let go of my ego's fears about how others might see me. I had been drawn to becoming an analyst and to becoming a shaman in part because I wanted to be special—seen as someone to be looked up to. Now I had to be willing to let all of that go so it would not hold me back from writing a new story for myself, one that was more pleasing to me and to Spirit. Although I had grown up with the term "God," I was starting to use different words for the same idea: Spirit or Source, for example.

I felt I was turning a corner and needed to take the next step into the unseen: starting to imagine the life I would lead next, the new story I was only beginning to conceptualize.

After my return from Peru, I found myself composing free-form poetry, allowing the flow of creativity and mystery instead of resisting it, trying to contain it, or stopping it because I couldn't see the practical value in it. I hadn't written poems since high school but now felt drawn to write them. I would end up including many I wrote during this period of my life in my first book, *Change Your Story, Change Your Life*, more than a decade after this transitional time in my life that began in the early 2000s.

One of the poems I wrote in my journal around this time captured my uncertainty about where my shamanic training, practice, and teaching would take me as I let go of a life of constant striving and began simply being present in the mystical experiences I was having:

LETTING GO
The struggle unremitting:
no movement, no resolution.
Suddenly, a letting go
a surrender
to the Source from which all springs.
Not knowing the outcome
but accepting
and trusting in whatever happens.
When do I let go
and You take hold?

I recognized I had to trust Spirit and this process of transformation and continue nourishing the self within me that might be called The Carl Who Is Seeking Greater Fulfillment and a Deepened Sense of Purpose. I believed that doing so would not only make me feel more alive but also in some way enable me to do more to help others who needed healing. The Wounded Healer archetype seemed to be influencing me strongly, and I sensed I was being pulled toward my destiny.

After I finished my four-part training and other advanced courses, I joined the staff and began to teach at the Four Winds Society's Healing the Light Body School. The trainings I facilitated alongside other teachers who were dedicated to the shamanic path—including Alberto—were rewarding. I saw students beginning to liberate themselves from old cultural conditioning about what they should and shouldn't do with their lives. Some would go on to become healers and teachers. Some would redefine their lives in other ways. Many had experienced health crises that had made them question the way they were living and their priorities. Others had achieved a great deal—good careers and relationships, for example—but wanted something more, something that spoke to them on the deepest level. I could see that shamanic training and practice were helping these students transform their lives in ways that were meaningful and fulfilling for them. That's what I wanted for myself, too.

"I am the fucking jaguar!"

My work with The Four Winds Society led me to develop a friendship with Alberto that ultimately became less competitive and more collaborative than many friendships between men are. Jaguar energy influenced this friendship and me, helping me let go of old stories about how men should relate to each other in order to be seen as strong and important.

In September 2003, Alberto and I decided to do a shamanic journey together using the sacred plant San Pedro. We looked forward to sharing an experience of communing with Source and nature outdoors while journeying side by side during a night-into-day retreat. I could not have predicted how in sync we would be during this journey. The barriers between his consciousness and mine seemed to become fluid, which made my own experience of journeying even more powerful.

Evening fell as we sat together on the mountain where we would do our work. We prepared for our journey by opening sacred space and, with that accomplished, agreed that our mutual goal was to learn lessons from the energies of jaguar and fire—both of which are energies of transformation. I had unwrapped my mesa and arranged the objects within the space we had demarcated. I had also placed some crystals around my mesa for protection and put a bottle of Florida water next to the rattle I had brought. I have used Florida water, which contains a mixture of essential oils and alcohol, in cleansing rituals, and I thought it might be of use tonight. Alberto had laid out his mesa, too, along with some shamanic tools he thought he might want to use.

In addition to discussing our intention for the journey, the two of us had talked about the *I Ching* and how it might help me to get some insights from Spirit. Those who use this ancient oracle system, which involves throwing yarrow stalks or coins, believe that Spirit and our questions interact to affect the throws. The patterns that emerge once the stalks or coins are thrown give us insights and messages. Alberto had brought a book of interpretations, and I had some coins I could use, so I began my oracle reading.

As I sat in sacred space, I posed this question: "How can I become more aligned with Spirit?" Carefully, I wrote down the results of each throw and then paged through Alberto's book to find the *I Ching* passages corresponding to the patterns of the coins I had thrown. My interpretation of the messages was that as a student of shamanism, I needed an experienced teacher and should try to maintain the right attitude toward learning. I should also remain conscious of my lack of experience and not ask too many questions or give up my exploration prematurely. With my analytical mind, I tended to quickly try to analyze shamanic experiences right after having them instead of simply allowing insights to arise in me organically. I was glad to have this extra nudge from the *I Ching* because it was helpful to remember my goal to simply be present in the experience and figure out later what it meant.

I also felt I was being challenged not to indulge any desire I might have to be seen as an expert and authority—and instead to let go of any fear that I would be exposed to be just a student and not as skilled as I wanted to be. I found it interesting that the message for me tonight was to let go of my ego's need to be the alpha dog. I shared with Alberto what I thought the *I Ching* reading meant, and that it seemed appropriate to my situation, with me as the student and him as the more experienced teacher. He knew I was used to being the boss at work or a teacher others looked up to—and respected that I was willing to be a student in this situation.

I believe doing my oracle reading helped make me more available to what I would experience that night as I worked with the energies of fire and jaguar.

Inviting in the Jaguar

The jaguar, a predator, contributes to the balance of the jungle by killing, which prevents overpopulation of other animals—a characteristic that would energetically affect me tonight. In essence, Alberto and I were asking the jaguar to help us to energetically kill off whatever we did not need—including any fear that might be holding us back in some way—so that we could be ready for something new. Just what needed to die was a mystery to us as we ingested the San Pedro with reverence for the power of this sacred plant. Together, we asked the jaguar and our fire to work with us, to give us strength and protect us. Remaining present in the moment of our experience, we sat together in silence before the fire we had built in a space outdoors with the night sky above us. I felt my everyday consciousness begin to give way to a more open state of awareness.

Alberto had given me a very old carved stone to work with, one he called a "jaguar stone." I held it in my hand as I sat looking into the flames before us. Later that evening, Alberto would tell me that the jaguar stone contained three energies: that of the stone itself, that of the jaguar, and that of the shaman who had infused the stone with his and the jaguar's energy in a ceremony that probably took place in Machu Picchu centuries before. At this point, I only knew the "jaguar stone" as he called it held some energies and had been a present to Alberto from a shaman—and that the carving on it looked a bit like a face.

Suddenly, a gale-force gust of wind came through, and we braced ourselves against it. It abated as swiftly as it had begun. Had it arrived to cleanse us, sweeping away energies we no longer needed?

Next, I noticed that the area surrounding us was filling with light from the ground up. Above us shone a dazzling array of stars and a full moon whose light pooled on the ground. I was still holding the carved jaguar stone Alberto had given me when suddenly my attention was drawn to the sensation of the rock in my hand becoming warm and pulsing like a beating heart. I looked down at it. To my shock, I saw the carved eyes were opening and closing.

"It's alive! It's alive!" I shouted to Alberto.

"Feed it, feed it! Before it feeds on you!" he exclaimed.

Quickly, he pressed into my other hand my bottle filled with Florida water, used for blessings, ceremonies, and cleansings. "Feed it! Hurry!" he cried. Knowing what he meant, I took some of the water into my mouth and sprayed it out in a mist toward the jaguar before it could devour me.

Instinctively, I knew the beast hungered for me just as I had hungered for its essence—the alchemical potential I had yearned for as far back as I could remember. My soul had craved nourishment, yet

I had denied it again and again. My heart pounded in fear, but then the jaguar's threat lifted like a fog and floated away into the night air. I felt the wet stone in my palm, sinister no more yet still alive, warm, and breathing. I realized the danger had passed.

Feed it. So simple.

It's said that the unseen world can exact a price on those who neglect their spiritual nature. Were the health challenges I had developed the result of this stingy starvation diet I'd inflicted on my long-suffering soul?

This much I knew: A sated jaguar has no reason to attack a human.

Feed it. Feed it well.

Thy will. My will. No more denial.

Despite feeling I had gained a crucial insight and escaped the danger that had been posed by the powerful jaguar energy I was working with, I remained somewhat on edge as the shamanic journey continued.

At one point, I became aware of energies attacking my energy field. Fortunately, the jaguar appeared in front of me and leapt at my energetic adversaries, dispersing them. Then it glided into a black pool of water and swam away. I realized that the jaguar that had wanted to feed on me was a powerful spirit animal serving as my protector, at least for now. I wondered how my new relationship with it would evolve. If the jaguar was my ally, how might he help me?

I looked over at Alberto and asked, "What does it mean when people say they have become one with the jaguar? Does their consciousness go into the jaguar or does the jaguar's consciousness go into them?"

In lieu of a response, Alberto began to shake his rattle. To my surprise, at that very moment, I knew the answer.

"Alberto!" I said. "*I am the fucking jaguar!*"

Somehow, I was inhabiting the jaguar's physical and energetic body as it inhabited mine. His helpful energy was there for me, inside my own energy field.

We were united.

Then, I found myself in an underground cavern where I was initiated into an ancient order of jaguar shamans who were helping me to receive the power of jaguar energy.

I was changing . . .

No longer in the cavern, now I was flying over the earth and looking down on a city thousands of years old. I sensed it was Mycenaean and noticed that its structures formed a pattern of squares and circles—a circle around a square that enclosed another circle, and so on. As I observed the city from above, I saw that one structure had a deep hole in it. Like an eagle, I could see far into the hole, into a place I somehow knew to be the holy of holies—the most sacred place, where one can experience Spirit directly and receive life-changing revelations. I flew down and was just about to enter it when Alberto lit a candle, yanking me back into ordinary consciousness.

I was disappointed to have missed out on such a wondrous opportunity, but then my consciousness shifted again. I was now at a place outside of a chamber, guarded by the Knights Templar, that I knew contained the secret of the Holy Grail. As I began opening the door to go inside, Alberto once again interrupted my shamanic journey to point something out to me.

A few words had snapped me back to ordinary reality—but it was okay because very soon, my journey continued. I quickly let go of my attachment to what I might have experienced and opened myself up to what was happening in the present. Later, as I thought about it, I came to realize the lesson of these interruptions and of my ability to shift back into everyday awareness when I was using San Pedro: that the line separating the reality of a shamanic journey and the reality in the world of our senses is very thin. One can bleed into the other. What's more, we have to accept that we aren't always in charge of which reality we are in. Journeys can end and begin abruptly. Maybe Alberto was supposed to interrupt me before my entering the holy of holies and before I walked through the doorway to enter the room where lay the Holy Grail. Maybe there was a reason I was yanked back to my place before the fire, listening to Alberto speak before he, too, returned to his journey state. Or maybe he was just interfering with my experience! Instead of being limited to one interpretation, I was aware of all the possibilities.

I intended to be accepting of whatever happened on my journey, but from an ego perspective, I wanted to know and understand everything. The truth is we can't know for sure what is random chance and what is destiny. Working with and trusting Spirit helps us to accept the uncertainty of our situations and the limits of our knowing and understanding. Since that San Pedro experience, I have come to believe that we will encounter the holy of holies only when we are ready, not before, and I'm okay with that.

Now I entered the transpersonal realm of the journey again. Several harlequin-type figures wearing masks and costumes with geometric, diamond shapes appeared in front of me. Something about them troubled me. They didn't seem at all friendly. I recognized they represented a robotic, ineffective way of moving through life—a way of being dead while still physically alive. After the journey ended, I would ponder this image and recognize its message for me: I needed to stop living as if on autopilot, without a sense of purpose and creativity. I wasn't writing my own story and claiming my own way of operating in the world.

Our journey continued, and Alberto suggested we do a nature painting together. In other words, we should let ourselves be drawn to natural objects around us and place them in the designated spot for the "painting," choosing the objects and their placement using our intuition. Nature paintings can give us insights into ourselves that are hidden from the conscious mind. Alberto asked me to draw four quadrants in the dirt, which I did. He commented on my precision. I said, "After all, I am an engineer!" and we both laughed.

Alberto drew a dove in one of the quadrants, and I drew a dragon in another. I watched mesmerized as my dragon come to life and began to gobble up Alberto's dove. When we realized we both were seeing the same thing, we laughed.

Then, I noticed some odd stripes on Alberto's face. I asked, "What are those markings?" He said he had received them energetically years ago during an initiation that had installed jaguar energy into his light body. I realized that the initiatory energies he had received had left their impressions on his energy field and that was what I was observing—jaguar markings.

The journey continued, and as I looked up at the night sky, I felt my attention drawn upward to a particular star. I reached toward it and saw light going from the star to me and back and realized we were exchanging energies. Of all the energies I had encountered since beginning this journey, the star's was the most gentle and benign yet the most powerful. I felt very comfortable communing with this kindly celestial entity and began to describe its beauty and qualities to Alberto.

"I know," he said. "I can see it, too. It's reaching down to you from the sky."

I asked Alberto if he would like me to give him some of the energy I was exchanging with the star. He said yes, and I held up my hand again to gather some of the energy to send it his way. When I pointed my hand toward him to transfer the starlight, the energy was so strong that Alberto stumbled backward a few steps, nearly knocked over by the power. Once again, we were having the same experience of the energy around us—seeing and sensing in sync with each other.

I suddenly became highly aware of the electromagnetic field surrounding my body. My field seemed to pulse and then fizzle as if it were being short-circuited. I felt anxious and concerned. Somehow, I knew that I needed to repair my field by weaving plant energy into my "fizzled" grid. I felt myself begin doing this, not questioning how this plant energy I needed showed up just as I realized I wanted to work with it.

Immediately after my energetic healing and repair, I felt my whole field start to come alive again. However, I had an inner knowing that the healing I'd experienced was not a quick, permanent fix. There would be more repair work to do in the future using plants. In fact, I would again use sacred plants for journeying. I would even go on to develop a new relationship with ordinary plants, modifying my diet to make it more plant based.

Soon after that plant-healing part of my journey, I returned to an ordinary state of consciousness again. I looked over and saw that Alberto had fallen asleep on the ground. Not yet sleepy, I sat before the fire and opened myself up to learning any lessons it had for me, sensing it might have some message I could benefit from. The flames in front of my eyes appeared to be like liquid. It occurred to me that I was watching all the elements transform themselves. The wood contained water, oxygen, and elements of the earth that were becoming fire and smoke—smoke that became one with the air drawn up into the sky, leaving behind ash, something people around the globe have used as fertilizer. The smoke would come down to earth again, embedded in rain—water that would help plants to break through the earth and reach skyward. Fire, I realized, renews itself over and over again, transforming continually. What seems dead is not really gone but merely nourishment for new life. Pachamama wastes nothing—even when fire seems to consume it.

I fell asleep at some point, and when I awoke, I noticed the fire had been reduced to mere embers. As I gazed into it, I began thinking about my call to do shamanic work and how important it was to me. I silently resolved to dedicate my life to my shamanic path. The very moment I had that thought, the embers burst into bright flames that leaped upward, as if the fire were reading my thoughts and responding, "Yes!" Pachamama was speaking to me through the fire, encouraging me to walk the shamanic path.

Soon afterward, I drifted off to sleep again, and as the dawn began to break, I woke up and looked around. To my surprise, I saw that nothing, not a single object I could see, had been blown away by that powerful wind we had experienced the night before. I walked around, sure that I must be mistaken, but I was not. It was bewildering not just to me but to Alberto, who by now had awoken, too. The wind that swept through with such intensity had seemed so real to both of us.

My bare feet sunk into the grass moist with dew as I went to check on my mesa. My glass bottle of Florida water was not even knocked over, much less shattered. My mesa stones had not been blown away but had somehow gently rearranged themselves into a different formation than the one I had left them in earlier. I was sure I hadn't touched my mesa after laying it out—and later, Alberto said he hadn't done so either. The new arrangement of my stones seemed to be giving me several messages: that the lessons of my childhood and family would continue to influence me but not nearly as much as they had. That I had new interconnections with the cosmos. That my relationships and sense of spirituality were changing. That I needed to get rid of my attachments if I wanted to find serenity and strengthen my commitment to my shamanic practice.

The interconnectedness among Source, me, and my mesa felt very real as I stood before it, alone and amazed at having experienced such a powerful and magically inspiring night.

The morning sun continued to rise above the horizon, enhancing my feeling of resurrection. I remembered having experienced initiatory energies as I was working with the jaguar during the journey. I knew something in me had been altered—and maybe something had died, giving way to this sense of rebirth and renewal. The jaguar energy had not fed on me after all. It had entered me and was now with me and perhaps would help me to achieve balance by letting go of energies that weighed me down and caused me to get caught up in a lifeless, harlequin-like way of living.

As I thought about all the shamanic work I had done so far, I felt that I was being drawn closer to Source in its many forms, including spirit animals. Tonight was the first time I had journeyed alongside another person and been aware during the journey that we were sharing experiences—of the jaguar in the stone and its pulsing and blinking, of the powerful wind that swept through yet left no damage, of the dragon consuming the dove in front of our eyes, of the star's energy I shared with Alberto only to see him knocked backward by its power. What was real and what was imagined?

Like any journeying experience, the story of that night on the mountain with Alberto could simply be a tale to tell others, nothing more. But for me, it was a deeply moving reminder that our individual consciousness is always connected with the minds of others even if we don't realize it. We are part of a great mind or consciousness shared by all. After tonight, this would no longer be simply a belief of mine I had first learned about when studying to become a Jungian analyst. Now, I had experienced it to be true and felt my oneness with all of creation.

As I mentioned earlier when explaining the ayni despacho ceremony, one of the core concepts shamans believe in is ayni, or reciprocity. We give and we take. We lose and we gain. Balance and mutuality are part of nature and core to the idea of ayni.

Shamans work with energy, letting go of some energies and bringing in others. You might need to let go of some energies to prepare yourself to bring in new ones. You might also want to relate to some energies differently so you are more conscious of their effect on you and you can begin to relate to them as allies rather than ignoring them or seeing them as negative influences.

Letting go of energies no longer serving you, or relating to them differently, might fuel big changes for you that lead to your writing and living according to a better story. You might want to think about what energies you are ready to let go of or relate to differently.

If you have an interest in shamanic work or other healing work that involves a relationship to Spirit and the earth's energies, you might also want to explore those topics.

My shamanic work and letting go of my old ideas about who I was and what a relationship to Spirit looks like helped me to become initiated into a new way of living. Initiations can be spontaneous or happen as a result of planning. Afterward, you feel different: You instinctively know you have undergone a deep change. As you think about your own life, you might want to identify any initiations you've undergone.

Questions for the Reader to Ponder

Fear. Fear can help us avoid unnecessary risks and make us aware of the need to take precautions to protect what we value. It can also paralyze us. What have you not done because of your fears? In retrospect, could you have actually done some of those things, or was it the wisest choice not to do them? How do you handle your fears today? Could you relate to your fears differently, reducing their paralyzing aspects? Could you begin to let go of them and bring in other energies for protection? What might those energies be? (If you don't know, you might want to do shamanic work to find out.) How do you know when it's right to move forward into unknown territory and when you need to back away? What can you do to keep on course when your fear tells you to quit?

Sacred sites. Have you visited any sacred sites such as Machu Picchu? How did you feel during your visit and afterward? Did you experience lasting changes in your life as a result of your visits? If you haven't been to sacred sites, would you like to go? What steps would you need to take to make it happen?

Initiations. Have you ever had initiatory experiences that caused you to feel you had a new relationship to Source? What effects did these experiences have on you? Did you make changes to your everyday life as a result and, if so, what were the changes? If you haven't had initiatory experiences or meaningful encounters with Source, would you like to? How could you make that happen?

Sacred plants, dreamwork, and other tools for transformation. Have you ever done work in an altered state and visited transpersonal realms, with or without the use of sacred plants? If you did not use sacred plants, what tools did you use to take yourself out of ordinary consciousness and into an altered state so you could experience transpersonal realms? What, if any, shamanic journeys have you undertaken? What did you experience as a result? Were the experiences transformational and lasting for you? How did they affect your worldview and everyday life? Have you had transformative dreams? Why were those dreams so powerful? Could you work with your dreams in new ways to make them more useful and glean more insights from them?

CHAPTER FOURTEEN

Bringing In

In 2004, Alberto offered me an opportunity to meet and work with some indigenous Q'ero shamans in Peru. There, he said, I could receive rites that would initiate me into their lineages: the rites of the Pampa Mesayok, Alto Mesayok, Curak Akullek, and the Mosok, all of which involved different types of energy. Subsequently, I was asked by the Q'ero to pass on these rites to others, and later, they were incorporated into what Alberto called the Munay-ki (MOO-nay KEY) rites, which he described as "blessings passed from person to person to person that initiate them into a new way of walking softly on the planet and harmoniously with each other."[11]

The ceremonies transferring these initiatory energies into me would take place at ancient sacred sites in and around the Sacred Valley of the Incas in the Andes Mountains of Peru. Alberto recommended that if I were to take this trip, I should bring a photographer with me to record the ceremonies for the Sanctuary Project, an endeavor to help preserve the shamanic traditions of the Q'ero people, whose way of life is dying out due to the pressures on them to adopt Western customs. He and I agreed that obtaining images must not interfere with the ceremonies and that none of the work should be staged for the sake of the photography. In addition, we would make no audio recordings. Christine Paul, an accomplished photographer with whom I had done my training at The Four Winds School, agreed to come along and take professional pictures. They turned out to be not only beautiful but also powerful. She captured some extraordinary moments.

At first, I questioned my preparedness and worthiness for such initiations, but then I thought about the shamans I would be meeting. Their way of life was dying, and their teachings about respect for the earth and living in mutuality with it needed to be shared with others.

If I could help bring forward the energies they had received as a result of their training and work, it would be an honor.

Despite all the detailed planning Alberto, Christine, and I did, the trip almost didn't happen. I was scheduled to leave for Lima on Tuesday, June 8, to travel to Cusco on Wednesday, and begin my work with the Q'ero elders on Saturday. On the Friday before my intended departure to Peru, I was hospitalized with an arrhythmia and remained in the intensive care ward Friday and Saturday. After the doctors determined I had not had a heart attack and had suffered no heart damage but had atrial fibrillation, I was discharged Saturday afternoon. Because of my arrhythmia, the doctors wanted me to cancel my plans. They were concerned about the severity of the conditions I might encounter in the high Andes and urged me to immediately start a medication regimen that would require frequent monitoring.

This trip had been in the works for several months and was very important to me. After agonizing over what to do and seeking other medical opinions as well as consulting my intuition, I decided to go after all and simply trust that everything would work out. One doctor did feel the risks were manageable. I admit I probably listened more to him than I did to his colleagues, wanting very much not to miss out on this extraordinary opportunity. As it turned out, I did not have any medical problems during my time in Peru.

Mutuality, Biting Insects, and Music

During the trip, I would come to feel a loving and respectful shared connection among Christine and me, the Q'ero shamans, our translator, and our driver. The shamans included Don Francisco and his apprentice, Basilio; Don Umberto and his wife, Donna Bernadina, along with their son and apprentice Rolando; Don Pasqual; and Don Mariano. All of them helped me feel at ease in unfamiliar places as I participated in rituals whose details I knew little about beforehand.

Some of the sites involved extensive climbs. I was concerned about whether I would be able to keep up physically and whether I might have another atrial fibrillation episode or even one more serious. The Q'ero were patient with me despite my need for breaks to catch my breath, and I gradually acclimated to the altitude. I have to wonder if the sacred and meaningful work I was doing somehow cued my body to keep up with the demands I was placing on it. This time, thanks to some orthotics and stretching exercises I'd been doing, my feet were better able to handle the climb up narrow mountain passes overlooking steep ravines. I managed to find the right balance between pushing myself and resting.

Prior to each ceremony, before the Q'ero joined me to commence the work, I meditated in solitude and prepared myself for what was to come. Every sacred site we visited had its own unique set of energies that had been experienced by the people who lived there as well as their shamans. Each initiation involved a different despacho and a different energetic transmission.

On the first day of our work together, the Q'ero and I hiked from Ollantaytambo to the Urubamba River, where the herbalist Doña Julia, who had hiked along with us, did a ritual cleansing of me and my energy field using water and smoke. I had my shirt off while being cleansed, and unfortunately, biting insects began to swarm around me. Everyone else was pretty well covered up, but those bugs ate me alive during the ceremony. I did my best to focus on the cleansing and not the distraction of slapping myself, too late to prevent many welts and a powerful urge to scratch. The Q'ero were amused.

Afterward, we went to Puma Marca to visit the Temple of the Puma (mountain lion) and did an ayni despacho for balance and reciprocity and to invite Spirit to be with us as we did our work that week. My Q'ero companions had learned it was my sixty-fourth birthday, and after our work was done, they decided to celebrate by bringing me an armful of flowers they had gathered from the mountainside. We had a good time talking about our families and laughing together, facilitated by our translator's skills—and by the beer we had purchased. The Q'ero elders told Christine and me they wanted to bestow Quechua names on us: They named her *Puna*, mountain flower, and me *Apuchin*, spirit of the condor.

The next day, Sunday, we traveled to a beautiful spot called Quillarumiyok, or the Temple of the Moon, a ceremonial temple of stone masonry built into a cave by the Inca hundreds of years ago. There, I received my first shamanic initiation: the Pampa Mesayok rites, which initiated me as a caretaker of Mother Earth. Throughout the experience, I tried very hard to make sure everything I said and did was appropriately sacred. I did not understand everything that was going on but attempted to be as present as possible to what was happening and to the numinous: Spirit all around us and within us, the stones, the tools being used in the ritual, and all the creatures and plants surrounding us. At the conclusion of the ceremony, I was given a *kuya* (KOO-yah)—a stone said to contain specific types of energies— to commemorate the initiation. I acknowledged it with gratitude, knowing how sacred a gift it was.

Throughout the ceremony, I had been kneeling for a long time and didn't realize that my legs had fallen asleep. Afterward, I tried to stand up—and fell flat on my face. It was humorous and embarrassing at the same time. My Q'ero companions were very kind, chuckling but helping me get to my feet and telling me not to try to walk until the circulation returned to my legs. It was a reminder that no matter how profound our spiritual experiences are and how seriously we take ourselves when we have them, we will experience moments that make us feel humble and vulnerable—and human. I thought of Don Pasqual, who spilled the wine during a despacho ceremony the last time I had been in Peru and how he had simply made a joke and moved on.

After I had gotten up from my fall, one of the shamans said, "Now we have to celebrate the new *paco!*"—the new shaman. We walked over to where our vehicles were parked and turned on a car radio. Music filled the air, and someone began to dance. Spontaneously, we all joined in. It was the perfect ending to the ceremony.

Caretaker of the Stories and Traditions

During that first day and into the second day, I ruminated about how I might not be deserving of these initiations. When doing the ceremonies, would I make mistakes—maybe put the wrong things in the despacho or place them the wrong way? Would I give the Q'ero a good impression of their northern brothers and sisters? I was used to being a boss or a Jungian analyst helping people to gain insights into the challenges they were facing. As a participant in unfamiliar shamanic ceremonies, I felt out of my element and vulnerable. I had resolved some of my concerns about my worthiness by reminding myself that the initiations would be beneficial not just for me but for as many people as possible. I was committed to sharing them with others as I went forward with my shamanic training and practice. Feeling humbled yet proud as I connected to each of the Q'ero shamans who were participating in these ceremonies with me, I was starting to believe that I had made the right choice to come to Peru for this sequence of initiations. With the weight of my worries gone, it was easier to fully open to the energies and initiations I was receiving.

The next afternoon, at the Temple of the Sun at Pisac in the Sacred Valley of the Vilcanota River, our group solemnly blew our intentions into stacks of three coca leaves as part of a despacho ceremony honoring the mountains whose terraces surrounded us. The Alto Mesayok initiation I was about to undergo would connect me energetically to a lineage of mythmakers and storytellers.

I hoped these initiations would help me write a better and more satisfying story for my own life. I felt the shamanic work I had been doing helped prepare me by challenging me to let go of my self-importance so I could humbly receive the blessings—the rites—that I would pass along to others.

Other rites I received on that trip would include the rites of the seer and the sage, which I accepted during my Curak Akullek initiation at Moray. Called the "belly of the Pachamama," this sacred site is known for its series of concentric circles used for experimental cultivation during the time the Inca Empire flourished. The energies I received there were of the ancient visionaries who could see future possibilities. With the rites I was about to receive, I was told, I would become a keeper of the traditions, a caretaker of my community and of the world. I thought about how as part of my ongoing shamanic training, I was learning to envision alternative, better futures and to help my clients do this for themselves.

On our last day together, our group went to Tipón at the base of Pachatusan, a place known for its fountains of sacred waters. Built by the ancient Inca to allow farming on the step-like terraces now covered in grass, the fountains consist of streams of sparkling clear water that tumble over carefully placed stones as it travels down the mountainside.

Here, I was to receive the Mosok rites of our becoming. I prepared for a very intense and long ceremony by cleansing myself in a sacred fountain.

As it started to snow, I reunited with the mountain that had instilled strength in me. I participated in creating one last despacho as the Q'ero, dressed in their brightly colored woolen ponchos, performed their ritual of evoking my potential. They anchored the energy of my potentiality in me by blowing smoke toward my chakras and tapping me with their mesas. The sound of the rattle filled my ears and was carried on the wind along with the smoke from a bundle of burning sage. At the conclusion of the ceremony, the Q'ero shamans presented me with a kuya from Huaman Lipa, a sacred mountain near their village. After we had closed sacred space, I placed the kuya in my mesa with my stones representing the direction of the east and new beginnings. My initiatory work involving the Munay-ki rites had ended.

Before leaving Tipón, I held a ceremony for the Q'ero shamans to bring closure to our work together and to honor its significance. I thanked them as a group for the work they had done with me. As they requested, I promised to share with others what I had learned. I addressed each shaman individually, giving them a blessing and a different animal energy embodied by a kuya that I had acquired for them from sacred places in North America. I then energetically transmitted the power of that animal and the intention for *yachay* (right thoughts), *munay* (right love), and *llankay* (right actions) into their various energy centers.

Even though we had a language barrier between us, by the end of the trip I had come to know the Q'ero elders better and felt affection toward each of them. They were astute and loving people who respected the earth and heavens and all of their energies. After this humbling and powerful experience in Peru, I would do further work with transpersonal energies. I would harmonize with them for the sake of repairing and healing what has been damaged—communities, individuals, and the earth itself.

I returned home feeling grateful to have undergone multiple energetic initiations thanks to shamans far more experienced than I was. I would go on to share the energies I had received with Westerners but also, it would turn out, with shamans on several continents—healers I would do work with as well.

Healing by the Numbers and Other Means

In the years after those first two trips to Peru and my first experiences with sacred plants, I continued to teach, do workshops, travel, and use shamanic tools for healing as well as meet masters of energy medicine. I also continued doing qigong, which I had begun to learn from Mrs. Chen, and in 2004, took a trip with her and some other qigong practitioners to China, as I mentioned before. One of the qigong healers we met, Jian, said he had a connection to what he called "the fifth dimension" (similar to Source or Spirit, as I call this energy) and would ask it to give him information about people he was helping. He explained that he received answers in the form of sensations in his hands. A sensation in a certain area—his thumb, perhaps, or the tip of his little finger—clued him into which part of the patient's body needed healing. The sensations also gave him information about when the health challenges began and what emotional experiences they were connected to. He believed that every physical ailment correlates with an emotional one—similar to Carl Jung's beliefs.

To clear the emotional experience at the root of the physical ailment, this healer would instruct his patients to recall the event and get in touch with their emotions about it. Then, they were to transfer those emotions to a ball of chi they could hold in their hands. Once they had done that, they were to fling the ball to the ground so that the energy would be absorbed by the earth. Jian had them do this over and over until they felt an emotional cleansing.

In shamanic work, energy containing information can be transferred into and out of the body intentionally. I was struck by that parallel as well as another one: This healer believed that past, present, and future all existed simultaneously in this fifth dimension, and by working with it, one could gain information and energies from all three. Here I was, halfway across the globe from the shamans in Peru, talking about the nature of time being nonlinear with a man who had no way of knowing what his brothers and sisters in the Andes and the jungles near the Amazon believed about time—or what Carl Jung believed about the mind-body connection.

On that trip, I also met another healer: Zhaohui, a woman who had fasted for spiritual reasons and told us she had not eaten, only drunk small amounts of fluids, for months. I found her very ethereal as she explained how she worked with numbers for healing. Patients would describe what they were experiencing physically, and Zhaohui would prescribe certain numbers for them to say—she called it "digital therapy." These numbers corresponded in traditional Chinese medicine to various energetic centers in the body and to antidotes for various physical and psychological ailments. She would tell a patient to keep repeating the numbers to bring about healing. I was intrigued once again to hear someone talk about an energy healing method that echoed ideas about energy that could be found in other cultures. The ancient Greeks, Kabbalistic practitioners, and people who were a part of other esoteric traditions believed numbers had specific energies for healing, too.

When I asked for more details, Zhaohui told me she felt that the healing power of the numbers had to do in part with the resonance of Mandarin Chinese. She said you could repeat the numbers in English but that using Mandarin Chinese was better. She gave examples of women with babies in breech positions, who, after repeating the numbers she prescribed, would have their babies turn and be head down in the womb. She said she had cured people with a broad variety of ailments through what she did.

Another qigong healer we met, Kang, based his healing approach on having people roll on the ground. He said this action reset the body's mechanisms into a new homeostasis that allowed for healing. He did rolling work with people who had cancer and with children who had psychiatric disorders and reported that many of them were substantially helped. Kang also said that he never had any of his cancer patients die after his treatment. Instead, they learned to coexist with their cancer.

There were some doctors in the group I was traveling with, and they expressed a good amount of skepticism about the claims we had heard. I completely understood their resistance, but I myself had experienced and witnessed inexplicable healings as a result of doing energy work. That was one of the reasons I had been drawn to shamanism. I listened to the doctors talk about the mechanisms by which the healings and health improvements could have come about. Some were fairly certain that the placebo effect was at play while others simply didn't believe what they had been told about the effects of qigong. The coming together of Eastern and Western healers on this trip certainly made me think even more about how I could participate in sharing techniques, wisdom, and energies with others.

In the years that followed, to some degree, my shamanic work became integrated into my work with clients as a Jungian analyst. I worked with people energetically to help them experience insights arising from the collective unconscious and the wisdom that is available to us when we are in nonordinary consciousness. I've assisted them in letting go of energies that are no longer serving them and bringing in new ones. I began writing down some of the stories clients, Four Winds Society students, and workshop participants told me about how my work with them helped them in their healing journeys.

In my shamanic practice, I have had many experiences of how we and inanimate objects are connected within the field of energy we all share. It's interesting to watch people in my office at the Replogle Center for Counseling and Well-Being pick a stone from my mesa, close their eyes, and share with me any impressions they receive. Often, what they experience is similar to the personal and transpersonal meaning that I have attributed to that stone.

Westerners may scoff at the idea of objects being imbued with energies that have awareness and can offer us helpful information. Animism is not part of the spiritual traditions and religions of most individuals and their families and communities. However, I have observed that after talking with people about this phenomenon of Spirit within objects, places, people, living creatures, and plants, many report they have experienced this themselves and want to know more. Others haven't experienced the phenomenon but are intrigued, and some of them express a desire to connect with hidden energies. I know that doing so will, potentially, reassure them that they are connected with something larger than themselves—something that has qualities of strength and healing they can draw on.

Sometimes, we have a strong inner knowing that we are in the presence of mystery and are interacting with the invisible world. This awareness can open us up to the possibility that energy from unseen realms can intervene in our lives in ways that benefit us. Once, when I was in a multiple vehicle pileup during a snowstorm near the Indiana/ Illinois border, I experienced what felt like an intervention from an entity that was looking out for me. Like many people, I had exited my car after the accident and was standing on the shoulder of the road, awaiting assistance. Out of the corner of my eye, I saw a car sliding toward me. Without knowing what lay on the other side of the guardrail, I leaped over it to avoid getting hit. I didn't know whether there was a long drop on the other side, but fortunately, there wasn't. I scrambled to my feet as I heard the car crashing into other vehicles that had been temporarily abandoned. A man who had been standing next to me, who had not jumped, suffered a broken leg.

I could have chalked up this incident to random luck, and I most likely would have years before, but somehow, I sensed I had been protected by some force that was looking out for me, a force I was meant to notice.

"We see a mountain protecting you"

A few years after my trip to China, Pat and I had an opportunity to travel to other parts of Asia as well as to Africa, Australia, and Europe with a group of people who wanted to visit areas of the world where cultural traditions were vanishing. As long as I was going to these faraway places, I decided to arrange visits with various shamans and healers. I hoped to discover what they believed about the hidden realms, energies, and our relationship to the earth—and learn how these healers worked. I also wanted to share what I knew. All of my meetings helped me deepen my understanding of energy medicine. What's more, I was fascinated to observe how other shamans picked up on energies I had brought into my light body as a result of the work I had done and the initiatory rites I had received.

In early October 2007, I met with Oktai, a shaman in Ulaanbaatar in Outer Mongolia. Through an interpreter, I told him what I did as a healer, and he told me about his work. We exchanged views about the nature of healing and about shamanism. Oktai explained that he saw Spirit permeating all things, including the sky—and he gave me a blue cloth for my mesa that he said would help me be connected to the sky's energy. Then he gave me a stone imbued with energy from his tradition, and I gave him a stone from my mesa that was infused with helpful energy.

After that, I traveled to the outskirts of Ulaanbaatar to a hill the locals called a mountain. There, I met two women shamans Oktai had told me about: Tuya and Esen. Snow was falling lightly, dry flakes that barely dusted the landscape, as the women and I drank yak's milk mixed with vodka to prepare us for our ceremony and healing work at the foot of the hill. One woman drummed and the other danced until they worked their way into an ecstatic state—which they later explained as being "possessed" by one of their shamanic spirit allies. Each of them separately did healing work on me. Both said they had difficulty penetrating my field and told me it was as if I had a big mountain, bigger than the "mountain" we were working with, protecting me.

Pachatusan, I thought.

When the shamans finished their healing work on me, snow began to fall more heavily, and the three of us drummed, rattled, and chanted in honor of their "mountain." We also expressed gratitude to Spirit in its form of a mountain. Our ceremony went on for some time as the snow began to stick and layer a blanket of white over us and the earth. I breathed in the crisp air, feeling my connection to the shamans, the land, and Spirit.

Hyena Energy

Later on this trip, I made arrangements to meet Fana, a prominent, well-respected shaman in Addis Ababa, Ethiopia. While there was no war in Ethiopia at the time, the nation was ringed by countries in varying degrees of civil unrest, many of which had been at war with Ethiopia at some point. When I and the group I was traveling with arrived in Addis Ababa late at night, the airport security was on high alert. Many armed guards slowly walked the floors, eyeing everyone who passed through. It took hours to get through security and customs. When we finally got to the hotel, we had to walk through metal detectors in the lobby. I saw many armed guards patrolling the grounds there, too.

After spending some time in Addis Ababa and its surrounding areas, I drove with my hired translator on paved roads that gave way to dirt and gravel before we finally arrived at the shaman's compound in a very poor section of the city. Fana wasn't there, and dozens of people were inside the compound waiting to see her for healing when she returned.

The translator and I went to a separate area as instructed, and Fana's son came out to see us. He spoke no English but offered us some *chat*, a mild narcotic that is chewed by people in Ethiopia and other parts of Africa. We placed some in our mouths, thanking him, and began to talk with him about conditions in Ethiopia and the world—and a little bit about what his mother did.

Then the shaman's son excused himself and promised he would see what he could do about getting me in to see his mother that day. Alone with my translator, I sat as he began to share with me some of his history, questions, and problems. He even told me some of his nighttime dreams that he had found disturbing. I asked him if he would like me to help him learn from them, and he said yes. Then, I walked him through the dialoguing process (which I described earlier in this book) so he could better understand what his unconscious was telling him. I'm struck by how we can be of service to others in surprising circumstances that can be synchronistic. If it weren't for our having to wait for the shaman we had arranged to meet, I might never have known that my translator was seeking healing. Afterward, he said he felt more relaxed and less anxious.

Eventually, Fana returned. Shortly thereafter, my translator and I entered a room that was divided by a large hanging carpet. To do her work, Fana sat on one side of the carpet while her clients sat on the other. I explained to her via the translator why I was there. At first, I sensed she was not just curious but wary—wondering who I was, how I had happened to get there, and what I really wanted. The Ethiopian government did not officially support shamanism, and she did not know who, if anyone, I represented. By telling her who I was and why I had come, I began to gain her trust. But the trust became more established when we talked about energy and each of us shared some of our own energy with the other.

I learned that in addition to being a shaman doing healing work for many people every day, Fana cared for orphans who had lost their parents in the violence in and around the city. She was an example of a powerful woman doing good for others in the midst of difficult circumstances, and I felt a kinship to her as a healer and shaman.

We talked for a long time. Her energy was so strong I could feel it traveling through the carpet toward me. I mentioned that to her—and she said she could feel my energy flowing into her, too. We shared our visions about life, healing, and what we did as shamanic workers, and found we had much in common. Fana said that like me, she also drew her energy from nature and from animal powers, which for her included the hyena. She then used those energies as conduits to connect her to transpersonal places from which she retrieved insights and energy to do her healing work. We gave each other blessings and shared more about our lives and experiences.

With her permission, I gave Fana energy from the mountains that were my sources, and in return, she gave me energy from her sources. At one point she started to make yipping hyena-like noises. The translator said she was paying me a great compliment by giving me some of her hyena energy. Fana said later that she had picked up on energies that were protecting me that she was unfamiliar with—and said that my enemies would have trouble trying to harm me because these energies were so strong.

By now it was evening and dark outside. I thanked Fana and left. Once I returned to my hotel, I became very sick, vomiting for a long time that night and into the next day. Perhaps it was a result of the powerful energy exchange I had experienced with this shaman—or maybe it was just from the chat I chewed! We often can't know for certain whether we are making up what we feel to be true—ultimately, we're the ones who decide what an experience means to us.

Another time, also in 2007, I traveled to Aboriginal lands in the Northern Territory of Australia, where an Aboriginal guide took me and others to a series of caves used by the Aborigines to bury their dead. There were ancient paintings on the walls of the caves that evoked powerful feelings in me of actually having lived in those times. Had I? After that trip, I had an experience during a San Pedro ceremony where I found myself back in Australia being initiated by Aboriginal medicine men and women. As part of this initiation, they cut me open and placed crystals into my abdomen. Their operation wasn't painful, and I found myself connected to a powerful crystalline-type energy that vibrated within me. Then I was flying with these medicine people, and I led us all to a sacred tree with spears in a circle around it. From our perspective overhead, we all looked down and imparted knowledge to the tree energetically and received knowledge from it in return.

I returned to Australia in 2011 and arranged to meet Harold, a well-known and sought-after Aboriginal medicine man. He worked in the Daintree Rainforest near Port Douglas in far north Queensland. I'd heard about Harold through the group that was arranging our trip. Because of my prior experiences in Australia and my initiations by Australian Aboriginal medicine men and women that I underwent during a shamanic journey, I felt an affinity to Harold before meeting him. On the day of our meeting, he said that he had dreamed about me before I came and recognized me as soon as I stepped out of the van and joined the crowd that was going to visit the rainforest that day.

He and I talked about our philosophies of healing and about the cosmos and the way it works. We agreed about many things, including that Spirit or Source is in everything, created everything, and is always active, energetically affecting everything on this planet.

Harold had been trained by his grandfather and told me about being out alone in the bush for many weeks at a very young age and doing a walkabout—which is similar to a vision quest, something I knew of from Native American traditions. He spoke of mystical experiences in places sacred to the Aborigines that he still visits from time to time to draw on the healing energies there to help himself and others. He also described how the Aborigines are familiar with plants and animals that have healing qualities—and others that are quite toxic.

I asked him about the process he uses when people come to him for help with a physical or emotional ailment. He said that first, he puts his hand under his armpit to coat it with perspiration. This is to protect himself from the energies he might encounter in the patient that could negatively affect his own energy field. Next, guided by training, intuition, and Spirit, he waves his hand over the part of the patient's body he wants to heal and extracts the energies causing the sickness or problem. Then he flicks his hand over a glass of water to transfer the energies into the liquid, which he carefully discards afterward.

Watching him work on a person who had come to him for healing, I could see the energetic essence of what he extracted take shape and coalesce in the water. It was a remarkable experience. He said that sometimes what formed was a milky substance; sometimes it was mucous-like or bloody. I thanked him for sharing his wisdom with me and letting me see him do his shamanic work. Before leaving, I gave him some stones with energies that I knew to be helpful in healing work. In exchange, he gave me an amulet he said had the same powers. I still keep it in my mesa, sometimes taking it out to use when I work energetically with others.

Over the years, I have become dear friends with some of the many shamans around the world that I have worked with. I've spent much time exploring ancient sites, doing ceremony, and having extraordinary adventures and experiences in North and South America—and doing extensive work with Alberto Villoldo, Marv and Shanon Harwood, and Theo Paredes. In all my travels, I have been struck by how all the shamans I've met have a deep connection to Mother Earth and work with her energies to promote healing. Like me, they all operate in realms of potential to bring about effects in the physical plane.

Since my training as a shamanic healer, I have done many journeys alone as well as with others. I have applied what I learned to my work with people who come to me for healing—some through The Four Winds Society, others through hearing of me by word-of-mouth or via the internet. Some have been analytic clients curious about how I might use shamanic techniques to help them access the wisdom of their unconscious. Those who seek me out typically have a physical ailment (such as cancer), feel lost and rudderless, suffer from anxiety or depression, are struggling with their relationships, or have a combination of issues they want to address with my help. Some want me to teach them how to do shamanic journeying and dialoguing.

I also do shamanic work on my own for my own healing. I start with an intention to connect to transpersonal realms rather than just relax or meditate, and I might choose to enter a specific realm, such as the Quiet, the place before creation where all exists in a state of potential. I use breathing exercises to draw my attention away from any distracting thoughts and to turn on my body's parasympathetic nervous system. That relaxes my body and mind while opening up my awareness. When I first began to do shamanic journeying, I listened to recordings of shamanic drumming to help me shift out of ordinary consciousness. Now, I typically do rattling as part of my ritual for leaving behind ordinary reality.

Whenever possible, I try to do shamanic work in nature, especially in places identified as having strong healing energies such as the vortexes at Sedona. That's near where my wife, Pat, and I worked together when she had her oozing incision from breast cancer treatment. Even before starting my shamanic work, I can feel the vitalizing energies in such power places.

No matter where I use shamanic practices, I always work within sacred space, opening it before journeying or doing a ritual or ceremony and closing it afterward. I am reverent as I call on helpful energies to support my work. I also cleanse my own energy field using breathing exercises or a rattle or a feather so I can be a clear channel for healing energies.

Sacred plants are a traditional tool for journeying, and while I have used them along with the power of my intention to receive their healing messages and energies, silently asking them for their assistance, I haven't worked with them in years. I believe the use of sacred plants is not necessary for people to be able to have a powerful, life-changing experience in the transpersonal realms. Simply being present in the natural world, maybe on a night when the sky is filled with stars and the moon is full, can shift your awareness. I have felt my consciousness change when I have observed a colorful sunset or a double rainbow over a lake where a mist drifts upward from the surface. The grandeur reminds me of my blessings and helps me experience a sense of gratitude and awe. These experiences remind me of that day on the neighbor's farm when I was a young boy and the colors of the sky, the scent of the grass, and the light surrounding the apple tree shifted something in me, opening me up to my first taste of the invisible world. It took me a long time to feel that sense of unity again, but thanks to shamanic work, I was able to make it happen.

Doing healing work for myself using shamanic and Jungian tools has influenced my well-being and maybe my health, too. I know that because of the training, initiations, and journeys I have done over the years, I have experienced psychological healing: I've been better able to integrate all parts of myself, to individuate as I find balance between my everyday responsibilities and my mythopoetic self's yearning for expression.

Having come so far in my life's journey and done so much work toward reintegration, now the question was, what was next in the story of my life? How could I live with an even deeper sense of purpose?

Reaching a turning point in my life at the age of sixty, I began to recognize that I wanted new experiences and to live my life differently, making shamanic practices a greater part of my story. I continued to learn more about shamanism and participated in a series of initiations to help me as a shamanic practitioner and a healer. I traveled far to learn from others and receive their gifts.

However far you are willing to travel out of your comfort zone or away from your home, your willingness to be vulnerable and open up to new ideas and energies might be key to living a more satisfying life.

Questions for the Reader to Ponder

Traveling to visit healers or shamans. Have you visited shamanic or energy healers in your own or other countries and been influenced by them and their energies? If so, in what way were you influenced? Have there been lasting changes in your life following such visits? If you haven't visited such healers, would you like to do so? How might you make that happen despite any obstacles that may seem to stand in your way?

Out of your comfort zone. Have you ever traveled out of your comfort zone to bring in new ideas, new resources, and new energies for transformation? What did you do? How far would you be willing to go to bring in something new? For example, would you spend money, travel to a remote area, or risk being seen as "too different" or "too out there"?

New ideas. Do you resist new ideas and ways of doing things? How might you bring in energies that would help you be more open and flexible? Are you resistant to ideas that seem to contrast with those you were raised with or are familiar with? Are these ideas from different cultures? How might you honor those cultures and allow them to influence you in a positive way?

CHAPTER FIFTEEN

Giving in Service to Others

A stent in an artery in my left kidney, an ablation to treat atrial fibrillation—these are just two of the procedures I'd had by my midsixties that reminded me of my mortality. I look in the mirror and sometimes notice how my face has changed over the years, and I'm aware that my interest in building financial security has lessened. I have entered a new phase of my life that might be described as the way of return. As the *Tao Te Jing* expresses so well, the way of return is about "emptying oneself"—giving back to the world accumulated wealth, knowledge, and experience in preparation for returning to Source. This stage and focus began with my teaching and learning more about shamanism and would lead me to experiences that altered the way I saw myself and my place in the world. Thanks to shamanic journeying, my consciousness expanded, and I now recognize I am a part of something far greater than myself that I'm always connected to. I aim to practice ayni with the world and echo the activities of nature, which is perpetually balancing and rebalancing itself. Because I have been given many opportunities, I want to make sure others have them as well. I feel drawn to helping those who are underdogs, who have caught an unlucky break or were born into much more difficult circumstances than I was.

My giving back has included teaching and offering shamanic workshops, sharing beneficial energies that I have received through my shamanic work, writing about shamanic and Jungian techniques for healing and personal transformation, and supporting various charities that seek to improve people's lives. I know from experience that becoming aware of our stories is the first step toward changing them for the better, and I hope I can play some part in freeing others from constricting stories that have kept them from living fully and authentically.

"What's your story?"

In the mid-2000s at The Four Winds Society, I assisted other teachers in taking a group of students all the way through the four directions in four different workshops. Even though Alberto and another teacher, Linda Fitch, did most of the actual teaching, I helped students learn the basics of shamanic work, answered their questions, and led some exercises during the workshops. In many cases, I worked with students one-on-one, incorporating my Jungian and shamanic training as I helped them gain insights and energies for their own personal healing and for healing others.

Eventually, I co-taught with other teachers more advanced classes on topics such as archetypes, soul retrieval (which involves working with the past), and destiny retrieval (in which you work with the future). Because the Four Winds Society staff handled all the logistics of registration, lodging, meals, and travel for the students, I could devote my time and energy to guiding people in developing their shamanic knowledge and skills. I wasn't interested in teaching on my own and having to deal with all the details of setting up workshops and classes. I continued teaching at The Four Winds Society until around 2008 when I stopped because I felt I had too many other commitments.

About five years later, an analyst friend of mine in St. Louis asked if I would come there to give a lecture on Jungianism and shamanism and follow it with a workshop the next day. The logistics seemed simple enough, the commitment wasn't too onerous, and I had always enjoyed teaching, so I agreed. I had a general idea of what I would say in the lecture but had to decide what the workshop would cover.

I considered many possibilities but finally settled on the idea of getting people to think about how they could bring their spiritual experiences into their everyday lives. The way I see it, each of us is living a life about which a story can be told, with chapters about our health, psychology, relationships, jobs, spiritual life, and ways of being of service in the world. Every chapter is part of the larger whole. If we can step back and examine our story, and be truly honest about what it is, we can start to make conscious choices about how we might change it. By accessing and working with transpersonal realms, we can gain energy and information to better overcome unconscious forces keeping us from writing and living according to a new story more pleasing to us and Source. My ideas about changing our stories became the core of the workshop and would eventually become the basis for other workshops and even books.

I had always been attracted to great stories and their meanings for people—how they shape individual lives and the lives of families and peoples. And as a Jungian analyst, I could see how stories we tell ourselves about our lives and our communities can hold us back or help us to grow and prosper. In retrospect, perhaps the Alto Mesayok rites had some influence on the work I would do in the years to come teaching people about the power of changing their story as a means of changing their life. The concept of a "story" can help people to see they have more power than they think to influence their lives and the people around them.

I remember a time when I was in Southern Illinois and stopped into a coffee shop to get some breakfast. There, as I ate my meal and drank a cup of coffee, I listened to the people around me talking and engaged in conversations with some of them. Many people were clearly holding on to the old stories about how good things used to be. Their tales, which reminded me of the stories of local people in Paris, Kentucky, seemed to give them strength in the face of tough economic times, inspiring hope and a belief that prosperity and well-being will return. I thought about how people all over the world break bread or gather around the fire, reconnecting with each other over stories with themes of good times returning.

When I later read author and venture capitalist J. D. Vance's best-selling memoir *Hillbilly Elegy*, I reflected further on the stories of people from the hills of Kentucky who came to the Midwest for good jobs many years ago. Vance was a working-class midwesterner who did physical labor, and when he saw some of his fellow workers not taking responsibility for their choices to skip work or show up late, he wondered why they didn't make the most of their opportunities. In his book, he expresses curiosity about why some people, like him, look for resources, however scarce they might be, and use them wisely to enact change in their lives while others seem to become stuck in a mind-set of victimhood.

I have wondered about that, too. How can people break out of a confining story and change their lives for the better? I believe many people have few opportunities and resources and that it's important to do what we can to change that, whether it's supporting charities or government programs or helping out people we know who are struggling. What if one of the resources many people are lacking is assistance in identifying the story of their lives and their role in it? As a Jungian analyst and a shamanic practitioner who has helped people access the wisdom of their unconscious, I've helped people identify stories they don't realize they're telling themselves. I know how important it is to acknowledge our choices, whether we made them consciously or unconsciously and despite any emotional pain that comes up when we look at them. Resentment and nostalgia for the good old days can be obstacles to moving forward.

What's more, memories can become altered as they're revisited. When we feel uncertain and unclear about where to go, we can start to idealize the past rather than look at it more objectively. We can also whitewash the story to make our role in it look more noble than it was in reality. Fears about the future are easier to manage when we let go of the stories about how the world around us has to be if we are going to be happy, safe, or fulfilled. If we live according to a story called "When we get back to the way things were in the good old days, all will be fine," we can become so caught up in it that we can't face our fears of the unknown. That's something we need to do if we are going to write a new story and begin living according to it.

As I thought about the workshop I'd be presenting in St. Louis, I wanted to be sure that the attendees who aspired to study shamanism would walk away with tools to change their lives in a meaningful way. My own shamanic experiences had awakened in me a sense of mystery and awe. But how did they affect my everyday life? By pondering this question and using my dialoguing technique to gain further understanding, I began to see ways to apply what I had learned. I was making small changes around the margins, such as in what I ate and drank and how I spent my time and energy. These actions were helping me let go of my old story like a snake beginning to shed its skin, to borrow an image from the medicine wheel. I was writing a new story of my life and living according to it. That's what I wanted for my students.

I decided I would ask my workshop attendees to take four core actions. First, they would identify and reflect on the story of their lives. Second, they would determine what they would like their lives to be going forward. Third, they would begin to examine why they hadn't been able to change their story. What obstacles had stood in their way—and how many of these were internal stories hidden in their unconscious? Fourth, they would learn how to access the transpersonal realms to gain energy and information to help them create a new story, freeing themselves from one they had not consciously chosen.

During the workshop, I described to my students such realms as the lower world, the upper world, and the Quiet (the place before Creation, where everything exists as pure potential). I then guided them on journeys to these places. Another one of my goals was to show everyone how their personal life stories and the stories of others affect and are influenced by one another. People often come to workshops for the purpose of self-healing, but I feel it's important to remind them that we are always interconnected with all that exists and that we need to think about our collective stories and how to change them as well. When one person's story changes, the shift can be felt by others—friends, family, and so on—even an ocean or continent away. It can even perhaps be felt by others in the past or future. I believe this is how the matrix works and how reality works at the quantum level.

At the end of the workshop, I had each person blow their intention for a new life story into a handful of stones—half of them white, half of them black. I then took these sixteen stones that had been infused with everyone's intention and dropped them on the floor. I asked everyone to come up one by one, and when they did, I said to each person, "How does this arrangement look to you? How does it feel to look at this pattern? What do you think it means?" They would answer, and then I told them they could consciously make changes to the stone pattern if they wanted it to better reflect their new life story. After each person in the group came up and moved the stones, letting their intuition guide them, they recognized that each person's desired new life story would affect and be affected by what actions others took. It's one thing to explain interconnectedness to people but another to have them experience it.

My students saw how their stories were impacted by both their inner, unconscious world and by the stories of other people in the outside world. Some said they could visualize wider possibilities for themselves than they had been able to before. Also, they realized they had to detach from their current stories and make different choices each day if they wanted to keep on track and stay connected to the energies they encountered when doing shamanic work—energies that could help them achieve the bigger changes they desired.

After the workshop, some people wanted to do further work with me. I hesitated at first. Did I want to set up a class, hold sacred space for so many people, and teach multiday workshops? And again, I had to think about what I would teach them. I could create a workshop around the medicine wheel and healing techniques, or I could continue to focus on using shamanic and Jungian techniques to anchor people's spiritual experiences in their everyday lives. I finally settled on the second approach and committed to doing a workshop, aiming to have eighteen to twenty people join me.

My first workshop was oversubscribed, so I held another one shortly thereafter for another group of roughly the same size. Each of these workshops lasted four days, and the workshop group met four times over two years, so it was no small commitment.

I had my students engage their stories through journaling exercises, answering questions such as "What is the story of my relationships?" I also asked them to engage their stories by writing poems or short stories about them or by answering questions such as "What color, sound, song, or animal is my story like?" I knew that posing questions such as this one would help them identify their story using both the rational and creative aspects of their brains.

I explained that we can be living according to a story that may have served us well in the past but might not be working for us anymore. There's nothing intrinsically wrong with a story such as "I'm a lone wolf" or "I'm the leader of the pack," but by becoming aware of it, we can stop mindlessly reacting to life in the way we always have and instead choose a new story that we prefer. Being a lone wolf, keeping your own counsel, might not be adaptive given the stage of life you are in, your commitments, your career and relationships—and so on. The leader of the pack might be weary and in need of focusing on the self instead of always taking the lead and feeling responsible for others.

The questions I asked my students to answer made them think about their unconscious beliefs about themselves and how they ought to live—and what their stories really were. Many people have difficulty being honest with themselves about their current stories, sometimes because they are ashamed or embarrassed. I believe that at least some of my students had a breakthrough in terms of facing the truth about the life they were living.

I also introduced the idea that often some part of us wants to change while another part resists it. If they hadn't been able to meet their goals or were holding on to habits and a story that was no longer working for them, I asked them to consider why. I taught my students that they could work with those resistant parts of themselves using techniques such as working with their dreams, journeying to transpersonal realms, and dialoguing. I knew that for many, identifying and working with their inner, unconscious obstacles to transformation would be key for them whatever their goals were: starting a new career, committing to a romantic relationship, and so on. I led them on a shamanic journey to the realm of death so that they could have a dialogue with this archetypal energy. Some were afraid to do the journey, thinking it would hasten their demise. But for most, the experience was paradoxically comforting because it helped them reaffirm that they wanted to live more fully and authentically, knowing that death will inevitably come at some point.

Once people accessed their unconscious, they often received energy and information from it, which helped them overcome any resistance they had to changing their story to a more fulfilling one. They learned that they could reframe the story of their past and present and alter how their story would unfold in the future.

After finishing my two groups of workshops, I held a final two workshops for those who aspired to teach some of my ideas. About forty people, including many shamans, participated. In my teaching, I included ideas for altering one's individual story, teaching others, working on behalf of the collective, and envisioning new ways to be of service in their communities.

Having recognized that people found these workshops to be valuable, I began to conduct more of them, in various places around the country. Some of my workshops were held at integrative medicine gatherings at Northwestern Memorial Hospital in Chicago, Illinois, where my students were physicians, nurses, and other medical professionals. I told them that I am a proponent of complementary, integrative, and functional medicine, all of which take a more holistic approach to healing than Western medicine. Many healers in the West do not work with the connections among our bodies and our emotions, our thoughts, and our spiritual natures. For those raised in the Western healing tradition, the lack of evidence for the effectiveness of energetic work like that done by shamans can make shamanic work seem "soft"—not evidence-based and therefore not valid. I made a point to cite research studies that supported the work we would be doing and I would be teaching about, knowing this would help the participants move past their resistance to alternative ways of healing.

I especially encouraged them to check in with themselves after doing energy work. What did they experience, good and bad? How might it help them in their everyday life? I was asking them to be more self-referential and take greater responsibility for their self-healing.

Some people would like to be told how to live happily ever after. I would, too! But I know it doesn't work that way. Ultimately, we have to be responsible for making the many daily choices that cumulatively determine if we live lives pleasing to us and Spirit.

When I have worked as a teacher, I've had to impart knowledge. As a company president, I had to solve problems, decide on what we were going to do, and then direct my staff to execute my plans. My initial attitude toward giving people advice had been influenced by my father, who too often was preachy and liked to tell others how they should live their lives. As an analyst and clinical psychologist, I've had to restrain my impulses to solve my clients' problems for them. I've learned that the best solutions are ones my clients find for themselves and that what's right for them is not necessarily right for me or others. I have brought that insight into my work with people studying shamanism who are searching for answers. I hope they can see that their inner wisdom has more to offer them than they might realize.

Working with the unconscious using what's called energy medicine—an umbrella my techniques fall under—can foster transformations in habits of mind and behavior. I don't just believe that; I have experienced it. Changing things at an energetic level can lead to changes at the physical level that can't logically be explained. As shamans say, often, healing comes before understanding.

When it comes to healing what ails us, Western medicine has its value. I have certainly benefitted from what it has to offer. However, as we become more globally connected, I believe Western medicine practitioners ought to consider exploring ideas and techniques from other healing traditions and integrating them into their work. Meeting and working with shamans on several continents helped me find some of the areas of commonality among healers from different cultures around the world. I believe I'm a more effective analyst and shamanic practitioner as a result. There can be great value in understanding the connections between energy and the body. Energy medicine practitioners who have this knowledge use it to work energetically to heal physical ailments as well as emotional ones.

I was glad that some of my workshop students reported feeling more confident they could achieve personal transformation and healing after doing Jungian-influenced shamanic work with me. My goal with all my students has always been to try to give them an experience that would make a lasting impact on them. I like to believe that in many cases, I have succeeded.

Growing a Foundation

When doing workshops, I often didn't charge tuition. When I did, it went to a charitable foundation Pat and I had set up, the Greer Foundation, which now supports a number of organizations whose missions are to improve others' lives.

The seeds of it all lay in Pat's involvement in some charities early in our marriage: People's Resource Center, which helps the disadvantaged with job training and emergency assistance; Family Shelter Service, which helps abused women and their children; and Wellness House, which helps cancer survivors and their families to get support on their healing journey.

The work these organizations did had impressed me, and I wanted to get involved.

When we first began working with charities, Pat and I helped out organizations that we happened upon—through presentations at our church or at the Replogle Center for Counseling and Well-Being, for example. Later, we became more intentional about which charities to support, focusing first on how to help underprivileged people who didn't seem to have a fair shot at creating the lives they deserved. Then we realized we also wanted to help veterans who were having trouble reintegrating into their communities after serving their country and help women who were victims of domestic violence.

I could have simply gone to charitable functions, made a pledge, and sent a check—and I did that sometimes. But I wanted a deeper connection to the organizations that were changing people's lives and a chance to use my experience, knowledge, and skills to collaborate with good people who were serving others. When I began to get involved in funding and helping nonprofit organizations, I decided not to serve on any of those charities' boards. I believed I could have more influence meeting with the executive directors than I would have working through a board to get a consensus. By speaking with executive directors directly, I've been able to offer my advice and let them decide on its value.

From the beginning, I liked to ask them, "Is there anything you haven't done yet that's part of your mission that we might be able to help with?" I made my funding contingent on them raising money I would match, knowing that would inspire them to find more resources, which would help them expand their programs' scope. Additionally, I offered ideas from my psychological and shamanic training I thought might be helpful to them and their staff or even to their clients. For example, I talked to some of them about using a fire ceremony or having leaders sit in a circle with a group they were working with rather than standing at the front of a room talking to people seated in rows of chairs.

Asking questions taught me a lot about what was going on in these charities and with the people they served. As an outsider, I can ask difficult and challenging questions of those who run these charities without getting embroiled in organizational politics. I ask what they are doing and why and compare their practices to what I've seen work in other charities with similar missions. I can then offer evidence-based suggestions as to what they might do differently.

Sometimes, the directors of the charities push back when they learn that the Greer Foundation only offers matching funds because they feel doubtful about their fundraising abilities. However, most of the charities discover that they can meet the match and exceed the amount of money they expected to raise. And although we give some multiyear grants, most groups reapply every year, so annually, they need to come up with specific programs or projects that require funding. We're asking the charities we work with to be more conscious about what they do and then translate that knowledge into concrete, specific programs or projects they can offer to those in need.

While dealing with the nuts and bolts of their operations, I don't want to quell the passion of the people in the organizations we support. Over time, I have found that many of the charities have been willing to accept my suggestions about improving their outreach and effectiveness. Many have ended up delivering their services to more people, with greater results—at the same cost. Executive directors I've worked with have said they appreciated my suggestions and my challenges. Even so, I am sure that at least some of the time, people have been frustrated by my efforts to get them to take things to the next level.

Through my conversations with executive directors of nonprofit organizations that serve victims of domestic violence, I found out that women who have abusive male partners too often don't leave because they financially depend on these men. That led to the Greer Foundation helping a charity that deals with domestic violence—Mujeres Latinas— to expand its entrepreneurship program for teaching abused women skills for starting and running their own businesses.

The People's Resource Center, which I mentioned earlier, offered a summer learning program in science for kids who lived in lower income neighborhoods. We thought the work the center was doing was valuable, but I asked how the number of kids served could be doubled. I helped them think through the logistics of attaining more staff, more buses for transportation, and more spaces in which to hold classes. I asked a lot of questions, listened to what they had to say, and made several suggestions. I think I was a catalyst to their expanding their already successful program and serving more people.

Health, Well-Being, and a Strong Foundation for Transformation

My experiences with the healing qualities of nature and with the notion of being in a reciprocal, balanced relationship with Mother Earth influenced our supporting organizations that protect the planet. Reforesting in Peru (something Pachamama Raymi does) and teaching inner-city kids how to grow crops on abandoned city lots (something Chicago Lights does) are two of them.

Pat and I were learning more about preventive health care and integrative medicine. Given our experiences with using shamanic techniques for helping ourselves deal with physical ailments, we decided the Greer Foundation should fund organizations that were health and wellness oriented. Wellness House, The Cancer Center, and LivingWell Cancer Center have programs we support—including nutrition and cooking classes; yoga, guided imagery, meditation, or tai chi sessions; and art therapy. People of means who develop cancer often have access to wellness classes that can help them fight the disease, but we wanted to be sure low-income people could take advantage of them, too.

One health-related charity we support is the Home Centered Care Institute (HCCI). This organization promotes the value of home visits by health care professionals so that patients don't spend excessive time in emergency rooms and hospitals. Saving the health care system millions of dollars, home visits are more beneficial and cost effective, and less emotionally stressful, than having patients get help while staying or living in a rehabilitation facility or a nursing home. The challenge is to get insurance companies, hospitals, and government agencies to recognize all of this and pay home care professionals adequately. By sharing some of the savings from home care, the medical system in the US will save money while providing better care, and the Greer Foundation is helping HCCI with this mission.

Some of our charities have missions that include providing shelter—to homeless veterans, for example, or to women and their children fleeing domestic abuse or children in unsafe home environments. Over 150 children and young adults under twenty-one reside at Mercy Home, which has been in operation since the late nineteenth century. Having a safe place to sleep at night protects them from the dangers of their neighborhood (and sometimes, the dangers of being with their family). The Mercy Home residents receive educational and psychological support as well as job training and attend a number of different Chicago schools.

Other charities we support protect vulnerable people around the world, whether it's women in Pakistan at risk of becoming victims of honor killings or albino people in Africa who are too often the victims of violence because of superstitions about them. Stephen's Children, founded and run by Mama Maggie Gobran, a Coptic Orthodox Christian, serves children who are the poorest of the poor in Egypt, and we help fund its mission. I first met Mama Maggie and learned about her work during a trip to visit healers around the world, when I ended up in a poverty-stricken neighborhood in Egypt. I saw for myself her sense of agape love and her deep dedication to helping children attain food, shelter, medical assistance, and education. Formerly a professor of computer science and a marketing professional in the business world, Mama Maggie changed her life's course to one of service and received the 2019 Secretary of State's International Women of Courage Award. Mama Maggie believes children should learn to better know themselves—their strengths, values, and dreams. It's a goal I believe is important, too. Mama Maggie is both a natural leader and a deeply spiritual person who has inspired countless people to help those less fortunate than themselves. I'm glad that our serendipitous meeting led to our becoming friends.

My engineering education gave me analytical tools that helped me build a successful career, so I thought about how we could help individuals from underserved communities get a college education in a STEM field. I decided to set up our first Greer Scholars program at Lehigh. We provide financial support for these students, but because I knew from experience that the Lehigh engineering program was very demanding, I wanted to do more than simply defray tuition costs. We also make sure that the Greer Scholars have access to tutoring, internships and research opportunities, cohort-building activities such as pizza parties and bowling outings, and conferences relevant to their fields. And we help them make connections to organizations such as the National Society of Black Engineers and the Society of Hispanic Professional Engineers. I believe all of our work for the Greer Scholars program has helped Lehigh's engineering department to focus more attention on keeping all engineering students continuing in their major and graduating within four years. The vast majority of Greer Scholars have done so.

Greer Scholars programs focusing on students in STEM majors are now not only at Lehigh but at six other universities and colleges. What's more, the program has expanded to support fourteen other nonprofit organizations, such as the Boys and Girls Clubs, that are working with high school students who are thinking of going to college and majoring in a STEM field. In some cases, we provide funding for these high school graduates to pursue degrees in other fields, go to trade schools, or pursue other avenues of post-high-school education. In keeping with the Greer Foundation's mission to help underserved groups, the scholarships consider the race and gender of applicants, and most of the scholars have been men and women of color. There are over 850 past and present Greer Scholars and at our current rate of adding students to the program, we expect that number to increase to 1,000 in a few years.

Another charity we support that helps low-income people is the Experimental Station. Located in the Woodlawn neighborhood on Chicago's South Side, this organization runs Blackstone Bicycle Works, a combined community bike shop and youth education program. Children from eight to eighteen learn about bike mechanics and repair and develop customer service and business management skills while building a sense of community. Kids participating in the program also have access to an on-site study lab, a homework area, and tutoring. The Experimental Station worked with us to set up a program that gives students access to ACT and SAT preparation so as to raise their test scores high enough to get them into the college of their choice. The original idea was that the Greer Foundation would then provide scholarship funding to help them get through college. However, the academic support and the ACT and SAT preparation program worked so well that some of the students ended up receiving full four-year scholarships, which meant that some of our foundation money wasn't needed. This success is a great example of the impact a simple program can have and how a small investment can produce big results.

As I became more involved with some of the charities, I realized that while addressing various social ills is important, preventing these problems is equally, if not more, important. For example, as part of their services, the ten or so charities we work with that address domestic violence provide abused women and their children with assistance such as shelter, legal assistance, medical care, counseling, education, job training, and job placement. But to help end the cycle of domestic violence in communities, many of these groups also conduct programs in schools, churches, and other organizations to change attitudes that cause people to get into violent relationships in the first place. They also aim to sensitize young people to signs of abusive relationships so they can extricate themselves from these situations quickly before violence erupts.

Studies have shown that when you teach kids in middle school and high school about the differences between healthy and abusive relationships, the girls are less likely to get into the latter not only when they're still in school but also in the future. Changing the attitudes of boys who are likely to be abusers is harder but not impossible. As it turns out, the best practice isn't to send a speaker to talk about teen dating violence to a large assembly of students for one hour. We have found that sending a male/female team into a classroom for one afternoon a week for an eight-week program, repeated over several years, is more effective. Such a prevention program develops trust between the team and the students and gives the students time to change their attitudes about relating to the opposite sex. What's more, when you help people change their attitudes about domestic violence, they may go on to educate others in their community.

The approach I'm describing has been pioneered by Between Friends in the Chicago area, where we have seen good results. We are encouraging other domestic violence agencies we support to emulate its work.

Many people may be pessimistic about how much you can really do to prevent domestic violence. My perspective is that if you work with 10,000 students and only 4 percent change their attitudes and behaviors, you can look at the 96 percent who didn't change or the 400 people who did. Four hundred people who will not become involved in an abusive relationship, affecting their health and well-being, their children, their employment, and their ability to contribute to their communities—that is significant.

The current way we treat and deal with domestic violence is necessary but results in far higher costs to society. Tally the workdays lost, the money spent on medical and psychological care for victims and their children, court and imprisonment expenses, and the cost of emergency responses that are borne by communities, along with the moral and ethical price of this chronic issue, and you can better understand why I feel very strongly about financially contributing to charities that help prevent domestic violence.

Some of the women served by organizations such as Between Friends have also been helped by the People's Resource Center. The Greer Foundation supports this organization that offers emergency grants—for example, if a person is one payment away from foreclosure. For want of just a small amount of money, a cascade of disasters can befall someone, so the People's Resource Center helps those in dire need of immediate financial relief.

A Contest Where Everybody Wins

The nongovernmental organization Pachamama Raymi, which we support, works with indigenous people in Peru to bring about innovations in ecological restoration, economic well-being, and human development, including preventive health measures. This organization's work is an interesting example of the many ways in which people can be helped with just a small amount of money—and how helping people can also help the land they live on.

The indigenous people living high in the Andes mountains of Peru have suffered from a high infant and maternal mortality rate, caused mainly by malnutrition and preventable intestinal and respiratory diseases. Traditionally, families sleep in smoke-filled rooms where they cook over a fire or stove that isn't properly vented. They also typically share living space with their animals and have limited access to fresh fruits and vegetables. Pachamama Raymi encourages families to upgrade their homes by installing pipes or chimneys that ventilate their cooking fires, thus preventing respiratory illnesses. They also suggest people sleep on raised platforms away from their animals, build a sanitary privy, and find healthy ways to dispose of their trash. Additionally, the families learn it's better to plant vegetable gardens and fruit trees rather than rely on low-quality, store-bought food. These changes to the villagers' lifestyles improve eating habits and respiratory and intestinal health. As a result, infant and maternal mortality have been reduced.

To increase local economic development, Pachamama Raymi helps families to start small businesses that raise guinea pigs (a popular food source in Peru), cattle, and trout and that make cheese. They sell all of these, along with excess garden produce, to people outside the village. The families participate in other types of entrepreneurial endeavors, too.

The pine trees the villagers plant reforest the area, protect the soil from erosion, and increase the value of the land. In the years ahead, these trees will become a valuable source of timber. In the meantime, mushrooms grow in a symbiotic relationship with the pine trees, and their sale provides an annual cash crop.

Pachamama Raymi supports villagers in learning from one another. Expert farmers from communities that have already generated changes come into villages new to the program to help families improve their living conditions and their farming and animal husbandry skills.

To further motivate people to adopt new habits and practices, Pachamama Raymi sponsors contests among village families. The judges are members of other villages. Those who achieve the greatest number of improvements in their homes, farms, surrounding environment, economic situation, or health practices win a small cash prize given out at a festival. Because the indigenous people revere Pachamama, the contest is not just about winning money but also about showing who best cares for Mother Earth. The original goal was to have 60 percent of the families in any village participate in these programs. But usually, more families are involved. We hope to maintain and even increase this rate of involvement in the future.

We usually give $5,000 for each contest per village, and often, the local municipalities give similar amounts. If a village has 400 families, each with six family members, and a participation rate of 60 percent, then six times 240 families, or 1,440 people, benefit from our $5,000 investment. By our spending less than $4 per person, we can see significant improvements in the health, economic well-being, and environment of the villagers. It's gratifying when such a small investment can yield such remarkable improvements in people's lives.

The charities I have mentioned represent just a small fraction of the more than 60 that we are working with and/or supporting. Given the number of organizations I'm involved with, I ration my time to ensure that I can help them strategize about how to use their resources to carry out their mission. When evaluating whether or not to keep supporting a particular charity, we consider whether the people running it have met the goals we have mutually agreed on.

As I reflect on why I initially began giving back through philan-thropy, I can see that along with being motivated by an unconscious desire to help the underdog, my support for charities is also an extension of my belief that we need to make our spiritual experiences practical. Through the foundation, we're involved with people who want to make a difference day after day, year in and year out, in the neighborhood, the city, and the world. I want to do whatever I can, with the time I have left, to help further their work.

A true shaman never takes anything from nature without giving something in return and never receives anything without offering profound thanks. This idea is core to ayni, and I consider my giving back to others through funding charitable organizations to be part of my shamanic work.

Becoming an Author

Around 2005, I began writing about my experiences of becoming a shamanic practitioner, recording the knowledge and insights I'd gained. Eventually, I wrote a book titled *Change Your Story, Change Your Life*. It was an added bonus that the original publisher, Findhorn Press, was associated with the Findhorn community in Scotland, a spiritual group dedicated to training people to be "light workers" in the world.

Change Your Story, Change Your Life carries out the theme of the workshops I have led: helping people change their life stories so they can live more soulfully and showing them how to bring their spiritual practices into their everyday lives so they can make practical changes in how they live. Translating workshop teachings and exercises into a self-help book to be used by individuals was an enjoyable challenge. I decided to follow up my first book with *Change the Story of Your Health,* in which I focused on how to gain insights and energies for physical healing and attain better health and well-being. I had noticed that many of those who appreciated the first book were healers, or people who were struggling with health issues, or a combination of the two. As I did in my first book, I encouraged readers to decide whether the practices I was sharing with them worked for them. I also provided research to help them better understand the theories that underlie why energy medicine seems to work. I believe that the foreword from Melinda Ring, MD, Executive Director of the Northwestern Medicine Osher Center for Integrative Medicine, as well as endorsements from other physicians, helped solidify the book's credibility with health care practitioners. And as with my first book, I received support from some Jungian analysts, too, which generated interest from other Jungians.

I went on to create audio versions of my books with a narrator bringing the words to life. This helped them reach an even wider audience in an era when many prefer audiobooks to physical ones. (They are also available as electronic books.) I've discovered much creativity is involved in finding ways to distribute and promote books in this age of rapidly changing information technology. I was able to partner with several people who assisted me in effectively marketing my books in all their various editions.

I also began writing articles related to the material and themes in my books, getting them published in magazines and on websites, including my own. I did some presentations and radio interviews to promote my books, and in the process of writing and publicizing, I also entered a new world of technology—doing Skype interviews using an iPad, for example. Prior to this, I did not use a computer, had never used email, and was not "connected." It's been a mixed blessing to become part of the internet age but a net positive for me. Writing and publishing have given me a chance to combine my shamanic and Jungian traditions in a way that reaches a far wider audience than would be possible through workshops or lectures alone. The writing process has given me a chance to reflect deeply on what I have learned—and pass on to others the knowledge and insights I've gained. Getting feedback from readers has helped me better understand how to tailor my message in ways that can help them feel motivated to begin the difficult work of identifying and examining their stories so they can write new and better ones. I'm enjoying this stage of giving back, knowing that even small actions I take on the way of the return, can potentially impact other people in significant ways.

Let's Not "Leave well enough alone"

In my practice as an analyst, I sometimes treated patients who were not keen to explore insights hidden in their unconscious. I remember one who started therapy to overcome his anxiety and depression. We talked about various aspects of his life, and he said he was afraid that if I kept asking him to explore what his unconscious was telling him, he would end up getting a divorce. He wanted to "leave well enough alone." My patient didn't realize that therapy or a therapist would not make him do anything he chose not to do. The therapeutic process would only give him more information. It was up to him to decide what he would do as a result. If he wanted to stay in the same marriage and in the same story, he could choose that.

When we change our stories, it affects the people around us. We hope it's for the better, but we can't guarantee that everyone will be happy about our new behaviors and attitudes. My hope is that people doing the work of personal transformation and healing will not be afraid of making thoughtful changes. If we make the unconscious conscious, we are better able to write stories of our lives—and chapters of those stories—that are far more satisfying than the ones written by our family and our cultural conditioning. What's more, we might be surprised at how positively the people we care about respond. They may even be inspired to change their own stories.

I'll continue to write as long as I feel what I have to say might help others. As with my workshops, I make no money personally from book sales. All proceeds go to support the charitable work of the Greer Foundation.

Giving back to others, experiencing my connection with Source, and spending time with the people I love—Pat, our kids and grandkids, and friends—are my highest priorities now. However, I still take time to contemplate questions such as *Where was I before I came into this life? Why am I here? Who am I? What am I? Where will I go after I die?* I have also been pondering what kind of legacy I want to leave. The books I have written—and the ones I plan to write—are a part of that. The Greer Foundation is, too. And to ensure that the foundation and its staff can continue their work far into the future, I have been doing succession planning.

I wanted my children and stepchildren to have sufficient funds to be financially secure and do extra things in their lives but didn't want to give them so much money that it repressed their initiative to build productive careers. I am proud that all of them have done so. They're all good parents and lovingly involved in their children's lives. Those working in the business world and the full-time moms, too, have what they feel are meaningful jobs. All of them spend some of their time giving back to others in some way.

I also didn't want my grandchildren to become "trust fund kids"—people who meander through life without purpose or motivation, knowing their basic bills will always get paid without any effort on their part. I'm glad to say that when I spend time with our six children and fourteen grandchildren at their homes or ours, up in Northern Wisconsin fishing—or someplace else, like Ireland, where we went on a family vacation not long ago—I can see they have good values.

Over the years, Pat and I have had some wonderful adventures traveling in this country and around the world, broadening our horizons and helping us appreciate the rich tapestry of how people live their everyday lives. As we have gotten older, we're doing less adventure traveling. We're playing tennis and golf less often, and we don't ski anymore. Instead, we're spending more time enjoying simple pleasures such as having coffee and reading the paper in our sunroom in the morning or sipping a glass of wine while watching a sunset or sitting by a fire. Pat continues to see clients as a Jungian analyst and is a successful author. We value discussing books, movies, and plays but also political, psychological, and philosophical issues. After more than thirty years of marriage, we have not run out of topics to talk about.

I wanted to make sure I had enough money for the things Pat and I wished to do, including travel. But over the decades, I have accumulated quite a lot of wealth and possessions, and it feels good to let go of some of it. In addition to contributing to charities, I have begun to sort through some of the things I own, passing some items on to my children and giving away or donating much of the rest. Some of the items had originally belonged to my parents or grandparents, and on closer examination, I realized I was never going to wear or repurpose my dad's neckties—and my granddad's tools were just rusty pieces of metal that were cluttering up my storage spaces. These made their way to some family members who wanted them—or were donated or tossed. It's funny how sentimentality can make ordinary objects seem more valuable and important than they are. I also let go of books on how to improve your golf swing or learn jujitsu, realizing that the "someday" I planned to use perusing them was never going to come—and that's okay. I'm able to close the door on some of the goals I once had that no longer are important to me.

Still, occasionally, I find it hard to let things go, believing I might need them in the future. Yet, at some level, I realize my kids aren't interested in receiving more things that they would have to pass on to someone else someday. All my medals and trophies, while important to me once, are not as meaningful to me now and are even less so to anyone else. They are tangible but their value is ephemeral. It seems to me that to share my wealth and experience to help those less fortunate in the world is the best legacy I can leave behind.

I have not "left well enough alone." I've done the work of becoming more self-aware, reintegrating parts of myself that I wasn't conscious of even when facing them made me uncomfortable, and I'm happier as a result. I'm no longer as constricted by old beliefs that were handed down from father to son, from grandparents to grandchildren, that I left unquestioned for many years. I no longer have to live according to the old story that I wasn't even aware of. Because of my experiences, I've found my thinking has become more nuanced and less black-and-white. I've become more willing to accept differences and accept people's right to make their own choices as long as it does not harm others.

Life doesn't have to be just one way. I believe we have to live and let live and help those in need, not just those in our own country but everywhere. Cultural and personal differences exist, but they do not have to form impenetrable barriers between people—or define us. All of us are influenced by our cultural conditioning in positive, negative, and neutral ways. When we examine where we came from and the beliefs that we inherited, we can make different choices—and hand down a different legacy to our children and grandchildren.

Doing work with archetypal energies has helped me to see the shadow and the light of any way of thinking or behaving. I discovered the best aspects of being prone to compartmentalization, for example, even as I discovered its shadow qualities for me. I learned to be more discerning about when to keep my own counsel and when to reach out and connect to someone to share what I am thinking, feeling, and experiencing. And I have guided others in questioning whether they could have a different relationship with the archetype of the fool, the warrior, the mother—whatever archetype was strongly influencing their life. Often, it's quite surprising to discover internalized messages that, when brought into conscious awareness and analyzed, are at odds with what we claim to be our values.

In attempting to heal that inner split between the conscious and the unconscious and accept all parts of me, all my selves, I've come to see that my mind created the illusion of separation from Source and from parts of myself. These "selves" often had qualities I didn't see the value in. But as I have healed and enlarged my worldview, I have come to realize that expressing my mythopoetic self means I am nourishing it and am no longer in danger of having it feed on me, having it eat away at me, which might have happened had I continued to deny it.

Sometimes, it has been painful to "re-member" the pieces of myself in my quest to experience unity with all my facets, reclaiming what I have forgotten or denied. I now recognize where some of my negative qualities originated, but that in no way excuses them. Honestly acknowledging my faults is a start, but the finish needs to include changed behavior. I see honesty as a tool for transformation. With each self-realization, I have tried to act differently going forward from how I have acted in the past. I'm striving to be less rigid and more flexible when it comes to seeing situations from a different perspective. I now realize that I need to continue to expand my ideas about what a good boss—and a good husband, father, and friend—should be.

I know that authenticity can give us more power over our lives and lead to greater happiness and fulfillment as well as a sense of wholeness.

What's the Rush?

For many years, I was too caught up in my own world to be fully present for other people—I was on the clock, feeling the pressure of time and agendas. It's clear to me now that sometimes, I was the one creating the sense of urgency. I wanted to get a deal done and move on to the next one before the opportunity fell through, not fully appreciating that there would always be another deal.

It's taken me years of inner work to start to see my interactions with others differently and to make noticeable changes in the ways I relate to family, friends, clients, coworkers, and business associates. As a boss who could come across as overbearing, I had to learn patience. In the past, I was probably not focused enough on fostering relationships. I am more aware now of how important it is to slow down and be sure I'm balancing my role as a boss (which I still am) with my desire to be understanding about an employee's emotions and personal life. People in positions of power and leadership need to figure out where that line is, which isn't always easy to do.

As my self-imposed clock has slowed down, I'm better at making the time to be present with others than I did years ago. Having fewer demands on my time and less of a desire to chase after an opportunity to make money helps, too. I also acknowledge that while I'd like to go back and change how I acted in some situations, hindsight is 20/20. People often say, "If I had it to do all over again, I would have stopped to smell the roses more often." But would they have? Don't we all try to do the best we can at the time given the many responsibilities we have to juggle?

Now that I am eighty, I continue to pursue my various interests, and while I have some health challenges, I am able to be active and enjoy my life. I believe that my health-related choices such as being physically active and eating healthfully have helped me stay alive and even thrive for so long. I also believe that the shamanic work I have done has contributed significantly. More than a couple of shamans have told me they saw a big protective shield around me—some guardian force looking out for me—and maybe what they were perceiving was real. I believe the shamanic work I have done and the rites I have undergone have helped me change my energy field and my destiny. The jaguar within has helped me to overcome fears that might have prevented me from living according to my own story, one I wrote consciously. It has helped me loosen the constrictions that might have caused me to stay on the same path and not make the changes that led me to where I am today: feeling I've lived a good life on my own terms.

Perhaps other things have positively contributed to my energy field, too. I have some good instincts and am not particularly anxious or fearful by nature, which reduces my stress. In a crisis, I can take a breath or two and, more often than not, act calmly. Martial arts probably reinforced my ability to remain emotionally nonreactive. Having good interpersonal relationships with friends and family is said to be health protective, even more so than not smoking, according to some research, so my remaining engaged with others has probably helped me foster good health, too.

That said, there are always going to be "suddenlies"—events we can't predict that interrupt our lives and demand our attention. Recently, just a month after having a stress echo test that showed no heart problems, I developed some heart symptoms so concerning that I went to an ER. After examining me, the doctors told me they saw no evidence of a heart problem. I was vacationing out of state, and when I got home a week later, I was still concerned, so I went to an ER again. Now I learned that my instincts had been right after all: The doctors said that three of my arteries were so severely blocked that I needed bypass surgery. Two days later, I had the operation.

The last thing I was expecting given the tests and examinations I'd just had was suddenly needing a lifesaving bypass, but these events reminded me that "suddenlies" happen sometimes with little or no warning.

The necessity of focusing on my health has made me more aware than ever of the importance of living with vitality day to day, moment to moment, making choices aligned with my priorities. I have accomplished a lot in this lifetime, but I still have ambitions—to write more books, for example, and to use my resources to help more people who are struggling with health problems or trying to find opportunities to change their lives for the better. There will be more "suddenlies" in the days ahead, I am sure, but I choose not to fear them. I have to accept that they will show up.

As I shape my legacy, I feel in sync with and guided by Spirit.

I am a fortunate man.

I'll close this book with lyrics from "Now the Day Is Over" by Sabine Baring-Gould, a camp song I used to sing as a child:

Now the day is over
Night is drawing nigh
Shadows of the evening
Steal across the sky

When the night of your life approaches, I hope your final sleep is sound, deep, and content, resulting from a life you have been pleased to have lived.

You may be at a stage in your life where you are starting to make the shift from acquiring to sharing—walking the way of return and facing the fact that your life is closer to its ending than its beginning. If you would like to do more for others, opportunities abound. However, you might feel that you can't make a significant difference because of your limitations—of time, resources, skills, and so on.

When you engage in service to others, you might find that you actually have more resources than you realized. You might also come to see as I have that life is enhanced by doing more for others and that helping even in what seems like small ways can potentially have a big impact. If you truly would like to engage in service to a greater degree than you are now, consider whether you are holding onto misconceptions about how much of a difference you can make.

If you are struggling to accept that you are closer to your life's ending than your life's beginning, you might want to work with shamanic and Jungian techniques for gaining insights and energies for healing and change so that you are not stuck in regrets.

Questions for the Reader to Ponder

Resources. Do you believe that if you give in service to others more than you are doing right now, it will drain you of resources? If so, where does that idea come from? Is it true for you? Why or why not? If you have engaged in service to others, do you find it replenishing and energizing in ways? Do you find it helps you recognize resources you might otherwise have overlooked? What if you were to experiment right now with spending more of your time giving and sharing instead of spending so much time acquiring and accumulating? What difference might that make in your own life and in the lives of others?

Charity. Have you donated time and/or material goods to charities in your life? If so, how did you choose each group, and what type of involvement have you had in their work? If not, would you like to start giving back to charities or other groups? What might motivate you to do so? How might you get involved in their work?

Simplifying your life. Do you have trouble letting go of accumulated possessions? If you want to do that, what, if anything, is holding you back? How might you go about simplifying your life? Could you do it in a way that would leave you feeling no regrets? Do you have trouble saying no to spending time in particular activities that aren't satisfying or rewarding anymore? How might you extricate yourself from these commitments without feeling guilty or ambivalent?

"Suddenlies." As you think about the "suddenlies" in life, are you prepared for them? How have you prepared yourself? Have you become better prepared for unexpected moments as a result of having faced shocking twists in the plotline of your life? Where has your strength come from when faced with a "suddenly"? Is there something you can do, or make happen more often, to remind yourself of that strength?

Legacy. As you reflect on your life, what kind of legacy would you like to leave behind? What would you like people to remember about you after you are gone? What have you accumulated in terms of material possessions and knowledge, experience, and skills that might benefit others? Have you acquired skills or wisdom that you would like to share with others via writing or teaching? What would prompt you to do so?

Your story. If you were to write the story of your life, would you be happy with your story, or would you want to change it? If you want the story of your life to change, what would you like your new story to be?

If you think it's too late to change, I leave you with this: I have seen people at the very end of life change their story and die a good death, free from the constrictions that have bound them since childhood, free to say "I love you" and to accept themselves and surrender to the mystery. Maybe you will choose to believe in your potential to do the same. I hope so.

End Notes

Chapter 10: The Mythopoetic Challenge
1. **Shosan quote:** "No matter how much you have learned and how much you know, if you don't know yourself you don't know anything. Indeed, if you don't know yourself you cannot know anything else." Thomas Cleary, *The Japanese Art of War* (Boston: Shambhala Publications, Inc., 1991, p. 45)

Chapter 11: Discovering What Has Been Hidden
2. **Carl Jung quote:** "the true value of individuation lies in what happens along the way." Daryl Sharp, *C. G. Jung Lexicon: A Primer of Terms & Concepts* (Toronto: Inner City Books, 1991, p. 69)

3. **Warrior archetype.** The book *King, Warrior, Magician, Lover* helped shape my thinking about my relationship to this archetype. Robert Moore and Douglas Gillette, *King, Warrior, Magician, Lover: Rediscovering the Archetypes of the Mature Masculine.* (New York: HarperCollins, 1990)

4. **Carl Jung's earliest memory of being in a pram.** Carl Jung, *Memories, Dreams, Reflections.* (New York: Vintage Books Edition, 1989, p. 6)

5. **Carl Jung quote:** "Am I the one sitting on the stone?" Carl Jung, *Memories, Dreams, Reflections.* (New York: Vintage Books Edition, 1989, p. 20)

Chapter 12: The Jaguar's Call
6. **Meeting of "the condor and the eagle."** In *Shaman, Healer, Sage*, Alberto Villoldo writes about how one of his Q'ero mentors, Don Manuel Quispe, passed on to him much of the wisdom of his people, encouraging him to share it:
"Anyone can be a soothsayer," Don Manuel explained. "We have been the keepers of a body of processes, of rites, that usher in who we are becoming as a people, as a planet. These processes are not only for the Indians, but for the entire world." Alberto Villoldo, Ph.D., *Shaman, Healer, Sage: How to Heal Yourself and Others with the Energy Medicine of the Americas* (New York: Harmony Books, 2000, p. 236)

7. **Alberto Villoldo's mentor Don Antonio working with the chakras.** The account of Don Antonio working with chakras originally appeared in *Dance of the Four Winds*, a book Alberto Villoldo wrote with Erik Jendresen, and also appeared in *Shaman, Healer, Sage*. According to both books, Don Antonio was working with a dying woman's chakras so her spirit could leave

her body, but chakra cleansing can also be done for releasing nonbeneficial energies—and I have done this as a shamanic practitioner. In *Shaman, Healer, Sage*, Alberto writes, "Simply because kidneys were named by Europeans does not make the kidney exclusively European. Similarly, the chakras are not exclusively Hindu." (pp. 51–52) He mentions, too, that Native Americans he met in South America called the chakras "*ojos de luz*," which is Spanish for "eyes of light," and "*pukios*," or "light wells" (p. 52). I described a process for cleansing chakras in my book *Change the Story of Your Health*. (Scotland: Findhorn Press, 2017, p. 176)

8. Psychedelics being studied as potential treatments for anxiety, depression, and tobacco and alcohol dependence. "Reviewed studies suggest beneficial effects for treatment-resistant depression, anxiety and depression associated with life-threatening diseases, and tobacco and alcohol dependence" https://journals.sagepub.com/doi/abs/10.1177/2045125316638008 Also, see pages 3 and 4 of Michael Pollan's book *How to Change Your Mind: What the New Science of Psychedelics Teaches Us about Consciousness, Dying, Addiction, Depression, and Transcendence* (New York: Penguin Books, 2018). Also, see this study for using psilocybin for treating alcohol addiction: https://journals.sagepub.com/doi/abs/10.1177/0269881114565144 More evidence that research has increased lately: https://beckleyfoundation.org/psychedelic-research-timeline-2/ also https://www.frontiersin.org/research--topics/5512/psychedelic-drug-research-in-the-21st-century

9. People who take certain medications could experience adverse effects. For example, ayahuasca combined with an SSRI could result in serotonin syndrome, a dangerous and even deadly condition. See: Jillian Kubala, "What is Ayahuasca? Experience, Benefits and Side Effects," *Healthline.com* June 26, 2019. https://healthline.com/nutrition/ayahuasca#bottom-line

10. DMT as "the spirit molecule." Author Rick Strassman coined the term "spirit molecule" in his book *DMT: The Spirit Molecule: A Doctor's Revolutionary Research into the Biology of Near-Death and Mystical Experiences* (Rochester, VT: Park Street Press, 2001), which was also made into a documentary.

Chapter 14: Bringing In
11. Munay-ki rites. Alberto Villoldo's description of the Munay-ki rites appeared in the foreword to my book *Change Your Story, Change Your Life: Using Shamanic and Jungian Tools to Achieve Personal Transformation* (Scotland: Findhorn Press, 2017, p. 14).

About the Author

Carl Greer, PhD, PsyD, is a retired clinical psychologist and Jungian analyst, a businessman, and a shamanic practitioner, author, and philanthropist, funding over 60 charities and over 850 past and present Greer Scholars. He has taught at the C.G. Jung Institute of Chicago and been on staff at the Replogle Center for Counseling and Well-Being. Learn more at CarlGreer.com.

CPSIA information can be obtained
at www.ICGtesting.com
Printed in the USA
FSHW021951020721
82938FS